LESSONS FROM THE TOP

How successful leaders tell stories
to get ahead – and stay there

Gavin Esler

PROFILE BOOKS

First published in Great Britain in 2012 by
Profile Books Ltd
3A Exmouth House
Pine Street
Exmouth Market
London EC1R 0JH
www.profilebooks.com

1 3 5 7 9 10 8 6 4 2

Typeset in Minion by MacGuru Ltd
info@macguru.org.uk

Printed and bound in Great Britain by
Clays, Bungay, Suffolk

A CIP catalogue record for this book is available from the British Library.

ISBN 978 1 84668 499 9
eISBN 978 1 84765 847 0

The paper this book is printed on is certified by the © 1996 Forest Stewardship
Council A.C. (FSC). It is ancient-forest friendly. The printer holds FSC chain of
custody SGS-COC-2061

FSC
Mixed Sources
Product group from well-managed
forests and other controlled sources
Cert no. SGS-COC-2061
www.fsc.org
© 1996 Forest Stewardship Council

LESSONS FROM THE TOP

GAVIN ESLER is an award winning television and radio broadcaster, novelist and journalist. He is the author of five novels and a non-fiction book, *The United States of Anger*. He currently presents *Newsnight* on BBC2 and Dateline London which goes out weekly on BBC World and the BBC News Channel, and is a regular writer and commentator across print media. He has interviewed leaders in their fields ranging from David Cameron to Dolly Parton, and Richard Branson to King Abdullah of Jordan.

For Amelia – in the hope that her generation
produces better leaders

The weakest possible excuse to include anything in a story is: 'But it actually happened.' Everything happens; everything imaginable happens. Indeed, the unimaginable happens. But story is not life in actuality. Mere occurrence brings us nowhere near the truth. What happens is in fact not truth. Truth is *what we think about* what happens.

Robert McKee, *Story*

Contents

A Message for the Reader

Everyone tells stories. It's one of the ways we connect with our friends and families. It's how we impress people when we apply for jobs and university places. It's what we do on Facebook and Twitter, and even how we go about the business of dating and finding a partner. Leaders tell stories too. They do so to attract, impress, control and retain their followers. Leaders have to possess many different skills, but without the ability to tell stories, they would have no followers and would cease to lead anyone. This book is about the power of such stories, based largely on leaders I have met. It is also about the great changes which have taken place in the kinds of stories leaders now feel they must tell in order to impress us in the twenty-first century.

We shall hear about 'leadership stories', the stories a leader tells, or asks his friends and followers to tell on his behalf. We shall move on to consider 'counter-stories', the stories told by enemies and opponents aimed at shattering the leader's image. We shall also consider 'pre-stories', the judgements we all make, for good or ill, before we meet someone, and which often need to be overcome if the leader is to impress us. We shall encounter storytelling techniques, including STAR moments – 'Something They Always Remember' about the leader or storyteller – and also what the Germans call the *Ohrwurm*, the 'earwig' which wriggles in your ear like the chorus of a pop song and which, however annoying, you just cannot forget. We shall come to understand how leaders, like novelists or Hollywood scriptwriters, hook us on the stories they tell by 'violating expectations', as some psychologists call it – telling us something surprising which makes us look at them in a different light, and which may or may not actually be true.

Throughout *Lessons from the Top* we shall learn which words to use and which to avoid when telling a leadership story. We shall understand how some leaders and their advisers use pictures to tell a story in a way that is more powerful than words, and how the use of pictures can deliberately mislead. We shall learn how a leader shapes a story from his or her origins to his achievements and then to the kind of leadership he intends to offer. We shall also learn why 'authenticity' is more important than 'truth' – and how 'authenticity' can be faked. And we shall come to understand how and why so many leaders try to persuade us that they are simultaneously 'just like us' while also being 'better than us', and therefore fit to lead.

All successful leadership stories involve three parts. First, the leader has to explain **'Who am I?'**, as a person. Then he or she outlines **'Who are we?'** as a group to followers or potential followers. Finally the leader tells us **'Where will my leadership take us?'** in our common purpose. A convincing leader will make these stories buzz in our heads in a way that is unforgettable. In modern democracies, with varying degrees of enthusiasm and skill, leaders will accept some kind of scrutiny from the media. But they also rise to the top by manipulating the coverage they receive on television and in newspapers, along with managing Twitter, Facebook and other storytelling tools, deciding when and how to appear, how much of their 'real' lives to share, and controlling the environment in which they will allow their leadership stories to be questioned. Throughout we will examine how profound changes to the media in the twenty-first century have transformed the kinds of stories leaders tell, or believe they need to tell, to impress their followers. This has already brought about a change in the kinds of leaders we have, and those who will emerge in the future.

This book, then, takes lessons in storytelling from the very top and offers them to those of us who aspire to lead, to do better in our careers or to prosper in our personal lives. Even if we do not aspire to a position of leadership, we are all followers of something or someone, of an ideal, a philosophy or religion, a football team, a rock star, a political party, a brand of computer, a fashion trend. Leaders are as selfish as the rest of us, perhaps more so. The stories they tell us are designed to make them look good. Such stories may be in the leader's best interests but they may not necessarily be in ours. This book offers all of us the keys to understanding, interpreting and, at times, debunking the stories leaders try to tell us and the ways they often mislead us for their benefit.

We are all storytellers, all followers, and often we are leaders in some way, or at least we aspire to lead. As we come to understand more about the storytelling process, I hope you will agree that, above all, *Lessons from the Top* is itself full of powerful stories.

Gavin Esler
London and Berlin, July 2012
Website: gavinesler.com
Email: gavin.esler@yahoo.co.uk
Twitter: @gavinesler

1 Lessons from the Top

Behind every great leader there is always a great story. Even not-so-great leaders understand the need to engage and impress their followers, customers, voters or audiences. They do it most effectively by telling stories about themselves, their origins, their vision and beliefs.

A leader must have many qualities. Vision, persistence, idealism, energy, determination, risk-taking, commitment and enthusiasm are among the most obvious. But a person may possess all those skills and more, and yet never be a leader. The indispensable skill for all leaders in business, politics, sport or any significant field of human endeavour is the ability to create followers and communicate effectively with them. All leadership demands followership. Whatever his or her other qualities, leaders or potential leaders will never have followers without the ability to articulate who they are, who they consider their followers to be as a group, where their views and expertise come from, and why, above all others, he or she is the right person to lead.

Bill Clinton understands the power of stories. That's why he managed to win the US presidency in 1992, transforming the Democratic Party from losers to winners, and how, against the odds, he came to survive the sex scandal over his relationship with Monica Lewinsky. Nelson Mandela also understands the power of stories. That's why, when he faced going to jail in apartheid South Africa, he turned up in court wearing the traditional clothes of the

Xhosa people, an African man representing his people against a white power structure. And that's also why as president of post-apartheid South Africa, Mandela attended the 1995 rugby World Cup Final wearing the Springbok shirt. The Springboks had long been a symbol of white supremacy. On Mandela's back the shirt immediately became a new symbol of inclusion, of a 'rainbow nation' and of a new kind of African leader. The shirt, like the Xhosa national dress, was not just an item of clothing. It was a storytelling device. In their very different ways Clinton, Mandela, Margaret Thatcher, Barack Obama, the British royal family and even terrorist leaders and organisations like Osama Bin Laden and the IRA all know that telling stories is the bridge between them and their followers, the essential connection that makes successful leadership possible.

During my years of travelling round the world, when I met Bill Clinton or Jimmy Carter, prime ministers and presidents, even monarchs like Queen Elizabeth II and King Abdullah II of Jordan, people would always ask me the same question: what is he, or she, really like? Generally they would not be asking about policies or ideas. Instead, they wanted to hear stories that captured the 'real' leader, his or her 'character'. The most effective leaders understand that these stories transcend matters of policy. Storytelling is how their leadership is often defined.

The Great Communicator

Let's begin by looking at Ronald Reagan, a US president of the type widely patronised and disliked in Europe, caricatured as a 'cowboy' and seen by many Americans to be divisive at home during his terms in office. When people asked me what he was like, I would normally answer without discussing his policies at all. Reagan's funding of armed counter-revolutionaries in Nicaragua, the Iran-Contra scandal which almost destroyed his presidency, supply-side economics, or his reputation in Europe as a warmonger, were the stories I reported as a journalist on television every day, but they were not, generally, what people want to hear as a guide to the 'real' man behind the public image. Instead, people would ask about Reagan's quirky sense of humour, his relaxed attitude to his job, his love for dogs, or the way he handled the assassination attempt which almost ended his life. I would respond with stories Reagan's deputy chief of staff Michael Deaver told me, or from other friends and White House contacts who saw Reagan frequently. Reagan's leadership story, Deaver always said, was that of a man comfortable in his own skin. For all the roiling public controversies over his policies, Reagan communicated an air of calm to everyone around him in the White House, and through his mastery of television, to the American people. As president, Reagan would stroll in to the Oval Office after a good breakfast, around nine in the morning. He would put in a few hours' work, then spend time with his wife Nancy in the late afternoon, leaving his staff to do their jobs. Sometimes he would take a nap after lunch. Not only did Reagan like dogs, but some of his pets were what Deaver called 'untrained mutts'. One morning at around nine o'clock, the president of the United States, with mutt in tow, breezed into the Oval Office and asked his high-powered team what was happening. There had been an urgent foreign policy crisis and the top players from the president's staff had worked through the night. They were tired and tetchy. By the time Reagan arrived, his advisers had spent many hours in earnest discussion, telephoning foreign capitals and checking military deployments. The dog began running excitedly round the room.

'Mr President,' one of the top aides snapped through gritted teeth, 'one day that dog is going to piss on your desk.'

There was a short pause. Silence in the Oval Office.

'Well, everyone else does,' Reagan responded. The dog continued to misbehave. The staff went back to work.

Not long afterwards, a friend of mine, a Washington-based TV cameraman, was scheduled to film Reagan at the White House.

The cameraman was the proud owner of a King Charles spaniel, the same breed owned by the Reagans. The interview was, as usual, slotted into a long day of official meetings which tended to bore the president, occasionally to the point of slumber. This interview took place in the Roosevelt Room, and when it was over Reagan bade farewell to the TV crew. At that point my friend showed him a picture of his daughter holding her pet spaniel. Reagan was clearly delighted but his aides ushered him away to his next appointment. The crew began to de-rig the TV equipment. Fifteen minutes later, Ronald Reagan re-entered the room, alone.

'Where's the man with a doggie like my little doggie?' Reagan enquired. My friend was astonished. Reagan produced a photograph showing him with his own dog. He signed the picture and handed it over, then the men in grey suits returned to the Roosevelt Room and took the most powerful man in the world back to the dreariness of his chores.

My friend never forgot this simple act. He told everyone he knew, who told everyone they knew, and now I am telling you. I suspect this story will stick in your mind, as it does in mine, while precise details of the Iran-Contra scandal, the Star Wars programme or Reagan's supply-side economics may fade. The big decisions leaders have to take, the policies they advocate, are often too complicated for us to fret about. Sometimes, as with Reagan, these policies may be considered divisive and contentious. But even a child understands what it means to be kind to dogs and gracious towards a visitor. As followers or potential followers, we tend to care more about character, judgement and temperament than we do about the minutiae of the decisions our leaders take. Successful leaders, or potential leaders in any field of human endeavour, understand this.

In Reagan's case, he and his team used such stories deftly to his political advantage. He once met a young foreign correspondent, a friend of mine, who sported a fine beard. At the end of their discussions my friend happened to mention that he would need to shave off his beard before returning to his office because his editor-in-chief had banned beards, considering them unprofessional. Reagan, who loved stories, clearly enjoyed this one. A few weeks later my friend was phoned by his editor-in-chief who demanded to know what he had said to the president. The editor-in-chief had been attacking the Reagan administration for being right wing and illiberal. Reagan responded that all that might be true, but at least he allowed a guy to wear a beard if he wanted to.

Now, it is not the purpose of this book to argue whether Reagan was or was not a good president, whether his policies were the right ones, or whether any of the leaders here were good or bad. That depends on your view of politics and world affairs. But Reagan certainly was a great communicator, one of the greatest tellers of a leadership story I have ever encountered, both privately in these examples, and publicly while in the White House. I suspect that stories about dogs and beards, like many other tales of Reagan's good humour, encouraged many Americans to think of him as a decent person, whatever their judgement about his policies and legacy. The important point is that such stories are generally not accidents. They are often created, massaged and retold to impress us about the leader's character and to encourage us to like and to follow him. In Reagan's case, it worked. Such stories helped him to be elected twice to the presidency, and to survive a profound scandal which could have driven him from office.

Ronald Reagan's image was crafted every day by the White House machine. When Reagan was shot and seriously wounded, we learned that he joked to doctors that he hoped they were all Republicans. He told his wife of the shooting: 'Honey, I forgot to duck' (a quote from an American boxer). These stories, told, retold and embellished by the Reagan team, made the president's character and temperament seem ideal for the Oval Office, even when we later learned that privately his staff considered him often inattentive, distracted and ageing fast.

Reagan's infirmities became part of the 'counter-story', that is, the negative stories used by his opponents and enemies to attack the Reagan presidency. The Reagan team knew such stories needed to be dealt with. As one member of Congress joked with me at the time: 'The president is deaf, falls asleep in Cabinet meetings and does not know what is going on. Thank goodness he is not running the country.' Significantly, that member of Congress, although a political opponent, admitted that he really 'liked the guy'.

The Leadership Paradox

Most modern leaders understand that there is a paradox at the heart of leadership. It goes back to the beginnings of democracy in ancient Greece. We want our leaders to be 'just like us', like Reagan with his dogs – the Greek word was '*idiotes*', meaning 'private person, layperson' (although potentially edged with contempt to suggest those not interested in politics) – but we also want them to demonstrate that they are 'better than us', so they can deserve the privileges of leadership, which the Greeks called '*metrios*'. As John F. Kennedy's biographer Robert Dallek put it, Americans today want simultaneously to mythologise and to debunk their presidents. We want our leaders to understand and have the interests of ordinary people at heart, but we would prefer that they avoid the weaknesses, vices and frailties of the rest of us. As the American presidential candidate Ross Perot told me repeatedly, Americans want to think that their leaders have boarded a plane, eaten a bad meal and lost their luggage, rather than being mollycoddled in first class or in a private jet. We want to look up to leaders, but also to feel that they are in some way our equals. And that paradox is where leadership stories come in. That's where the leaders shape the facts of their lives to impress us, connect with us emotionally and make us like them. That's also where they lie and cheat, telling what Huckleberry Finn called 'stretchers', distorting the truth to suit their own purposes, rather than ours.

As we will see, throughout history leaders and their followers have always understood the power of such stories and counter-stories. Sometimes these can be effectively summed up in a word, phrase or headline. Jesus of Nazareth was 'the Son of God', but he was also ridiculed in the counter-story as 'the King of the Jews'. England's Queen Elizabeth I was 'the Virgin Queen' who turned a negative counter-story – that she was without a husband and hence without an heir – into a positive leadership story by insisting that she was married to her country. Catherine the Great, Charles the Great, William the Conqueror (Guillaume le Conquérant was formerly Guillaume le Bâtard, or William the Bastard – now *there's* a sharp bit of rebranding), Richard the Lionheart, and Edward I, the 'Hammer of the Scots', all recognised that even a monarch who might assert the divine right of kings still needed a leadership story of some kind to impress his or her subjects, rival monarchs and perhaps ambitious nobles in court. It's true of more modern rulers too. Bismarck was 'the Iron Chancellor'; Mussolini and Hitler 'Il Duce' and 'der Führer' (the Leader) respectively. North Korea's Kim Jong-il was variously 'Dear Leader', 'Our Father' and 'the General'; Haile Selassie was 'the Lion' of Ethiopia; and so on. As the historian Mark Mazower points out in *Dark Continent* the twentieth century, at least from 1914 to the end of the Cold War in 1989, was a period when the survival of the institution of democracy appeared to be in doubt.

But since 1989 democracies, with all their flaws, have flourished from Brazil to Greece, Spain to Turkey, Chile to Tunisia and Peru. The collapse of communism has meant that political differences since 1989 tend to be about practicalities and effectiveness – 'what works' – not grand contests between competing ideologies. Consequently, democratic elections are sometimes disparaged as beauty contests for ugly people. Those who depend upon the popular vote have needed to be especially energetic in trying to implant in our minds versions of their leadership story, because 'Who am I?' often makes them stand out more than relatively minor policy differences.

Italy's former prime minister Silvio Berlusconi understood the power of stories to win elections. He used some of his billions in wealth to distribute to every home in Italy at election time a booklet which told his version of his personal story, explaining in heroic terms how 'Il Cavaliere' (the Knight) achieved such extraordinary business success. In 1993 Berlusconi created a new political party, Forza Italia ('Forward Italy'), cleverly named after the chant Italians use to support their national football team. Margaret Thatcher repeatedly told a leadership story that she was 'a grocer's daughter from Grantham', and then was fortunate enough to be called by a Soviet newspaper 'the Iron Lady', a counter-story she immediately seized and made her own. The first time I met Bill Clinton in 1991, when he was still a governor, he made sure that he described himself to me as 'the boy from Hope', helpfully trying to write my headlines for me. Such leadership stories go far beyond politics. The football coach José Mourinho tried to shape his leadership story as 'the Special One'. Others have found that their leadership stories, for better or worse, are written for them by the media, and they need to make the best of it.

The Royal Bank of Scotland's Sir Fred 'the Shred' Goodwin and BP's Tony Hayward were destroyed not just by their misjudgements in business but also by their inability to keep control of their leadership stories and neutralise the counter-stories in a hostile media. Hayward had to leave BP not because he handled the aftermath of the Gulf oil spill incompetently in technical terms. The real reason he had to go was that he did not convince people he was genuinely concerned and contrite. He did not tell an appropriate story. Other business leaders such as Warren Buffett, 'the Sage of Omaha', or Jack 'Neutron Jack' Welch, Ryanair's Michael O'Leary, Microsoft's Bill Gates, Apple's Steve Jobs and Virgin's Richard Branson find they have a natural gift not just for making money but also for making headlines through telling stories. Many of them have shaped their leadership stories by writing autobiographies or cooperating with those who will portray them sympathetically. The script for so many leaders' biographies follows the same pattern as the one told by Bill Clinton, which we will examine in detail later: humble beginnings, conflict with authority figures, unconventional choices and ultimately the triumph of the leader's will.

The personal stories of truly great business leaders become inextricably part of their brand identity. Victor Kiam famously so liked the shave from Remington razors that he bought the company. Richard Branson has constantly presented himself as the cheeky anti-establishment outsider, even as his Virgin business empire grew from music to vodka, trains to planes and possibly into space, and he received a knighthood from the Queen. The beard, the open-necked shirts, the slightly hesitant manner on television, all became part of Brand Branson storytelling. The same is famously true of the guiding genius behind Apple, Steve Jobs. As he prepared to launch a new product, one of the world's richest and most powerful men would appear rather like a geeky university professor in jeans, open-necked shirt and trainers. But as his biographer Walter Isaacson reveals in great detail, Jobs managed his life-story with the same attention to detail he gave to Apple products, even to the point of insisting (repeatedly) that Isaacson was the man to write the book. Isaacson's account is warts and all, but as Jobs was dying he could be assured of his legacy, a leadership story about his rise from nothing, summed up in one of the book's opening sentences: 'In August 2011, right before he stepped down as CEO, the enterprise he started in his parents' garage became the world's most valuable company.'

How Leaders Do It

Changes in the worldwide media in the last few decades, particularly since the end of the Cold War in 1989, have contributed to a new confusion between leadership and celebrity. These changes mean we can expect different types of leaders to emerge in future. Some of them – Arnold Schwarzenegger, Silvio

Berlusconi, Jesse Ventura, Boris Johnson and Ronald Reagan – have already translated celebrity into power. Others – Donald Trump, George Soros and Alan Sugar come to mind – move in the other direction, translating their business leadership and power into celebrity. And still others, like President Sarkozy and his wife Carla Bruni, have become quite literally a marriage between the two. New technologies and new media mean new pressures on leaders and new opportunities and dangers. Leaders of countries with state-controlled media – Egypt, Libya and Tunisia – were overthrown in the 'Arab Spring' of 2011 partly because their opponents used the social media to communicate damning counter-stories about Hosni Mubarak, Colonel Gaddafi and Ben Ali.

At the same time, democratically elected politicians have seized on Twitter and Facebook to tell new types of stories about themselves, their leadership, and what they clearly hope will be a more intimate and personal relationship with what Twitter calls their 'followers'. This is all-pervasive. I follow, among others, a senior officer at the British Ministry of Defence who offers news about British troops and their operations, a well-known footballer or two, a couple of newspaper editors and numerous politicians. Celebrities like Lady Gaga and Angelina Jolie feature in this book because I believe their success offers lessons to genuine leaders, but the confusion between leadership and celebrity goes further. It infects the professionals, spin doctors, media consultants and others, whose job is to help the leader confect the appropriate leadership story in order to sound 'authentic'. This has created new demands for leaders to 'open up' their personalities to journalists, to 'humanise' themselves in ways which even a few years ago would have seemed shameless, prurient and unwise. Some do it well. The British prime minister David Cameron tried to defuse the damaging counter-story that he is a posh, wealthy Etonian who joined an ultra-posh Oxford dining club, the Bullingdon, and married into the aristocracy. He does this by constantly reminding us that he is 'Dave' Cameron, an ordinary bloke at home in jeans and T-shirts, someone who just happens to be prime minister and a multi-millionaire, but who has in fact spent a lot of time in National Health Service hospitals seeking treatment for his ill son, takes his wife on holidays on a budget airline or to Cornwall, and likes nothing better than cycling to work. Pictures of Cameron on a bicycle are easy to find on the internet, because they tell the 'right' story. But while David Cameron also enjoys riding horses at his country house in the Cotswolds, pictures of the prime minister on horseback are very difficult to discover. Presumably this is because, like the famous picture of David Cameron in a white tie and tailcoat at an exclusive Bullingdon supper, such photographs would tell the 'wrong' story.

While David Cameron is a gifted storyteller, others are hopeless, including Cameron's immediate predecessor, Gordon Brown. Brown has an extraordinary personal story of near blindness and significant academic achievement, and yet he has never managed to connect with the British people. Unlike Cameron, Gordon Brown could not explain in any attractive sense the most basic part of a leadership story: 'Who am I?' This new twenty-first century confessional culture, as we will see in detail later, demands an answer to that question. Explaining 'Who am I?' has encouraged leaders like Barack Obama to write about his former use of cocaine, David Cameron to discuss when he had sex with his wife, and Cherie Blair, the wife of Tony Blair, to talk openly about forgetting to use contraceptives when conceiving their son Leo at the royal estate in Balmoral. Blair, the most successful Labour party leader in history, a man who won three general elections by a landslide, is a master of the power of stories. Whatever you think of his policies and achievements or lack of them, Tony Blair stands alongside Clinton, Thatcher and Reagan as one of the greatest political communicators in the English-speaking world since the Second World War. In his autobiography *A Journey*, Blair reflects on the trends I have suggested above and what he calls 'the pace of modern politics and the intrusion of media scrutiny – rightly or wrongly, of an entirely different order today than even fifteen or twenty years ago'.

This new intrusiveness in the media and the search for supposed authenticity and intimacy in storytelling affects all of us. With more than half a billion people worldwide telling stories about themselves on Facebook, and millions more trying to communicate on other social media, with President Obama and Prime Minister Cameron using Twitter to keep in touch with followers, we can all learn from these masters of communications how to present ourselves, how to tell stories and how to avoid serious errors. Be warned: throughout this book, some of the stories the leaders tell are true, some have elements of truth and some are simply phoney. In most cases the question of truth is less important than whether the stories are effective. And, as we shall see, leaders understand that to be effective their stories often do not need to be true at all. They just need to seem 'authentic'.

Leadership Stories Mean Control

Storytelling is like singing. It's a skill that we all possess but also one we can learn to do better. If you are a deputy bank manager who wants promotion or a teenager who wants a good job or university place, you can learn lessons from the great masters to use in your own lives. Should we trust Apple because Steve Jobs' leadership story marks him out as a cool kind of geek? Should we trust Virgin products because Richard Branson took risks in business and at the same time dared to fly round the world in a balloon? Should we trust Ronald Reagan because he was self-deprecating, kind to strangers and liked dogs? How do we understand what is going on underneath the carefully prepared narrative of the clever, manipulative and often devious people we are expected to follow? How do we read the code of an increasingly complex and invasive media, and sift through the negative messages in a counter-story to figure out what really lies behind the stories we are being fed?

Failed leaders and despots also understand the power of stories. Robert Mugabe in Zimbabwe is an obvious example, along with Colonel Gaddafi in Libya, and Saddam Hussein in Iraq. As each man came to sense that their rule was near the end, they repeated the self-aggrandising legends that their lives had involved years of sacrifice and dedicated patriotic service to their grateful people. As Colonel Gaddafi put it, such people 'loved' him to the end. The events surrounding his gruesome death suggested this was a somewhat optimistic view.

Democratically elected leaders like Tony Blair and George W. Bush handle things differently. Once out of office, they write reputation-enhancing autobiographies and engage in lucrative speaking tours to persuade us that their legacies are good, their decisions wise, their hearts pure, despite the problems caused by their policies. Twenty-first century leaders of all types, cultures and backgrounds, from Gaddafi to Obama, from the government of the People's Republic of China to Bin Laden, understand that a leadership story is fundamentally about one thing: control. Leaders want to influence the way we think, the way we vote, who we might kill, what products or corporations we admire, what we consume and how we worship. The leader hopes to manufacture an attractive image of who he or she is, or claims to be. He wants to make it stick in our minds like a catchy tune that we cannot help but hear, and which drowns out any possible criticism. We will examine just how he does this in the following chapter.

Leadership Lesson: Leaders have many qualities, but if they cannot tell stories then they cannot communicate with their followers; consequently, their leadership will fail. The twenty-first century has seen great changes in the ways leaders communicate and hence in the stories they tell. We all tell stories, even those of us who do not aspire to any kind of leadership. We can all learn lessons from those who tell stories most effectively: leaders.

Followership Lesson: We are all followers of something or someone. We need to understand how to deconstruct the stories leaders use to impress us. They have become more adept at crafting stories to make us think well of them. As followers we need to become more adept at figuring out whether these stories are misleading so that, in the words of the old song by The Who, we 'won't get fooled again'. Above all we must remember that for many leaders 'truth' is often less important than 'authenticity', or at least seeming to be authentic.

2 How to Tell a Leadership Story: The Earwig and Lady Gaga

Leaders need stories. They always have and they always will. They adapt their storytelling to the best technology of their day. In the case of Jesus, it was to offer parables and deliver a sermon on a mount so that as many people as possible could come and listen; St Paul wrote letters; Abraham Lincoln took part in public debates; Franklin D. Roosevelt used radio; Barack Obama appears on Oprah. But something has changed profoundly in the past thirty years, not just in the media technology available to leaders and the rest of us, but also in the kinds of stories leaders believe they have to tell to grab our attention, and in the new ways they strive to control the stories we hear about them. To understand the changes of the new media world of the twenty-first century, we first have to understand what has not changed in the need to tell and listen to stories, and how they are implanted in our minds. What follows are the secrets of telling a leadership story.

For thousands of years leaders have used stories to assert, confirm and extend their power, demonstrate their supposed wisdom and secure their reputations among their followers. Leadership stories are not designed as entertainment, although the best ones are often very entertaining. They are about control. Most leaders know that if you control the stories people tell about you, then you control much of what they think about you. Listen to news reports about coups or attempted coups anywhere in the world, and in the early stages there will always be an attempt to secure the TV and radio stations. Coup leaders know that stories matter because they are the easiest form of social control. And what is true for a leader of a military coup is also true for the leader of a religion, a democratically elected government or a business, though there are more subtle means than sending in the army.

The secret weapon of storytellers throughout the centuries has been to create a story which sticks in the mind, just as a successful musician will write a pop song with a melody so powerful that you cannot get it out of your head. Germans call this an *Ohrwurm*, literally an 'earworm', or 'earwig', which won't stop wriggling, whether you like it or not, until it worms its way into your brain. Successful leaders work hard at creating an 'earwig', or they employ others to do it for them. They spend a great deal of time wondering how to communicate their leadership story and subvert the counter-stories told against them. One of the great growth industries of the past thirty years has been in 'communications specialists' – PR companies, publicists, speech writers, ad men, strategists and 'spin doctors' – but leaders have always enlisted help from advisers or acolytes to tell their stories. We learn about Jesus through a group of storytellers we call the Apostles. The rulers of ancient Persia, Greece and Rome employed bards as storytellers to sing of their (supposed) exploits. But when it comes to the creation of an 'earwig', it is not surprising that those with an interest in how leaders communicate in the twenty-first century should choose as instructive models those who have created pop songs that we cannot get out of our heads. Two academics from Antwerp business school, Jamie Anderson and Jörg Reckhenrich, together with Martin Kupp of the European School of Management and Technology, produced a case study in 2011 called 'Lady Gaga: Born This Way?' The authors assert that Lady Gaga is 'one of the first pop stars to have truly built her career through the internet and social media'. She was estimated to earn around $100 million in 2011, and has what the authors call 'leadership projection'. They say that Lady Gaga tells 'three universal stories', which are similar in nature to the stories told by all great leaders, as we will see throughout this book.

Who Am I? Who Are We? What Is Our Common Purpose?

As mentioned in Chapter 1, every leader begins with a personal story, a way of answering the question 'Who am I?' Lady Gaga tells us repeatedly that she was the weird kid at school, though she also turned out to be highly driven and creative. She describes herself as 'a freak, a maverick, a lost soul looking for peers'. Secondly, every leader's story involves a group narrative, a way of explaining 'Who are we?' In Lady Gaga's case 'we' are the outsiders. She calls her fans 'my little monsters', and in her leadership story she is 'Mama Monster' who keeps in touch with her offspring on Facebook and Twitter. Thirdly, all leaders offer a collective mission, the answer to the question 'Where are we going?' or 'What is our common purpose?' Lady Gaga tells her followers that together they can change the world. She promotes a positive message about gay rights. This 'leadership projection' is what most of us would call storytelling.

Every successful leader featured in this book follows Lady Gaga's technique of telling those three universal stories, about themselves, about the group they wish to lead and about the future of their leadership. Whether such stories are true or false is often a question of belief rather than proof. Imagine if in the Old Testament Moses had appeared one day and ordered the Jews to start behaving in a certain way. He had been out in the desert and after a bit of thought he had come up with ten rules. Even if the rules were good ones, would his followers have done as Moses demanded? Possibly. But Moses did far more than just produce some rules. He told his people a story. He said that God himself had given him Ten Commandments, inscribed on pieces of stone. By framing and shaping the Ten Commandments as a story, Moses ensured that the rules were much more likely to be remembered, accepted and obeyed. Like religious leaders throughout history, he also confirmed his own power and influence by claiming a special relationship with the Divinity. This is one of the most ancient and most potent universal stories: Who am I? *Moses, your leader.* Who are we? *We are Jews, the Chosen People.* And what is our common purpose? *To live according to the Commandments God has given us, and to return to the Promised Land.*

The kings of Israel told stories to justify themselves as the chosen leaders of the chosen people, sanctified by God, a practice copied through the ages by kings and khans asserting their divine right to rule, pharaohs, popes and tribal leaders around the world. The Greeks and Romans in their myths, plays and poetry told stories not just about their leaders being linked to the gods, but also about their own shared histories as people. How much more engaging and unifying for Romans that their city was founded by Romulus and Remus, boys suckled by a she-wolf, rather than merely an accident of town planning, a city grown up around a settlement at a fertile, navigable point on the River Tiber. As later Roman rulers might have put it: Who am I? *Civis Romanus Sum, I am a citizen of Rome.* Who are we? *The children of Romulus and Remus.* What is our common purpose? *To conquer and rule the known world.*

The stories leaders tell about themselves and their people, and the stories people tell about their leaders and themselves, are central to all cultures and all times since the beginnings of recorded history, and probably before. Cavemen undoubtedly told stories of their hunting prowess; they certainly illustrated them in the Lascaux caves. We can be sure that prehistoric storytelling went beyond mere facts to ego-boosting tales that enabled successful hunters to make claims to lead their tribes and take the most wives. The great storyteller Philip Pullman is among those who have suggested that mankind created language so that we could tell stories to one another. One of today's most influential Hollywood figures, the screenwriter and creative-writing teacher Robert McKee, puts it slightly differently in *Story*:

Story is not only our most prolific art form but rivals all activities – work, play, eating, exercise – for our waking hours. We tell and take in stories as much as we sleep – and even then we dream … the story arts have become humanity's prime source of inspiration, as it seeks to order chaos and gain insight into human life. Our appetite for story is a reflection of the profound human need to grasp the patterns of living, not merely as an intellectual exercise, but within a very personal, emotional experience.

McKee also points out, in a Hollywood context, something which touches on the craft of storytelling throughout history:

Given the choice between trivial material brilliantly told versus profound material badly told, an audience will always choose the trivial told brilliantly. Master storytellers know how to squeeze life out of the least of things, while poor storytellers reduce the profound to the banal. You may have the insight of a Buddha, but if you cannot tell a story, your ideas turn dry as chalk.

We pay attention to the Buddha precisely because, like Moses, Jesus or Muhammad, he combines *both* great insight *and* great storytelling abilities. It is a quality shared with other great leaders.

I, Caesar

Julius Caesar was one of history's most effective and relentless 'Who am I?' story-controllers. He was so concerned about the way history would regard his exploits that in *De Bellis Gallicis* he wrote about 'Julius Caesar' in the third person, as if he were objectively assessing the career of someone else. He gave the weight of historical judgement to recent events in which he himself was the key player. Not surprisingly, Julius Caesar the author and commentator thought 'Julius Caesar' the warrior to be an excellent fellow. Equally unsurprisingly, Caesar omitted the counter-stories put about by his many rivals – that he had amassed a large personal fortune in the service of Rome and that behind his accounts of his heroic exploits was the larger ambition of a potential tyrant who sought to gain popular support for his power grab.

Winston Churchill did not go quite as far as writing about himself in the third person, but no modern world leader has so extensively chronicled his successes and glossed over his missteps as Churchill himself. In his writings Churchill constantly shaped his leadership story. He tends to underemphasise his views on independence for India, the reasons behind his inability to connect with voters in his landslide electoral defeat in 1945, the terrible fiasco of Gallipoli, and his consistent (but wrong-headed) belief that the Mediterranean constituted the 'soft underbelly' for liberating Europe rather than the Normandy beaches. Churchill carefully rehearsed his speeches, shaped and crafted his image, and made sure that his version of 'Who am I?' drowned out the more critical counter-stories. Churchill's grandson, Nicholas Soames, once asked: 'Grandpa, are you the greatest man in the world?'

'Yes,' said Churchill. 'Now bugger off.'

A story no one would ever forget, and a judgement suggested less succinctly in Churchill's own writings.

Many modern leaders have followed Churchill and Caesar in recognising that one of the best ways to control a leadership story is to write it yourself. The shelves of bookshops groan with the often turgid memoirs of leaders determined to justify their decisions, argue against counter-stories and explain their sometimes unrecognised genius. Some leaders, in the words of the Irish rugby captain Willie John McBride, manage to 'get their retaliation in first', by publishing autobiographical books even before they have achieved anything very much, defining their image before the news media takes an interest.

Hitler's pre-emptive shaping of his leadership story is obvious even from the title of the book *Mein Kampf* (*My Struggle*), published in the 1920s when he was still an obscure figure on the far-right fringes of Weimar democracy. It's a tedious work except for the chapter on propaganda, which is Hitler's considered account of how to communicate a leadership story, in his case recounting his service as an Austrian who enlisted in the German army and fought in the trenches of the First World War, the personal embodiment of the idea of Großdeutschland (Greater Germany). As we will see, this is just one of the many examples of a 'Who am I?' story in which the leader tries to persuade followers that he, and his nation, are one and the same. It's a fiction of course, but as the playwright Jean Anouilh puts it, 'Fiction gives life its form,' or perhaps more accurately, stories give life its meaning.

In modern democracies a serious political leader, significant business titan or cultural leader without a 'Who am I?' storytelling biography has become a rare beast. Richard Branson's autobiography, *Losing My Virginity*, ties his personal story intimately into his business leadership and brand name, the implication being that one of the shrewdest financial brains in the world was at some point a naive business 'virgin'. Top level sports stars like Andre Agassi, Michael Jordan and David Beckham are not leaders in any conventional sense, but they are so wealthy and influential they appear almost to be the CEOs of their own leading 'brand', which happens to be themselves. Agassi, Jordan, Beckham and countless other sportsmen and women have published autobiographies that shape and control their own stories, ramming home on every page anecdotes which appear to reveal their 'true' character, as they see it. Even a topless model, Britain's Katie Price, also known as 'Jordan', has turned her 'Who am I?' story into a commodity, chronicling her own life with the relentless enthusiasm of Samuel Pepys, if not quite with his literary flair. Jordan is very far from being a leader, but the banality of her achievements suggests Robert McKee is right about the importance of story. In the twenty-first century, trivia well told will always capture the imagination better than profundities badly told, as Jordan's success demonstrates. If a topless model can produce a series of best-selling autobiographies by the time she is thirty years old, all of which market her one product – herself – then what opportunities might there be for a real leader in our celebrity-obsessed culture? And what dangers for those who may have talent but who find such intimate 'Who am I?' storytelling difficult to do?

From Fergie to Royalty: 'Just Like Us'

Sir Alex Ferguson, the Manchester United coach, is, unlike some of the above examples, a true leader. He has the most successful track record of any manager in the most competitive football league in the world, the English premiership. But one of the reasons Ferguson is so successful is that he rigorously manages and polices his own leadership story. That story, as he himself tells it, is of a self-made, competitive, tough-minded boy from working-class Glasgow, the shipbuilding area of Govan. He is said to encourage his team by shouting in the faces of players in a manner some (anonymously) describe as like being subjected to the blast of a hairdryer.

Even some of those who owe their positions of leadership to being the son and grandson of kings have taken time to explain their 'Who am I?' story in an autobiography. The 'earwig' of King Abdullah II of Jordan, for example, is that he is a reluctant leader, someone who would have been happy with a more ordinary life, but who nevertheless cannot resist his destiny and duty. When I met King Abdullah, I was struck by his personal humility. In his autobiography he replaces the mystique of monarchy with factual details of his childhood, his friends, his military career and even how he came to fall in love and marry. When he married Queen Rania they honeymooned in the United States, where, he writes in *Our Last Best Chance* (2011), 'we bought a Visit USA Air Pass which allowed us a month of unlimited economy class travel … Occasionally when they heard we were honeymooners, check-in staff would upgrade us to business class.' Note Abdullah's storytelling ability. He was upgraded to business class, in his version of events, not because people knew he was the future King of Jordan but because staff heard that he and Rania were honeymooners. In his pleasure at paying an economy fare but obtaining an upgrade, King Abdullah is 'just like us' – except of course that he isn't. He is the King of Jordan. But if the story connects his privileged royal life with ours, the 'earwig' has worked.

Abdullah is eloquent on the dangers his family faced, turning what could be a story of royal privilege into one of sacrifice and danger: 'My mother never left the house (in Jordan) without a Kalashnikov in the passenger seat and a small Colt revolver in the glove box.' Later he details the toughness of his military training, including at the hands of a British drill sergeant in England: 'Mr Abdullah, there's something I have been meaning to tell you,' the English sergeant tells the future king. 'You're always going to be in the shit. It's just the depth that's going to vary.'

Leaders, even those destined to inherit the throne of their country, often feel the need to relate how they overcame a complicated childhood and a troubled adolescence by relying on a strong family, strong values and a strong personality. Barack Obama, in his pre-emptive autobiography, recounts how he had to deal with the problems caused by an absent father, an unconventional upbringing and the temptation of drugs. Bill Clinton had a father who died before he was born; then he had an adoptive father who was an abusive alcoholic and a brother with a host of personal problems. The implication of these stories is that Obama and Clinton's past 'Who am I?' difficulties help them to empathise with your problems and mine, making them better leaders.

Part of the charm of Nelson Mandela's story in his inspirational 'Who am I?' account *Long Walk to Freedom* is precisely this kind of empathy. Mandela dwells on his roots and origins in the countryside. He chooses to tell us repeatedly how inadequate or unskilled he was, how shy and unable to communicate with girls, how awkward in social situations, how inexperienced in politics or in forming what was to be the armed wing of the African National Congress. We are left with the impression of a modest, likeable and yet determined fellow. His artlessness is artful. Hostile commentators have shaped Mandela's story differently, focusing more on the personal failures within his own family, the extremely unsettling stories about his ex-wife Winnie, and some of the less savoury characters with whom he was associated in the ANC. Mandela, however, got his retaliation in first.

The Story Event

In his how-to book for screenwriters, Robert McKee offers the key to all such 'Who am I?' leadership stories, from the time of Moses to Mandela and beyond. McKee writes of a 'story event' which he says 'creates meaningful change in the life situation of a character'. All this is 'achieved through conflict' with a change for the character (or leader) 'from the positive to the negative or the negative to the positive'. If you thought David Cameron was a Hooray Henry in the Bullingdon Club, for example, a young and irresponsible toff who owed his job at Conservative Central Office to a phone call made on his behalf by a family friend who worked for the Queen, then clearly all his gilded youth did not prepare him for the 'conflict' of the terrible health problems and death of his son Ivan. In McKee's terms, Cameron's 'Who am I?' story went from positive to negative, and then back to positive again with the news that Samantha Cameron was pregnant with another child. In the case of President George W. Bush the 'story event' achieved through conflict was his embrace of Christianity and his decision to stop drinking alcohol.

With Obama and Clinton, it was a more traditional tale of rising through conflict from what could have been a disastrous childhood. The personal story that the German Chancellor

Angela Merkel tells, however, is one of repeated conflict as an outsider who came inside. Merkel was the daughter of a Lutheran pastor from northern Germany, but now leads a largely Roman-Catholic-influenced grouping with strong support in Bavaria and the south of Germany. She lived under communism, yet now leads Europe's most successful capitalist country. She is from the old East and yet her country's political and economic power lies in the West. She is a woman in a country that formerly had only male leaders, some of them aggressively masculine; and she is a scientist by training in a political class that tends to lean towards arts or social sciences. At every stage Merkel's narrative fits the McKee 'story event' principles, as a tale of achievement through conflict, but with variations suitable for modern Germany, which requires that such 'conflict' be low key. Merkel uses stolidity, perseverance and homeliness to her advantage, something that is summed up in her own nickname (one that to many Germans has also become an 'earwig') – *Mutti*: mummy.

The Risks of Emotional Commitment

So, to recap: how do they do it? How do all the significant leaders here create a story that sticks in the brain – the 'earwig' – and control it in the face of critics and counter-stories? From Moses to Obama, from Caesar and Hitler to Churchill, Clinton and Blair, from King Abdullah II to Angela Merkel, leaders follow the route academic researchers have described Lady Gaga as taking. They begin just as you or I might do when we introduce ourselves to strangers, potential employers, dating partners, university admissions tutors and others: we answer the question 'Who am I?' and we frame our answer in terms which, we hope, will make us look good. Some of us do this in more personal terms than others. Lady Gaga has the 'ability to build emotional commitment' by telling her personal story, according to the academic authors who have studied her success. They claim they have found her techniques useful in trying to identify future business leaders. But there are significant risks in telling a highly personal 'Who am I?' story, since it may encourage a highly personal counter-story attack, as we will see later in Chapter 9, *Story Wars*. First we need some lessons from the great masters of storytelling, the ones who create the 'earwigs' that have the power to move us all.

Leadership Lesson: Leaders tell stories they hope will stick in our minds like earwigs wriggling in our ears. Typically they begin with their origins and personality by answering the question 'Who am I?' It is the one part of their story they should find most easy to control.

Followership Lesson: The stories leaders tell us are not facts. They are not accidents. They are narratives deliberately shaped to engage our attention. Leaders, even great and admirable ones like Nelson Mandela and Winston Churchill, emphasise the parts of their life-story that they want us to hear and gloss over the parts that are not to their advantage. So do the rest of us.

3   Words, Pictures, Action: Lessons from the Masters of Spin

Spin, like sin, has always been with us. So have spin doctors. Even if the name is new, the role is as ancient as leadership itself. As we have seen, leaders have always tried to manage the stories they tell about themselves, and control the stories others tell about them. Often they seek help from followers to do so. Some followers, like St Paul, shape the leader's story to such an extent that they emerge as leaders in their own right. Nowadays shaping stories for leaders has become a profession. These paid advisers may call themselves by various names: public relations consultants, communications directors, marketing managers and, pejoratively, spin doctors. They are twenty-four-hour PR people. They know, or claim to know (for they are adept at spinning stories about their own usefulness), how to get positive stories in newspapers, how to keep damaging stories out of newspapers and how to ensure that the stories the leader tells will make the most impact. This chapter is about three of the most influential storytelling experts of recent times: Newt Gingrich, Michael Deaver and Alastair Campbell. I have chosen them because they each teach a significant lesson from which we can all learn.

It is difficult to say the word 'spin' nowadays without a curled lip and a scornful tone. A spin doctor is someone who tells or embellishes a leadership story to try to influence the way we think and behave. By definition, the word 'spin' in its political sense points to a lack of truthfulness or authenticity. Associated with the so-called 'father of spin' Edward Bernays, the phrase 'spin doctor' became popular in the 1980s, and the *New York Times* was one of the first publications to use it, stating in its coverage of the October 1984 presidential debate between Ronald Reagan and his opponent Walter 'Fritz' Mondale:

> A dozen men in good suits and women in silk dresses will circulate smoothly among the reporters, spouting confident opinions. They won't be just press agents trying to import a favourable spin to a routine release. They'll be Spin Doctors, senior advisors to the candidates.

These advisers were of course 'spinning a yarn', telling a story, for the benefit of their leaders. There is nothing inherently wrong with that process. Some of the most influential and admired world leaders, Jesus and the Prophet Muhammad among them, owe part of their reputations to followers who deliberately used stories to shape opinions, make converts and alter behaviour in support of their religious leaders. St Paul was among the most successful of religious spin doctors. He occupied a leadership role within the early church and profoundly influenced its teachings. Religious scholars debate how far Christianity was shaped directly by Jesus and how far by Paul's retelling of the Christian story. Storytelling is never neutral or objective. The Gospels of Matthew, Mark, Luke and John, together with the writings of St Paul, have broadly the same purpose but each has a different emphasis and point of view, and there are some apparent contradictions. You can no more separate the storyteller from his version of the story than separate the dancer from the dance.

Avicenna, Maimonides and Thomas Aquinas are among the most interesting of religious thinkers and yet, at their core, they are also trying to influence the stories we tell about their religious faiths. Jews, Christians, Muslims, Hindus, Buddhists and Sikhs all repeat the inspiring moral stories from their holy books, scriptures, parables and *hadith*, paying particular attention to the stories attributed to the leaders of their faiths, but as they retell the stories, they reshape them. While 'spin' is nowadays considered to be among the Dark Arts, there is nothing inherently wrong with a leader, or one of his followers, trying to communicate, explain or extrapolate from a leadership story, to place an emphasis on a particular part of that story, and to do so in the most effective way possible. What is wrong is lying or deliberately misleading people. We are about to discover, yet again, how profoundly things have changed in the last few decades.

Spin Cycle

Newt Gingrich, Alastair Campbell and Michael Deaver can all teach leaders, and the rest of us, how to construct an effective leadership story, deftly answering the questions 'Who am I?', 'Who are we?' and 'What is our common purpose?' They show clearly how we can make the best of what we've got, how we can minimise our weak points and how we may be able to exploit those of our opponents. They also suggest how we can transform our own leadership story to bring about change, and to bring people with us. We'll begin with Gingrich, because he is particularly insightful on the words we should use.

As he began running for the presidency of the United States in 2011, Newt Gingrich defined 'Who am I?' in his own inimitable way: 'God wanted me to be a bear, not a gazelle'. These ten words give a hint of Gingrich's storytelling genius. He reminds God-fearing Americans that he too is a Christian believer, and depicts himself as a slow-moving, stolid and powerful bear rather than a quick and flighty gazelle. This is, to mix up our animal metaphors, a classic Gingrich 'earwig'.

Newton Leroy McPherson was born in Harrisburg, Pennsylvania, in 1943 and took the name Gingrich when his mother remarried. He was the principal architect of a document called *Contract with America*, published in 1994, a brilliant piece of political salesmanship which led to the Republican landslide in elections that year. Subtitled 'the bold plan by Representative Newt

Gingrich, Representative Dick Armey and House Republicans to Change the Nation', *Contract with America* talks glowingly of a 'meaningful mandate for change' and 'a common-sense agenda', and is an object lesson in the significance of vocabulary, whether you aspire to lead a country, write a job application, make a sale or plan a presentation to impress your bosses. It also reveals how important it is to be aware of what political strategists call 'dog whistle' politics, the use of certain words which, like a dog whistle, trigger an almost immediate response.

'Bold', 'meaningful', 'mandate' and 'change' are four of the positive words that Gingrich often uses when telling stories about his own side – 'Who are we?' – although what these words actually mean is open to interpretation. The *Contract* then moves on to 'What is our common purpose?' It praises 'individual liberty – economic opportunity – limited government – personal responsibility – security at home and abroad'. Again, who can argue against this motherhood-and-apple-pie common purpose? Every word is positive, unobjectionable and vague. Gingrich understands the power these words can have. In 1996 he and his colleagues in GOPAC – a political action committee chaired by Gingrich and on which he was the leading intellectual light – privately circulated a document to Republican candidates which speaks of 'Language, a Key Mechanism for Control'. Control is the important point. Gingrich realised that if he could control the words people use to describe leaders, political parties or common purpose, then he could control his leadership story, and if he could do that, he would also control the political debate. Gingrich's document lists two sets of words, which, he noted in a covering letter, are 'from a recent series of focus groups where we actually tested ideas and language'. Here's a selection from the first list – 'Optimistic Positive Governing Words', which 'can help give extra power to your message':

candid, care, challenge, change, children, courage, debate, dream, environment, family, hard work, legacy, liberty, opportunity, peace, proud, reform, share, tough, we/us/our ...

Anyone reading the biographies of the American leaders I mention in Chapter 5 will note how many times these 'optimistic, positive, governing' words, or similar ones, appear, and how often they also appear in Bill Clinton's speeches, or those of Barack Obama and George W. Bush. Such words are strongly value-loaded, which means they are useful to any political ideology in any culture because they are like mirrors: we see in them what we want to see. They are frequently used by British politicians and, in translation, in the speeches of Angela Merkel, Silvio Berlusconi, Vladimir Putin, Nicolas Sarkozy and, for that matter, Fidel Castro. If you excised those twenty or so words from the speeches of David Cameron, Tony Blair or most political and business leaders, there would in many cases be very little left.

Now here are some thoughts from the GOPAC document on the 'contrasting' words Gingrich and his colleagues suggest should be used to describe your opponents (Who are they? What is their purpose?), followed by a selection from this list:

Remember that creating a difference helps you ... Apply these to the opponent, their record, proposals, and their party: bureaucracy, cheat, collapse, corrupt, crisis, cynicism, decay, destroy, destructive, failure, hypocrisy, incompetent, selfish, sick, steal, traitors, urgent, waste ...

The list goes on and on, reading like America's haemorrhoidal Fox News network where everything is an 'outrage', and where waste, corruption and hypocrisy cheat us towards perdition. This time the dog whistle is designed not to make us salivate, but to bark in fury.

It's worth emphasising that these lists are policy-free. Gingrich is not telling his Republican candidates how to decide which policies they advocate or how to explain them. He is merely offering words to describe Republican ideas as 'tough' or 'courageous' while the Democrats pursue policies which must be 'corrupt' or 'wasteful'. It is an all-purpose storytelling toolkit. It is hardly surprising that, as Tony Blair observed in his memoirs, journalists and voters are not much interested in policy when the Gingrich vocabulary used by so many political leaders fits any policy, any situation, any political party and any culture, from Iran, Ireland and Israel to Idaho and Iowa. The power of leadership is the power to tell and shape stories about yourself ('dream', 'hard work', 'proud') and about your opponent ('crisis', 'failure', 'traitors') using the vocabulary that you choose. Choosing the vocabulary means choosing the ground on which you will fight, like a football team playing in front of a home crowd. It is a way of maximising control.

But there is a catch. Voters are increasingly cynical of politicians who shovel value-loaded words around like a farmer shovelling manure. What worked in 1994 for Gingrich is losing its power in the twenty-first century.

Hope is me – Fear is you

In the 2010 British general election the Conservative Party suggested the British people had a choice between 'hope' (Conservatives) and 'fear' (the Labour Party.) This was a simple but effective use of a similar message delivered by the Labour leader Tony Blair thirteen years earlier. In 1997 Blair declared that it was Labour that represented 'hope', whereas the Tories exemplified 'fear'. Then in May 2011 in the campaign to change British voting practices towards the alternative vote system, the new Labour leader Ed Miliband re-trod that old favourite and said voters again had a choice between 'hope' (Miliband himself, and changing the voting system) and 'fear' (the Conservatives, who wanted to keep the same old system). The constant peeping of tired dog-whistle words can, of course, become irritating, especially if voters could not see why the old voting system was somehow associated with 'fear' while a new and more complicated one offered 'hope.' As soon as the general public begins to wonder if such an emotive vocabulary is being mis-used, then it fails, rather like a once powerful antibiotic which has been prescribed too often and so loses its effectiveness.

For Gingrich, the blowback came quickly. Bill Clinton also understood that language was a key mechanism for control. From 1994 onwards Clinton struggled with Gingrich at every stage to define US politics according to his own vocabulary, or to steal Republican language and put it to use for his own benefit. In 1995 Clinton declared that 'the era of Big Government is over', echoing precisely Republican sentiment in Republican words, annexing his opponent's definition of 'our common purpose'. Then, when Gingrich's Republican Revolutionaries refused to agree a budget, the US federal government was forced to close down due to lack of funds. Public servants were not paid. Clinton's Democrats took Gingrich's slogan 'Contract *with* America' and altered it to 'Contract *on* America', making it sound like a mafia hit. By changing just one word, the Clinton team masterfully suggested that Gingrich was killing the country by provoking the longest government shutdown in US history. And when a right-wing fanatic blew up the Oklahoma City federal building and killed more than 160 people, including children in a day-nursery, Clinton suggested that it was the inflammatory anti-government words used by Gingrich and his friends that had encouraged right-wing extremists to physically attack the institutions of the United States and kill people. The *coup de grâce* for Gingrich came when he fell into a trap of his own making. He suggested to reporters that he had been snubbed by President Clinton on a flight back on Air Force One from the funeral of the assassinated Israeli prime minister Yitzhak Rabin. Clinton had refused to invite him into the presidential quarters on the aircraft to continue their important budget discussions. Helped along by Clinton's own spin-team, the media reports suggested that Gingrich was not as he presented himself in his fine words – 'change', 'bold', 'hope' – some kind of doughty revolutionary bringing about fundamental change to the way America was governed. In complaining about Air Force One, many Americans saw Gingrich as just another crafty politician on the make, concerned more about his own ego and comfort than the high minded struggle about the future direction of the United States.

In Hollywood movie storytelling, the gap between what a character *says* and what he *does* is called dramatic irony. In leadership storytelling it is called hypocrisy, and derided as 'politics as usual.' Gingrich sounded petty and started to lose credibility, which meant he also lost the struggle to define the political battleground and control of the vocabulary of change. It cost him his job, while Bill Clinton kept his. The key message from Gingrich is nevertheless vitally important in story-telling. The words that a leader uses about himself, his party or his country, are at the core of his leadership, but if voters believe a politician is merely mouthing the vocabulary dreamed up by focus groups and clever rhetoricians, they will rebel against what seems phoney and manipulative. Back in 1984 Gingrich observed in *Window of Opportunity*:

> People are not, in general, stupid, but they are often ignorant. In their ignorance they often tolerate ignorant news reporters who, in turn, tolerate ignorant politicians. The result is an ignorant politician making an ignorant speech to be covered by an ignorant reporter and shown in a forty second clip on television to an ignorant audience.

Gingrich's analysis is characteristically robust, but his ability to turn it into a successful leadership story has always been problematic because of the gap between what he says and what he does. In his ill-fated 2012 campaign he again tried to lead a Republican party committed to 'family values', although he himself has been married three times and admitted to adulterous affairs. When the supposedly ignorant audience suddenly becomes informed of the rhetorician's tricks and recognises his hypocrisy, then ignorance rapidly turns to irritation.

'New Labour, New Britain'

Spin Master Number Two is Alastair Campbell. Once a vital component of 'New Labour', which has seen the most successful electoral period ever for the British Labour Party, Campbell is a master of strategy as well as of communications. He is also a polarising figure. Every time I interview him I receive emails saying he should never be allowed to appear on television because, the complainants say, Campbell is cynical and manipulative. As Labour's communications director, Campbell was Tony Blair's trusted friend and confidant, and he would recognise instinctively the lessons I outline in this book. He would also understand immediately the usefulness of the vocabulary lesson from Newt Gingrich, and the dangers of a senior politician being associated with something so obviously manipulative. Campbell is credited with inventing the 'New Labour, New Britain' slogan, as part of his attempt to ensure that the words 'New Labour' and 'change' were bonded together in the public consciousness, something vital for any leader's story-telling vocabulary, as we will see in detail in Chapter 8. Tony Blair describes Campbell as profoundly important to him, someone who, while remaining loyal and supportive, was able to offer criticisms that questioned Blair's own judgements and made the prime minister think carefully about the decisions he was about to take. Campbell's role in Blair's leadership story has echoes of Harry Hopkins, Franklin D. Roosevelt's aide in the 1930s and 1940s. FDR once said that what was important about Hopkins was that he never wanted anything personally, no honours or favours, beyond the chance to be of service to his country and his leader. Campbell could have forced his way into becoming an MP or a peer in the House of Lords, but he didn't.

The Campbell counter-stories are of bullying and ruthlessness. He is widely believed to be the model for Malcolm Tucker, the intimidating Scottish hard-case spin doctor played by Peter Capaldi in Armando Iannucci's TV series *The Thick of It* and the feature film *In the Loop*. But however much of a hate figure he has become for some people, Alastair Campbell remains one of the greatest and most successful political communicators in British politics since the Second World War.

The Golden Rule: objective, strategy, tactics

I first met Campbell in the early 1990s. He was then political editor of the Labour-supporting tabloid the *Daily Mirror*, and I have met him often in different venues, formal and informal, ever since. At a conference for National Health Service leaders I attended a few years ago, Campbell explained, in terms that everyone from a nursing sister or doctor to a university applicant, assistant bank manager, military commander or even a prime minister could understand, that any significant act of leadership has three parts: objective, strategy, and tactics. Successful leadership means getting these three parts in the correct order, and understanding how they relate to each other.

First, Campbell said, you must be absolutely clear about your objective, what I have earlier called 'our common purpose'. Campbell's objective in 1997 was to ensure that Tony Blair's New Labour Party was elected to government. Secondly, Campbell said, you must shape your strategy by ensuring that every part of it is directed towards gaining your objective. Campbell's strategy was to redefine the Labour Party – 'Who are we?' – in the eyes of British voters, in order to make it electable. 'New' Labour was, Campbell's strategy insisted, no longer the tax-and-spend, bad 'Old' Labour that had lost countless elections, but a fiscally conservative, hard-headed party fit for government. Finally, Campbell instructed the NHS workers, you must employ whatever tactics are necessary to enhance that strategy and deliver results towards the objective. For example, you might get Tony Blair to say (repeatedly) that he is 'tough on crime, tough on the causes of crime' as part of the strategy of changing Old Labour to New Labour. Or you might adopt broadly the same spending plans as the Conservatives, to show that New Labour is not a tax-and-spend party. In Campbell's analysis, the tactics must be developed *only* to support the strategy, and the strategy is there *only* to secure the objective. What you do *not* do – and Campbell was very clear about this – is let clever tactics distract you from the strategy; nor do you let the sophistication of the strategy blind you to the overall objective. You keep your eyes on the prize. Winning is not the most important thing. It is the *only* thing. That's why people keep score. That's why Tony Blair was electorally the most successful Labour leader in history.

Campbell's analysis of objective–strategy–tactics is exactly the same as defining 'What is our common purpose?' first (objective), then shaping the 'Who are we?'(strategy) part of the story to fit that objective, and finally to shape the 'Who am I?'(tactics) as a series of stories to fit the overall plan. You can also find variations of the objective–strategy–tactics idea in military textbooks from Sun Tzu and *The Art of War* in the sixth century BC to Carl von Clausewitz in the early nineteenth century, or in management textbooks and the leadership stories of prominent businessmen and women. In *Obliquity* (2010), John Kay of the London Business School examines the roundabout methods people use in order to be successful. He recounts a visitor to a cathedral who asks three stonemasons what they are doing. One says, 'I am cutting this stone to shape.' He was your tactics fellow. The second has a sense of the grand strategic vision: 'I am building a great cathedral,' he says. But it is only the third who recognises the true objective: 'I am working for the glory of God.' He, of course, is the leader. Any stonemason who competently cuts stone that does not fit into the overarching cathedral design is useless. Any architect who designs a cathedral but does not recognise it is for the glory of

God is also missing the point. The leader's job is to make everyone understand their individual role ('Who am I?'), telling stories so that everyone on the team understands where they fit in ('Who are we?') and what the real objective should be ('What is our common purpose?'). Campbell got it. That is why he, and New Labour, were so successful.

Picture This

So, if Gingrich teaches us the importance of vocabulary and Campbell offers a lesson in priorities, then the third of our great modern masters, Michael Deaver, can be said to have understood the power of pictures over words. As Ronald Reagan's White House deputy chief of staff, he had special responsibility for managing Reagan's image. He oversaw the Reagan vocabulary while avoiding the overt manipulation we have seen Newt Gingrich demonstrate, and ruthlessly organised Reagan's leadership story in terms of objective, strategy and tactics.

Reagan was elected in November 1980. He took office in January 1981 and was shot and wounded by a deranged gunman, John Hinckley, in Washington just two months later, on 30 March 1981. As Reagan's speechwriter Peggy Noonan put it, the counter-story inside the White House itself was that after the shooting Reagan tired easily and could be profoundly inattentive. But he was also a man whose personal charm was so extraordinary that after titanic political struggles with the Democratic House Speaker Tip O'Neill, O'Neill confessed how much he liked Ronald Reagan personally. They would sit and tell Irish-American humorous stories to one another. A successor to O'Neill, another Irish-American Speaker, Tom Foley of Washington State, told me the same thing. Foley said that Reagan's charm amounted to a kind of political genius. Even many of his enemies liked him. Michael Deaver used this Reagan charm as a political weapon, putting together one of the best communications teams ever seen.

One of the stars of that team, Peggy Noonan, had started

writing for radio and then for one of America's leading TV news anchors, Dan Rather of CBS. Her transition to writing for another great performer, the president of the United States, proved seamless. Deaver made sure that Reagan, despite his many weaknesses, always looked 'presidential', appeared calm and sounded good, especially in times of great trouble. When the space shuttle *Challenger* blew up, the speech written for Reagan by Noonan is one of the most movingly delivered pieces of oratory of the twentieth century. Noonan, in her own account, *What I Saw at the Revolution*, explained how the system worked. The aim was to ensure that on every occasion Reagan appeared to be the embodiment of the United States itself: optimistic, cheerful, resolute. It was always, as one of Reagan's slogans put it, 'Morning in America'. This meant that the many tens of millions of Americans who loathed Reagan's policies – and who therefore disagreed profoundly with Reagan's notion of 'our common purpose' – could still, like Speakers O'Neill and Foley and many others, respect and even like Reagan personally. You do not just elect a president, Noonan observed, you elect a staff.

After the Hinckley assassination attempt, the White House staff made sure Americans learned and loved the story, mentioned in Chapter 1, that Reagan, while badly wounded, had joked to emergency-room doctors that he hoped they were 'all Republicans'. It also became part of Washington folklore that Reagan told his wife Nancy, 'Honey, I forgot to duck' (a line the boxer Jack Dempsey had said to his wife after his defeat in the ring by Gene Tunney). Reagan is then supposed to have quipped to hospital staff, 'All in all, I'd rather be in Philadelphia' (another quote, this time from the actor W. C. Fields, facing the prospect of his own death). These words – whether he actually uttered them or not – rapidly became part of the Reagan legend, and to maintain that leadership story over the next few years, his staff faithfully sheltered him as best they could from the scrutiny of troublesome journalists, lest his weaknesses were cruelly revealed. One TV reporter, Sam Donaldson, became the stentor of the Reagan years, bellowing out questions which Ronald Reagan either did not hear or pretended not to hear. But instead of undermining Reagan, his obvious frailty added to the Reagan charm. He was regarded by many Americans almost as British people regarded the Queen Mother: as beyond politics, and certainly beyond answering impertinent questions about the government that he was supposed to lead. When he ran for re-election in 1984 against the Democrat Walter 'Fritz' Mondale, the Mondale camp tried to use the counter-story that Reagan was too old to be president. The Reagan team, led by Michael Deaver, understood that this counter-story was more damaging than any policy differences. 'Reagan is too old' was an 'earwig' which had to be killed. In the 1984 presidential debate with Mondale, Reagan destroyed it in just two well-rehearsed sentences:

'I want you to know that also I will not make age an issue of this campaign. I am not going to exploit, for political purposes, my opponent's youth and inexperience.'

The audience laughed. Even Mondale laughed. The 'earwig' died. Reagan won the election by a landslide. Deaver laughed last and longest.

Many Voices, One Story

After Reagan's re-election, I met many members of his administration, including the Defense Secretary Caspar Weinberger, the Navy Secretary John Lehman, Secretary of State George Shultz, National Security Advisor General Al Haig and Chief of Staff James Baker III. The Reagan team was a grouping of strong men (and a few women) who operated like competing barons fighting internal wars and settling scores, while trying in public to appear united behind an ageing president. They quarrelled incessantly over the content of Reagan's speeches, because, as Noonan asserts, when the president himself formally made an announcement, the words he used were like Holy Writ. Michael Deaver was a key player in all this. His job depended on understanding the power Reagan had as a storyteller. While the policymakers quarrelled over the words – since these affected their own departmental interests – Deaver focused on the power of pictures.

The veteran US journalist Lesley Stahl illustrates the point. Stahl covered the 1984 Reagan re-election campaign and reported on the contradictions between what Ronald Reagan said, and what his administration actually did, the gap between his avuncular nature and the harshness of some of his policy choices. Reagan had a reputation for contradicting himself, or saying things which seemed nonsensical. During his first presidential election campaign in 1980 Reagan had claimed that 'approximately 80 per cent of our air pollution stems from hydrocarbons released by vegetation, so let's not go overboard in setting and enforcing tough emission standards from man-made sources'. Senator Ted Kennedy and others at the Democratic convention ridiculed Reagan for blaming 'killer trees' for destroying the planet. When tackled about such contradictions, holes in his leadership story or his stretching of the facts, Reagan responded, with typically disarming shrewdness, that in his administration it looked as though 'the right hand does not know what the far right hand is doing'. Again, everybody laughed. The 'Who am I?' Reagan story – that he was Mr Nice Guy – habitually trumped the hard heartedness and confusion in 'our common purpose'. Reporters called him the 'Teflon President': nothing bad ever stuck.

In 1984, as Lesley Stahl recounts in her autobiography *Reporting Live* (1999), she used pictures of President Reagan in typically amiable form visiting a nursing home, and the Special Olympics for children with disabilities. Stahl accurately reported that Reagan opposed funding for public health schemes similar to the nursing home and had cut funding to children with disabilities. Just as with Gingrich's complaints about Air Force One, Reagan's appearances at the nursing home and the Special Olympics had an air of hypocrisy which Stahl exposed, although she worried that this major piece of brave, high-quality journalism would cost her dear:

> I knew the piece would have an impact, if only because it was so long: five minutes and 40 seconds, practically a documentary in Evening News terms. I worried that my sources at the White House would be angry enough to freeze me out.

After the report was broadcast a senior Reagan staffer called Stahl from the White House.

'Way to go, kiddo,' he said. 'What a great piece. We loved it.'

Stahl was amazed. 'Didn't you hear what I said?' she responded.

The senior staffer told her, '*Nobody* heard what you said.' (My italics.)

Stahl wondered if she had heard that correctly. 'Come again?'

'You guys in Televisionland haven't figured it out, have you? When the pictures are powerful and emotional, they override if not completely drown out the sound. I mean it, Lesley. Nobody heard you.'

Nobody heard you. The epitaph TV reporters hate most. What viewers *saw* was a five-minute long report showing pictures of the president at a nursing home and with disabled children, all the time looking 'authentically' concerned, interested and presidential. The Reagan team understood – even if the people in 'Televisionland' were slow to catch on – that you cannot buy such valuable coverage. A former BBC radio colleague of that era used to lecture me endlessly: 'Nobody cares what you wear on the radio. And nobody cares what you say on TV.' When it comes to telling a TV story, Deaver knew that most of us are led by the pictures rather than by the reporter's words. The 'authenticity' of what we see is stronger than the factual truth of the words, policies and apparent hypocrisy.

Manipulating reporters in this way became standard practice in the Reagan White House. Deaver turned creating a 'photo opportunity' into an art form, a skill that was adopted in London by Mrs Thatcher's team and became commonplace around the world. When Reagan made announcements about environmental policy, on which he had a poor record, Deaver and his team would find suitable backdrops in the American West. Reagan looked handsome in a plaid open-necked shirt, and he would be set against a photogenic background, some red rock canyon, river or forest, perhaps riding a horse, Mr Rugged Individualism, identified, as always, with the land of the United States, the embodiment of his nation and its cowboy myths. Reagan could have announced that the Grand Canyon was to be turned into a cement factory, but the pictures told a different leadership story – just as Michael Deaver knew they would. He understood that leadership storytelling is twenty-four hours a day, 365 days a year and 360 degrees in scope.

Research on the impact candidates make during job interviews suggests that the power of the visual image often matters more than words. Some candidates are thought suitable or unsuitable even before they open their mouths. On television, the visual medium of our times, the impact can be even starker. Famously, the Americans who tuned in to the radio to listen to the televised 1960 presidential debate between Richard Nixon and John F. Kennedy thought that Nixon had 'won', whereas those watching the TV thought that he had 'lost' because he sweated and looked ill at ease. In Britain, any politician who puts himself up for scrutiny in an interview on the Radio 4 *Today* programme needs to be master of the subject, while any leader who – like Ronald Reagan – makes a speech on TV against his chosen background can count on the visual image to help control his leadership story.

Leadership Lesson: Leadership stories demand the careful use of words: a positive vocabulary about the leader, and at times a very negative vocabulary directed at rivals and competitors. On television, pictures can be even more important. Telling a leadership story is like Snakes and Ladders. Making a speech in a controlled environment is a Ladder, something likely to enhance the leader's reputation. But giving an interview, especially on an argumentative radio programme or to a newspaper journalist, is potentially a Snake, because it is very difficult for the leader to control.

Followership Lesson: Listen to the words carefully. Look at the pictures even more carefully. Be aware that these words and pictures are not accidents. They are like dog whistles. The aim is to make you salivate or bark, without necessarily explaining why you should.

4   The Globalisation of Gossip

This chapter is concerned not with what we can learn from leaders, but with how changes to the media have altered the way in which they communicate their stories to their staff, their customers, their voters and supporters or potential supporters around the world. The media landscape has changed more quickly in the past thirty years than at any time since the invention of printing. Most of us use the phrase 'Information Age' to explain the technology or delivery systems for the explosion of information available instantaneously in the twenty-first century. But there's a catch. Much of this information is unreliable, distorted, easily manipulated or lies. In our search for stories we can trust, we are therefore often much more receptive to the things leaders tell us that seem 'authentic' and convey something personal about who they 'really are'. But how can we know for sure? As we will discover, 'authenticity' can be faked. That is especially dangerous in a world in which gossip has become globalised.

Here are some examples of the stories that modern leaders have told. All have something in common. Each story, offered voluntarily by a leader, would have been seen even a few years ago as too private for a leader to tell and too prurient for a newspaper or TV programme to publish.

Story One: In April 2010, David Cameron, the man who was about to become prime minister of the United Kingdom, gave an interview to the *Mail on Sunday* magazine. He was asked whether he had ever committed adultery. Cameron replied that he had not. Have a look at my gorgeous wife Samantha, was his retort. 'Why would you?' he asked. He was also asked about when the couple had had procreative sex, and Cameron answered that it was at Christmas 2009. Samantha Cameron's pregnancy was one of the more charming stories of the May 2010 British general election campaign. Fecundity among leaders ticks the box that journalists call 'Human Interest'; spin doctors love pregnancy stories because babies are good news, and remind voters that leaders are 'just like us'. Not even the most devious politician would fake a pregnancy (as far as I know). But would anyone in the 1980s have dared ask Mrs Thatcher about her sex life? Or when she conceived her children? Would Mrs Thatcher have shown Cameron's good humour in answering such questions?

Story Two: President Barack Obama, in his 1995 autobiography *Dreams from My Father*, revealed that as a young man he smoked marijuana and tried cocaine. Obama offered the information before some investigative reporter or political rival could dig it up as a negative counter-story. It was 'authentic' – as with a pregnancy, why would he lie about drug use? – and it was 'just like us', in the sense that he was admitting a human frailty, although only after he had rejected and overcome it. Stories about redemption are extremely popular with spin doctors. George W. Bush turned the negative counter-story of his alcoholism and bad-boy ways to his advantage and emphasised the redemptive power of religion. Obama got his retaliation in first, by creating a positive pre-story of just saying no to drugs, thirteen years before he would run for the presidency. It meant that by 2008 the drug story was old news. Nevertheless, can you imagine John F. Kennedy voluntarily discussing his use of painkillers? Or Winston Churchill being forthright about his dependency on alcohol?

Story Three: Max Mosley was the boss of one of the world's most popular sports, Formula One motor racing. In February 2011 he explained in a lengthy interview with the *Financial Times* that he enjoyed consensual sadomasochistic sex with prostitutes. This interview came after a libel case in which Mr Mosley had successfully sued the now defunct British tabloid newspaper the *News of the World*, which had sensationalised the sex story. Mr Mosley became a strong campaigner for privacy legislation. The author of the in-depth *Financial Times* feature admitted that despite this personal interview on private matters, she never felt she got to understand what Mr Mosley was really like. I have met and interviewed Mr Mosley a number of times and have found him an eloquent and effective advocate of privacy legislation, but I could not say what he is really like either.

Story Four: During the 2010 British general election campaign, Gordon Brown, the man David Cameron defeated, talked movingly on television about the death of one of his children, while his finance minister, the Chancellor of the Exchequer Alistair Darling was asked in a televised encounter with the interviewer Piers Morgan whether he was good in bed. A few months before the election, Nick Clegg, the leader of the Liberal Democrats, who was to become Britain's deputy prime minister, was asked how many women he had slept with. He settled on a number around thirty.

Now: all these stories clearly form part of our increasingly confessional culture. They have become commonplace to the point of being unremarkable. But can you really imagine Ronald Reagan being asked how many women he had slept with? General de Gaulle? Mikhail Gorbachev? Richard Nixon? Can you imagine a well-known business or sports personality of thirty years ago, the Max Mosley of his day, willingly discussing his sadomasochistic use of prostitutes? More astoundingly, can you imagine the *Financial Times* a few decades ago wanting to tell such a story?

Some newspapers have always been interested in the private lives of leaders, but what they reported in the past was much more limited than now. In the 1930s British newspapers were circumspect about the abdication of Edward VIII and his love for

Wallis Simpson. As we saw in the hit film *The King's Speech* (2010), even the stuttering of Edward's successor, George VI, was a matter for embarrassment rather than revelation.

But by the 1990s British newspapers showed much less caution over Princess Diana and Prince Charles, printing, among other things, apparently bugged intimate conversations between Prince Charles and his then mistress, now wife, Camilla Parker Bowles and, in the case of one tabloid, a double-page spread featuring pictures of all Diana's alleged lovers. Fifty or sixty years ago when a leadership story turned on matters of sex, such as the Profumo affair in 1963, it tended to be in the context of a serious political scandal or a breach of national security. John Profumo was Secretary of State for War. He was having sex with Christine Keeler, who was also sleeping with the Russian naval attaché, at a time when war with the USSR seemed possible, even likely, and espionage was an extremely serious matter. Significantly, the Profumo affair was not uncovered by muck-raking journalists. It was raised publicly in the House of Commons by a Labour MP, George Wigg. A journalist asking a leading politician how many women he had slept with was not deemed acceptable in 1963. Apparently it is now.

Each of the modern leadership stories I have recounted above reflects the significant social and cultural changes of the past thirty years, changes in attitudes to privacy and sex, changes in the media, and a consequent change of emphasis in what we expect from our leaders in terms of the stories they tell. There has been a shift from a media more focused on substance, competence and policy – with, say, Churchill, de Gaulle and Roosevelt – to a media obsessed at all levels with character, confession and charisma (or lack of it), with Cameron, Obama, Gingrich, Sarkozy, Berlusconi, Brown, Clegg and the others. Above all we have shifted towards a search for 'authenticity', the desire to read and hear the 'real' story behind our 'real' leaders and their 'real' lives, to find out what they are 'really like'. This opens the door to significant manipulation by media advisers as they offer to trade access to the leader in exchange for favourable coverage.

The Internet, competing twenty-four-hour television news channels, the convenience of BlackBerries, iPhones, iPads, Facebook, Twitter, Google, Wikipedia, YouTube, emails and so on, did not exist thirty years ago. No one had ever heard of an 'app'. But the new technology is only the most visible part of the story. When the *form* of information delivery changes, so does its *content*. The publication of the vast trove of documents known as WikiLeaks was made possible only because so much information can now be stored on a small piece of hardware. In the past no one individual could ever have hoped to carry away so many pages of information on US diplomacy as Bradley Manning did. Such secrets would have remained hidden for decades, perhaps for ever.

Many well-known figures are responsible for these profound changes in the media. You might start with Tim Berners-Lee, the inventor of the World Wide Web, or the media barons we have already discussed, including the Australian-American Rupert Murdoch, or Italy's Silvio Berlusconi, or Julian Assange of WikiLeaks. You might also think of media strategists and manipulators like Tony Blair's communications director Alastair Campbell or Ronald Reagan's Michael Deaver. You might throw in the Saatchi Brothers, Microsoft's Bill Gates, Apple's Steve Jobs, Facebook's Mark Zuckerberg and the creators of Twitter. But a largely unknown creative genius stands behind some of the most significant and least understood trends in our modern world. He is an old-fashioned Spaniard called Eduardo Sánchez Junco, and he helped to change the stories that leaders tell all across the world.

Hola! Eduardo

Eduardo Sánchez Junco was born in 1943 and brought up in Barcelona. His father Antonio was editor of a newspaper. In 1944 his mother came up with the idea for a magazine showing the beautiful things of life, a magazine which, given the nature of fascist Spain under General Franco towards the end of the Second World War, would have to be cheerful, respectful and accurate. *Hola!* was born, better known to most English readers nowadays as *Hello!* When Eduardo assumed control of *Hola!* he took a moderately successful family project and turned it into one of the greatest publishing sensations of the last fifty years.

At the time of his death in July 2010, his name was unknown to most people outside publishing, but his magazines were famous around the world. *Hola!* and its clones reflect the rapid changes in public taste in the last few decades, and by reflecting taste, they have also transformed it. By the early 1990s Sánchez Junco and others, including Oprah Winfrey, Phil Donahue and Jerry Springer, had pioneered a confessional style that encouraged celebrities and then politicians and other leaders to talk publicly about matters which once would have been regarded as private and even shameful: drug abuse, adultery, prostitution and sexual affairs. The consequences have been profound. Sánchez Junco's part in the transformation of our taste, combined with the new technology of the Internet and mobile phones, has seen trivial stories told around the world in an instant. I call this phenomenon 'the globalisation of gossip'. It has accelerated the collapse of any notion of privacy. These factors taken together have contributed to a sea change in the ways leaders in every field of human endeavour, from Formula One's Max Mosley to those at the White House, the Élysée Palace and Buckingham Palace, now try to manage their leadership stories. American commentators talk of the 'Oprahfication' of American culture. A more accurate analysis would be to speak of the Juncofication or Junkification of journalism and of culture around the world.

The Junkification of Journalism

Hola! was launched as *Hello!* in Britain in 1988, and has since spread to seventy countries, including Brazil, India, Canada, Malaysia, Russia, Thailand, Morocco and Turkey. This magazine and its competitors, including *OK!*, *Now* and, you may think, any magazine with an exclamation mark in the title, have a confessional-celebrity tone which easily crosses over into TV and radio. Oprah Winfrey, whose career also took off in the 1980s, pitches her shows at a similar level: upbeat, cheerful, personal, and generally not significantly challenging to her guests or the audience. The words 'amazing' and 'fascinating' occur frequently on Oprah Winfrey's website, and a typical aspirational storyline might invite you to 'meet the billionaire mom and author', or learn 'the best way to turn failure into success'. There is of course nothing wrong with aspiration or, in my view, with Oprah Winfrey. I have interviewed her and found her thoughtful and inspiring. She was eloquent when talking of her support for the good causes she espouses, especially literacy as an escape from poverty, and she is a shrewd businesswoman and an engaging interviewer. And she actually *listens* – unlike many other chat-show hosts, who often use guests merely as a foil for their own egocentric genius. But the trends Sánchez Junco and Oprah Winfrey unleashed have changed the way stories are told, first by celebrities, then by people in power, and now by the rest of us.

Sánchez Junco spoke of his magazines as 'the froth of life' ('*la espuma de la vida*'), 'always tasteful and discreet'. The articles are bubbly, anodyne and collusive, a bargain between consenting adults, and are beautifully illustrated. The photographs tend to flatter the subjects and their possessions, rather like eighteenth-century portraits of the European aristocracy or landed gentry with their dogs, horses, guns, houses and land in the background. All these positive storytelling opportunities on *Oprah* or in *Hello!* were to strike a chord with leaders and their media advisers, who were constantly searching for glossy, sympathetic, *controlled* contact with tens of millions of readers, listeners and viewers. A former editor of a British magazine similar to *Hello!* explained to me that many of the celebrities who 'open up' to these 'froth of life' magazines allow pictures of their homes, families and supposedly 'intimate' moments to be published because in return they receive often quite significant amounts of cash and the guarantee of positive publicity. It is the twenty-first century equivalent of an eighteenth-century commissioned painting where the artist chooses to soften lines and avoid the subject's blemishes. The result is something which often reads like free advertising. That's because it *is* free advertising – a fact that leaders, especially politicians and their advisers, understand. Even sending in the tanks to surround the radio and TV stations after a coup does not achieve as much positive media coverage as a puff piece in a celebrity magazine. But, of course, it has come at a price. It could be a bargain with the devil.

Celebrity as Commodity

The genius of Sánchez Junco was to understand that celebrity would become a tradeable commodity, bought and sold like coffee beans or copper, although differing from real commodities in that it can be manufactured from otherwise useless ingredients. The case of the topless model Jordan is an obvious example. She has become, in one of the clichés of this new media world, 'famous for being famous', but this dismissive language underestimates her skill at expertly commodifying her life story. Jordan is most certainly not a leader, but she does tell her trivial story brilliantly. She took the first step essential in every leadership story by explaining 'Who am I?' to anyone who showed an interest, and has now become a best-selling author of novels which are ghostwritten by someone else. You could see this as moving from fact to fiction, but it is simply the substitution of one type of storytelling for another. As Robert McKee puts it in *Story*:

The weakest possible excuse to include anything in a story is: 'But it actually happened.' Everything happens; everything imaginable happens. Indeed, the unimaginable happens. But story is not life in actuality. Mere occurrence brings us nowhere near the truth. What happens is fact, not truth. Truth is *what we think about* what happens.

Stories, including biographies and autobiographies, are contrivances, not accidents. They are manufactured, not stumbled across like lumps of coal or gold found naturally occurring in the environment. Leaders, and their advisers, slowly began to notice that something was changing profoundly in our culture and in the kinds of stories people wanted to hear and be told. The question was how could leaders take advantage of it? The answer was to be more personal, more intimate, and to claim to be more 'authentic' when answering the question I have often been asked about all the leaders I have met: *What is he really like?*

Screaming for Attention

A former Fleet Street editor commented on Sánchez Junco's 'froth of life' achievement worldwide: 'Gossip was therefore transformed from a whisper over the garden wall … into a scream for attention on the spot-lit drawing room sofa' (*Daily Telegraph*, 15 July 2010). The sociologist Professor Stuart Hall puts it differently. Hall calls such stories a 'personalising transformation' for the celebrity or politician involved, making us think better, or at least differently, about them. Imagine, therefore, because their media advisers certainly do, a world in which presidents of the United States, prime ministers of Great Britain or Japan, chancellors of Germany and chief executives of multinational corporations like BP and Microsoft can avoid the inbuilt hostility and negativity of the White House press corps, the international press commentariat and those despicably cocky interviewers on the BBC. Imagine a world without what the professionals call 'the media filter' provided by journalists. This is a world in which leaders can get their messages across through intimate 'Who am I?' moments with soft interviewers in nice magazines or a spot on a sofa on an uplifting TV programme, without being asked anything too awkward, except to talk about those bits of their 'real' life that they agree to discuss, to 'share their pain'. Forget the policies, economic catastrophes and wars. Pass the Kleenex as we observe their 'personalising transformation'.

Leaders, and their advisers, spotted one other benefit from 'froth of life' journalism. Sánchez Junco paid, it is reported, £1 million for paparazzi pictures and negatives of Diana, Princess of Wales, sunbathing topless. You have not seen these pictures in his magazines. He never published them. What Sánchez Junco did do was to buy them up to prevent others from doing so, burnishing his reputation as a decent fellow in a sea of sharks, and contributing to his own leadership story. A new generation of media fixers have learned from Sánchez Junco. They sometimes go under the name of 'reputation managers', or PR advisers. Part of their job is to broker deals between celebrities and the highly competitive celebrity-obsessed magazines and newspapers. The editor of one such magazine told me, 'Most of their job is to keep stories *out* of the newspapers.' How do you do that? I wondered. One way, he said, is 'by offering them something else that they can print – something that is more in your client's interest'.

One of the most insightful and best known of this new breed in Britain is Max Clifford, a leader in the field. Clifford's own 'Who am I?' story is that of a man in touch with ordinary people and popular taste. He once talked to me about how he made a point of asking the opinions of people he met in a chip shop about phone hacking and other matters, to get a glimpse of how people were reacting to the big newspaper stories of the day. Clifford believes he acts ethically in his clients' interests, and on several occasions he has expressed to me his loathing for journalists who hack into phones in pursuit of gossip. He himself was a target of hacking and received significant compensation from Rupert Murdoch's News International. When I asked Clifford if phone hacking could ever be justified, he said that it possibly could in the case of terrorists or paedophiles, but that was it. He readily admits a large part of his job is, as I have described, not selling stories to newspapers but the opposite – trying to keep damaging counter-stories out of newspapers, while promoting the more positive stories his clients are keen to tell. Political spin doctors have told me they admire Max Clifford's talents, and have learned from him how to handle some of the pitfalls facing a leader in trouble.

One other media figure – and a leader of sorts – provides a shrewd assessment of how this new media landscape has transformed leadership in the twenty-first century. He is a leader in pornography, Larry Flynt, the proud publisher of *Hustler* magazine and a well-known campaigner for freedom of speech. Flynt, played by Woody Harrelson in the movie *The People vs Larry Flynt* (1996), has become a scourge of sexual hypocrisy in the US Congress and elsewhere. Harrelson effectively captured Flynt's Flyntiness. When I talked with Flynt about his book *One Nation Under Sex* (2011), which documents the hypocrisy of American leaders over sex scandals, I asked him for his explanation of this new, more intrusive age of globalised gossip. He suggested that the end of the Cold War played a big part, and that we were reverting to earlier models of scurrilous reporting. 'Nineteenth-century newspapers also considered the sex lives of politicians fair game,' Flynt writes in *One Nation Under Sex*:

> because a candidate's personal history was seen as a barometer of how he would behave in public office. Not until the early twentieth century did journalists adopt a professional code of ethics that prohibited reporting on the private lives of politicians … The rise of tabloid journalism and the end of the Cold War, however, freed the press to once again report on White House sex.

Historically, in Europe and the United States, pamphleteers and scurrilous journalists – including Benjamin Franklin – regarded the private lives of people in power as legitimate targets. But from the start of the First World War in 1914 right through to the fall of communism in 1989 the world was more or less at war, first with Kaiser Wilhelm, then with Hitler, Mussolini and Japanese militarism, and finally in the Cold War with the Soviet Union and communist China. Throughout most of this past century of conflict, editors of newspapers, radio and TV programmes in democratic countries recognised that, as Flynt put it to me, 'it was important that they protect the president … they were part of the establishment'. Flynt argues in his book that 'the media's current obsession with political sex scandals is actually not a new phenomenon but a return to the roots of the American political tradition. Bloggers are the new pamphleteers.' Benjamin Franklin would have understood the popularity of bloggers like Matt Drudge and Perez Hilton, as well as of *Hello!* and Oprah Winfrey. The difference in the twenty-first century is that the 'pamphlets' – now blogs or Tweets, or TV reports and pictures uploaded easily on to YouTube – are available instantaneously worldwide. The globalisation of gossip has consequently had a profound effect on leaders and their advisers. It is an opportunity, but it is also a burden. I want to return to the stories from the 2010 British election with which I began this chapter, to demonstrate how stories and storytellers have been changed by this new 'froth of life' media world.

Sailing or Sinking in the New Media Sea

For weeks in early 2010 the future of the United Kingdom was in the balance between Gordon Brown's outgoing Labour government and the two opposition parties, David Cameron's Conservatives and the Liberal Democrats of Nick Clegg. The election was a watershed. It brought Britain something very unusual: a coalition government. But it also emphasised what is truly new in the new politics, new media and culture. On the day in April 2010 when the general election was called by Prime Minister Brown, every British voter knew that the United Kingdom faced the most difficult economic situation for almost eighty years – rising unemployment, a potential debt crisis, failing European economies – and was involved in an unpopular war in Afghanistan. On his TV chat show, Piers Morgan, the former editor of the tabloid *News of the World* and *Daily Mirror*, interviewed the man at the heart of many of these problems, the British Chancellor of the Exchequer, Alistair Darling. Morgan's career spans both those 'red-top' tabloid newspapers and also the reality TV show *Britain's Got Talent*, and in his latest role he has taken over from Larry King as an interviewer on CNN. They discussed the sobering political situation, but Morgan also asked Alistair Darling whether he was good in bed. Later, Morgan said: 'Asking Alistair Darling if he was good in bed was difficult, but I did it. The more shameless you are as an interviewer the better the interview. I have no shame about asking anyone anything. But then I am shameless.' (*Observer* 4 April 2010.) As it happens, asking people if they are good in bed cannot be that difficult for Piers Morgan since he has also put the same question to the Labour leader Ed Miliband, the Liberal Democrat leader Nick Clegg, and the opera singer Katherine Jenkins.

During the 2010 election campaign the wife of David Cameron, Samantha, (or 'Sam Cam' as the British tabloids like to call her) appeared in respectful confessional interviews, sharing her joy, grief and private moments. We were to find out that she was pregnant. As previously noted above, the *Mail on Sunday* Magazine included a lengthy profile of David Cameron.

'The thing I really want to know about the baby, quite cheekily, is how on earth did they find time to conceive?' wrote the journalist Cole Moreton.

'Look,' Cameron replied, 'all I can promise is that I was there at the time ... I think you might have worked out that it was a Christmas baby.'

Moreton asks whether he has ever been unfaithful.

'I haven't been, as a matter of fact. You've seen the photographs. Why would you?'

The future prime minister, we learned from 'Sam Cam', loves to cook. He is not very good with the washing-up. He enjoys watching *Godfather* movies. And so on. What is important in all this Juncofied journalism is not the triviality of the leadership lives we are being fed, nor the dubious taste of those who are doing the feeding, but the fact that in the space of a few years, direct questions and answers about the private lives of people in power have gone from being unacceptable to commonplace and to *compulsory*. Journalists who ask these questions nowadays know they will probably be answered. Issues which once upon a time might have been a peripheral part of our national conversation – gossip – have *become* the conversation. If a leader like Cameron or Brown does not engage with globalised gossip, then they risk being seen as remote, cut off, not 'like us'. If they do engage, they find the banalities of their lives are repeated every hour by twenty-four-hour news, as if, in some way, they help us voters to decide how to choose our next leader. Interestingly, David Cameron does still try to draw lines of privacy. He was happy to say he was not interested in committing adultery, and was polite about an enquiry as to when he had procreative sex with his wife, but he has always refused to give a straight answer about whether he has used illegal drugs. Nor will he comment about the extent of his family wealth, which some estimates put at £30 million. But in all these cases the sphere of what is considered 'private' continues to shrink, while that which is assumed to be 'public' continues to grow.

What has not changed is that once again a leader is telling a story that focuses on making public those elements of his personal life which make him look good, keeping as much as possible of the rest hidden, and all the while distracting us from the job that he is supposed to be doing, which is not procreation or entertaining us with stories, but running the country. A friend of Cameron told me that Cameron himself was particularly alarmed about the story that showed him cycling to the House of Commons but revealed he was followed by a car containing his shoes and change of clothes. Cameron understood that this was more than a dent in his image as someone who was environmentally friendly. It suggested a kind of hypocrisy or double dealing which can fatally damage a carefully crafted leadership story. That is why the first months of 2012 have been so difficult for David Cameron and his Chancellor of the Exchequer George Osborne. The March 2012 Budget made a few technical adjustments to taxation, minor in themselves, and a headline-grabbing cut of the top rate of tax for the most wealthy, from 50 to 45 per cent. But the supposedly 'minor' changes were presented even in the Conservative-supporting press as a 'granny tax' on older people and a 'pasty tax' on cheap hot food, measures which hit the relatively less well-off, while the Chancellor cut taxes on the most wealthy. It came after revelations about party donors paying huge sums to have private dinners with the prime minister. One Conservative MP Nadine Dorries commented: 'I think that not only are Cameron and Osborne two posh boys who don't know the price of milk, but they are two arrogant posh boys who show no remorse, no contrition, and no passion to want to understand the lives of others – and that is their real crime.' Even those within the Conservative party who regard Ms Dorries as a maverick understood that this criticism of the two most important leaders in the party was extremely damaging – 'out of touch' and 'not like us,' men whose real weakness was not any particular policy but *the kind of people they were*. Every attempt by Cameron or Osborne to suggest otherwise seemed merely to reinforce the idea that they were being less than 'authentic'. Cameron claimed to have eaten a pasty at a train station fast food outlet which does not exist. Osborne claimed to be shocked at how little tax some wealthy people were paying, while in the *Financial Times* How to Spend It magazine (21 April 2012) his own father was discussing his enjoyment of face cream costing £39 a tub and his desire for a desk which cost £19,000. In other words, Osborne's father would happily pay roughly two-thirds of the average British annual wage for one piece of furniture. One commentator called the desperate attempt to remember when David Cameron had last eaten a pasty 'plebbing'. The Eton and Oxford educated prime minister was trying to look like the common people, the plebs, but failing dismally. Another Conservative commentator told me that Cameron's inauthentic attempt to look 'just like us' risked undermining what the commentator saw as the government's great achievements because it seemed so phoney. In any event, the public demand to know about the 'real' leader through some of the trivia of a leader's life, is a worldwide trend, though in different cultures the manipulation is, as you would expect slightly different.

Gaddafi and the Lion King

While twenty-first century British and American leaders love to present themselves as family men, some leaders want to impress us with their intellectual credentials. Colonel Muammar Gaddafi of Libya and Osama Bin Laden fall into this storytelling category. A few years ago, when Gaddafi feared for his safety, he lived in three identical and very well-appointed tents in the desert. Each tent, of course, was more than accommodation. It was a storytelling device, emphasising Gaddafi's supposed humble nomadic roots. An Arab journalist friend who visited Gaddafi in that period told me that in each tent there was a reception area for guests set out with books, including heavyweight intellectual tomes such as Francis Fukuyama's *The End of History* (1992), Samuel Huntington's *The Clash of Civilizations* (1996), the Quran, and Gaddafi's own contribution to political thought, *The Green Book* (1975). Such books were laid out in each tent so that the guest could not possibly miss them. Osama Bin Laden, as we will see in more detail later, similarly made sure visitors to his cave at

Tora Bora could see his impressive collection of scholarly Islamic literature. In London, a Russian oligarch, a multi-billionaire with a somewhat thuggish reputation, recently invited me to meet him in his offices. The office was full of grand books. On his desk and tables were displayed some of the finest and most expensive art books I have ever seen. The oligarch, in fact, was quite well read. The same could be said for Gaddafi and Bin Laden. But in each case they wanted every visitor to be sure to know it.

In France, which gave the world the concept of the 'intellectual', such bookish pretensions are an essential part of a leader's storytelling toolkit. In the run-up to the 2012 presidential election many of the major candidates published competitive accounts of their thoughts. On the left, François Hollande gave us *The French Dream*, in contradistinction of course to the American dream. His former partner Ségolène Royal, who ran in 2007 for the presidency and was considering having another try, published her work, the snappily titled *Letter to All Those Resigned and Indignant Who Want Solutions*. The centrist hopeful François Bayrou published *2012: State of Emergency*. On the right, Dominique de Villepin offered *Our Old Country*. In France, however, with their strict laws on privacy, such works tend to be less about 'Who am I?' than about the other two parts of the leadership story: 'Who are we?' as Frenchmen and -women, and what is our role or common purpose in the world. Not, perhaps, that such details matter. As the *Economist* noted on 10 September 2011 of the rush to publish in France:

> These days few books by serving politicians sell well. Last year (2010) not a single one made it into the top 30 ... Politicians today write books more as 'marketing tools not literary works', says Francois Leotard, a former culture minister.

The *Economist* also reported that one politician who had not produced a new book – though he had written a pre-election work, *Testimony: France in the Twenty-first Century* – was the sitting president Nicolas Sarkozy. But a French writer who had lunch with Sarkozy, Franz-Olivier Giesbert, said that the president had reinvented himself as *un homme serieux*, quoting Camus, Sartre, Proust, Maupassant, Corneille and Racine over the course of the meal. And – in keeping with the era of globalised gossip, in 2011 President Sarkozy produced something even better than a book of political philosophy. He and his wife Carla Bruni had a baby.

Tony Blair is, once again, an astute commentator on the new media world and how it has helped change leaders and leadership since the end of the Cold War. In *A Journey*, he writes:

> The pace of modern politics and the intrusion of media scrutiny – rightly or wrongly of an entirely different order today than even fifteen or twenty years ago – mean that decisions have to be made, positions taken, strategies worked out and communicated with a speed that is the speed of light compared to the speed of sound.

In the jargon, these are changes to the 'group narrative', 'common purpose' or 'collective mission' parts of a leadership story, which can be complicated for a leader to explain. That's why, in this new, intrusive, confessional media landscape, leaders so often fall back on answering questions about their private lives that would have been unthinkable thirty years ago.

'Who am I?' is the one question we assume a leader is capable of answering with unimpeachable authority. The changes in what we have come to expect from our leaders since the days of the Profumo affair in 1963 have been so gradual that we barely notice them. But they are also so profound that at the end of his first, troubled year in office, facing the worst set of challenges of any American president since Roosevelt in 1933, Barack Obama chose to appear on Oprah Winfrey's Christmas special. Obama, his wife and their two photogenic daughters cheerfully discussed what it was like to have Christmas in the White House, offering not so much a State of the Nation account as a state of his personality and family. I have yet to hear anyone say that Obama was wrong to add his extra bubbles to the froth of life.

Leadership Lesson: The twenty-first century Information Age has seen a transformation in the way we receive news, and also in the kind of news we read, see and hear. Gossip has become globalised. Even obscure people can suddenly become famous. Privacy is dead. Celebrity culture has changed what we expect to see and hear about those in the news. The end of the Cold War has brought a new intrusiveness into the lives of our leaders – or, as Larry Flynt argues, a return to much older traditions of eighteenth- and nineteenth-century pamphleteers. Politicians, business and other leaders have recognised that they have to adapt the way they tell their leadership stories to compete in this new media market. So do the rest of us.

Followership Lesson: The challenge for all modern leaders is to find a 'personalising transformation', a way of appearing more human, more sympathetic and more 'authentic' in the world of globalised gossip. As followers we need to remind ourselves that just because leaders are increasingly prepared to talk about their supposedly 'personal' lives, this does not give us any clues about their competence, honesty or even their openness. Just because we have often seen pictures of David Cameron on a bicycle does not necessarily mean the cycling Cameron is somehow more ' authentic' than David Cameron riding a horse. It merely means that the cycling Cameron is the story that he and his advisers are more interested in telling us.

5   The Origin of Specious

Here is a group of professionally told leadership stories which reflect the increased appetite for 'Who am I?' tales by leaders. They come from some of the most famous people in the world over the past twenty years. All are American. All became, or aspired to become, or have been tipped to become, the president of the United States. Each leader is striving to sound 'human' and 'authentic', as the introductory act of a leadership story aimed at American voters. In each case the leader is searching for the Ohrwurm, *the 'earwig' that will stick in your mind and make you think well of them. Each leader tells an 'origin' story – like Moses being found in his basket in the bulrushes – rooted, we are encouraged to believe, in the childhood years before spin was necessary or even possible. I have heard many leaders tell their 'origin' stories, from President Ollanta Humala in Peru and Daniel Ortega in Nicaragua, to a billionaire Gulf prince talking of his simple life in the desert, or the followers of Deng Xiao Ping quoting proverbs from his childhood in Sichuan. Some of these stories have the power of myths. They have been so massaged and shaped that I have come to think of them in terms of a bad Darwinian pun: the Origin of Specious. Can you guess, from these brief extracts taken from their autobiographies or biographies, who these American leaders might be?*

Here's Leader A:

> For four years, I lived with my grandparents. They didn't have much money. Nobody did ... I spent a lot of time in the country

with my great-grandparents, who by any standard were very poor. But we really didn't know we were poor because we cared for each other, we didn't make excuses, we believed in the American dream and were the backers of family and hard work.

Here's Leader B:

Mom and Dad rented a tiny wooden house built in 1898 on the corner of First and Main … we added a couple of dogs and a cat … My first clear memory of school was when my kindergarten teacher wheeled a black and white television into the classroom so we could watch American astronauts land on the moon … Even watching taped images of an American astronaut walking on the moon stirred in me an overwhelming pride in our country – that we could achieve something so magnificent. A similar feeling stirred in me as my class recited the Pledge of Allegiance. I felt proud and tall as we pledged our hearts every morning … I knew those words held power. And not just those words. I developed a love of reading and writing early on.

You might be beginning to wonder if I have cheated. Are these really different people? They sound almost identical. They appear to live in the same small-town America, populated by the same hard-working, decent folk who lovingly look after each other while overcoming material hardship.

Here's Leader C:

M. was a small town, with small-town values. We learned to respect our elders, to do what they said, and to be good neighbours. We went to church. Families spent time together … No one locked their doors … It was a happy childhood. I was surrounded by love and friends and sports.

Leader D has a similar story. This is taken from an unauthorised and somewhat critical biography:

The best evidence of his sense of destiny stands on the corner of 29th and Olive … [Leader D's] father built the trim little brick bungalow in the 1920s when 29th Street was the edge of town. It's still an attractive house in a well-kept middle class neighbourhood … [Leader D] turned his ordinary youth into a virtue. His was a triumph of the system. In America, pluck and vision can still win out over class and privilege. 'The secret of America is common people achieving uncommon things,' quoth [Leader D]. He told stories that celebrated the essential goodness of small-town America, sometimes with a splash of wry humour. In any of his stories, listeners can close their eyes and imagine the scene as a Norman Rockwell painting.

When I visited Leader D's office in the 1990s, he certainly did tell me 'stories that celebrated the essential goodness of small town America'. He proudly showed me his own Norman Rockwell paintings and talked of his humble childhood. The irony, of course, is that Norman Rockwell originals are so expensive that none of the middle-income small-town characters depicted by Rockwell could afford to buy his art. Only a very rich person, like Leader D, has enough money to purchase these sentimental portraits of American 'ordinariness'.

Now briefly from Leader E:

Sundays meant attending St Margaret's Church, where we had our own family pew … my folks always worked on the bazaar, the bake sale and the annual dance, where you could let your Episcopalian hair down …

These five leaders are three white males, one African American male and one woman. They have very different identities, very different origins and yet suspiciously similar stories. They spent their formative years in New York City, Arkansas, Alaska and two very different small towns in Texas, and yet their leadership stories celebrate identical virtues of humility, patriotism, thrift, family, faith, optimism, and perseverance in the face of all obstacles. It's not quite Moses in the basket, but with minor changes you could cut sections of one leader's story and paste it beautifully into another, down to the grandparents and pets. Each of these leaders is supposedly from the 'common people' aspiring to do 'uncommon things', as Leader D puts it. Like different brands of pasteurised and homogenised milk, the cows may be different but the milk always tastes the same. What is surprising is that not only do they define 'Who am I?' in very similar terms, but superficially they also define 'Who are we?' in a similar way. Each aspiring presidential candidate repeats the attractive American myth-making story that the modern United States is a country inhabited largely by community-minded people with the small-town family values of *Little House on the Prairie,* even if intellectually they are aware that many of their fellow citizens have family values closer to that of *The Simpsons.*

So who are these leaders?

The Boy From Hope

Leader A is President Bill Clinton, and the extract is taken from *Clinton: Young Man in a Hurry,* by Jim Moore (1992). Clinton, as I mentioned in Chapter 1, talked frequently of himself as the 'boy from Hope', the small town of Hope, Arkansas, where he was born, a place riddled with those semi-mythical small-town values. (When I visited Hope for the first time on a hot day in 1992, a local woman came out of her home to offer me freshly squeezed lime juice because I looked 'like I could use it'; she also wanted to find out what I was doing. Her warm generosity to a stranger and her nosiness indeed amounted to genuine small-town values.) Clinton's attempts to control and fashion his leadership story, as Julius Caesar and Winston Churchill had done, continued, and in 1996, when he was seeking re-election, he published a book called *Between Hope and History.* The reality of his origins is a bit different, however. Clinton had grown up partly in Hope, but also in the flashier surroundings of the spa and gambling town of Hot Springs, Arkansas, and he had studied at some of the best universities in the world, Oxford and Georgetown. But when it comes to answering the 'Who am I?' question, 'the boy from the gambling and spa town who went to Oxford' is less useful for late-twentieth-century leadership storytelling and presidential myth-making than the cutely worded and aspirational 'boy from Hope'.

Clinton is the leadership figure who, more than any other, symbolises the transformations in twenty-first century leadership, particularly the end of privacy in public life and the age of globalised gossip. As the first US president to be elected after the Cold War, Clinton was the first president since the nineteenth century to feel the full heat of the new media culture, and the new muck-raking pamphleteers – bloggers like Matt Drudge, who broke the Lewinsky scandal, and others. And, like the other leaders here, Clinton uses a description of his childhood to put himself at the heart of how Americans see themselves: 'we cared for each other, we didn't make excuses, we believed in the American dream'.

A STAR Is Born

Leader B is Sarah Palin, former governor of Alaska, vice presidential nominee of the Republican Party in 2008 and darling of the right-wing Tea Party Movement. With her constant Tweets, Palin is more like Lady Gaga than an old-fashioned politician, the poster child of the megaphone media age. And just like Lady Gaga, Palin relentlessly presents herself as an outsider, a 'rogue', although not quite as 'Mama Monster'. In her autobiography *Going Rogue: An American Life* (2009), from which the above extract is taken, Palin (or a ghost-writer) cranks up the 'Who am I?' myth-making and, just like Clinton, puts herself at the heart of her vision of 'Who are we?' as Americans. She writes glowingly of her childhood in Alaska, right down to her father taking her on hunting expeditions where he would, among other things, gouge the eyeballs from a dead moose and put them into little Sarah's hands. She observes that she likes Alaskan wildlife – especially on her plate next to the potatoes. Moose eyeballs in the hands or moose-burgers on the plate may not help when it comes to balancing the budget or dealing with Iran's nuclear programme, but such 'froth of life' stories deflect from Palin's inadequate scholarship and coherent policies. At the Republican National Convention in 2008 she wowed delegates not with her ideas but with 'froth of life' details of her personal life and leadership story. She told the world that she was a devoted 'hockey mom' who had risen to become Governor of Alaska. To roars of laughter she explained the difference between a hockey mom and a fighting dog, a pitbull: 'Lipstick.' Tough enough to be president? *You betcha.*

Sarah Palin is, in fact, just a different type of Mama Monster, a conservative Alaskan Republican version of Lady Gaga in her dress made of meat telling her own stories about being an 'outsider' to help her get to the top and to make her seem unforgettable. Palin's method (again, just like Lady Gaga's) is to use what the American presentation expert Nancy Duarte calls 'STAR' moments. STAR is an acronym for Something They Always Remember. (We will explore this in more detail in Chapter 7.) Palin's performance at the Republican convention was indeed unforgettable, even though behind the scenes some in Senator John McCain's team were scathing about her lack of substance. But the important 'Origins of Specious' storytelling point is that despite their positions at opposite ends of the American political spectrum, Sarah Palin could easily echo Bill Clinton's words 'we cared for each other, we didn't make excuses, we believed in the American dream'. Whether you believe any of this classic American political boilerplate is another matter. And what Palin and Clinton mean by these words could not be more different.

In the winter of 2010 I followed Sarah Palin's *Going Rogue* book tour to the heartland states of South Dakota, Nebraska and

Iowa. Palin talked about her all-American values ('we believed in the American dream') as if they were under constant threat from the institutions of government itself. Clinton, on the other hand, dedicated his political career to considering how government could nurture and make possible the values of community behind the American dream.

When I talked with Palin supporters on the *Going Rogue* tour, they never once mentioned any policy associated with her campaign. Instead they repeated that Palin was unlike 'the crowd in Washington' and was instead 'just like us'. Palin's rise to prominence was based on defining 'Who am I?' as 'Who are we?' – ordinary Americans under threat from *Them* in Washington.

'My folks were smart,' Palin writes of what she claims was her father's decision to put the television set in an unheated room of their family home in small-town Alaska, 'less TV meant more books. From *The Pearl* to *Jonathan Livingston Seagull* to *Animal Farm* and anything by C. S. Lewis. I would put down one book just long enough to pick up another.' Palin concludes with the thought: 'The library on Main Street was one of my summer hideaways.' All this may be 'authentically' part of Palin's leadership story, just as the display of books in Colonel Gaddafi's tent may indeed have been part of his strong intellectual life, but it strains belief to imagine Sarah Palin to be a fan, in any genuine sense, of George Orwell, beyond the set text she had to read at school. (His days with anarchists in POUM fighting Franco? His perception of politicians as potentially Big Brother, or the Pigs who take over from the Humans in Animal Farm?) More revealingly, when Palin was asked soft questions during the 2008 presidential election campaign about her favourite reading material and quizzed on specifics about newspapers by the journalist Katie Couric, she was unable to recall any titles, even those of the newspapers to which she supposedly turned as a source of news and information. In 2010, on Twitter, in connection with the row over the supposed plans to build a mosque near the site of New York's 9/11 attacks,

Palin called on peaceful Muslims to 'refudiate' the plans. On Fox TV she called on Barack Obama to 'refudiate' suggestions of racism in the Tea-Party movement. When challenged on her use of words which do not exist, Palin suggested that the English language was a living organism and like Shakespeare she was inventing new and vibrant expressions. At no point did the moose eyeballs, odd vocabulary or pervasive air of Know-Nothing ignorance damage Palin's credibility with her followers. Quite the reverse. They emphasised her position as an 'outsider' and cemented the relationship of 'Who am I?' to 'Who are we?' Her followers told me that Palin's mistakes meant that she was more 'real', more 'human', more 'like us', more 'an ordinary person, a mom', and consequently more in touch with the 'real America' than the liberals and sell-outs in Washington with all their book learning, university degrees and proper grammar.

The Palin phenomenon, like the success of Ronald Reagan and George W. Bush, is widely misunderstood, especially in Europe. In their work *The New Psychology of Leadership* (2011) S. Alexander Haslam, Stephen D. Reicher and Michael J. Platow explain how simplistic storytelling may allow a leader to bond with an audience. The authors cite the moment when Ronald Reagan, who was running for re-election in July 1984, turned on his Democratic rivals. He was in the South, in Atlanta, Georgia, and talking of the Democrats at their convention in San Francisco, California:

> You know, those folks who are writing off the South out there in the fog in San Francisco, they were busy talking and filling the air with eloquent-sounding words; as a matter of fact big-sounding words. But a lot of those words contained what Winston Churchill called 'terminological inexactitude'. That's a nice way of saying they said a few things that weren't true.

Haslam, Reicher and Platow go on to explain how Reagan, like Palin and George W. Bush, often 'uses folksy language to position himself as the blunt man of the people up against a sophisticated but alien elite ... There is much complexity in being a simple "man of the people". ... his words were an artful construction of identity posing as an artless description of reality.' The authors bang home their point with an internal campaign memo from Richard Darman, assistant White House chief of staff, setting out Reagan's overall storytelling strategy:

> Paint RR [Reagan] as the personification of all that is right
> with or heroized by America. Leave Mondale [his opponent in
> 1984] in a position where an attack on Reagan is tantamount
> to an attack on America's idealized image of itself – where a
> vote against Reagan is in some subliminal sense, a vote against
> mythic 'AMERICA'.

Note the use of the word 'mythic'. Darman was in no doubt that Reagan was telling a story, about himself, his leadership, his audience and also this mythic 'America', which he claimed to represent. Reagan characterises the Democrats as 'those folks' – *Them*, the Other – while he identifies himself with 'we', the right thinking people, *Us*.

This attempted identification of the leader with the nation can be found in different times and different cultures, and can be seen in the leaderships of Benito Mussolini in Italy, Emperor Hirohito in Japan, Joseph Stalin in the USSR, Winston Churchill in Great Britain, Colonel Gaddafi in Libya and Nelson Mandela in South Africa. In America it is not just the property of Republicans. An internal memo in Hillary Clinton's 2008 campaign from her chief strategist Mark Penn shows how he wanted her to characterise Barack Obama:

> His roots to basic American culture and values are at best
> limited ... Let's *explicitly own 'American'* in our programs, the
> speeches and values. He doesn't. [my italics]

Owning 'American' is the point of all these leadership stories, that's why so many of them sound the same, give or take a few moose eyeballs.

Dubya

Leader C is George W. Bush (Bush Junior), the forty-third president of the United States, and the extract above is taken from his autobiography *A Charge to Keep* (1999). Like all the other leaders here, George 'Dubya' presents himself as if his, too, were the story of Moses in the bulrushes, or more pertinently Abraham Lincoln, who rose from lowly beginnings in a log cabin to power in the White House. In Bush's case, his 'Who am I?' tale of a small-town upbringing as a humble lad from Midland, Texas is politically convenient but simply laughable. George W. Bush is, of course, the son of President George H. W. Bush, the former director of Central Intelligence, a man who for decades was a Republican Party grandee, chairman of the Republican National Committee, and envoy to China, with a family home in Kennebunkport, Maine. Bush Senior was for eight years also vice president of the United States, residing in a grand mansion behind the British Embassy on Massachusetts Avenue before he moved up a notch to the White House, and was himself the son of a very wealthy US senator, Prescott Bush. The family was so well off that as a young boy George H. W. Bush was said to have been chauffeured to school in a limousine during the Great Depression.

George Dubya might well praise the 'small-town values' of Midland, Texas, in his childhood, but he does not dwell upon his family's great and inherited riches, their wealth of political and business connections and the pervasive racism and segregation in the town in which he claims his origin story. Many African Americans regard George Dubya's account of his childhood as more Mythland than Midland. Black people did not, for example, get into the country clubs where the Bushes and others played golf and tennis, except to wash the dishes and mow the golf course fairways. Even as late as the mid 1990s I played golf with the first African American member to be allowed into an exclusive Texas country club used by the Bush family, in cosmopolitan Houston. I was in the company of the Reverend Kirbyjon Caldwell, of Windsor Village United Methodist Church, a 14,000-member (at the last count) mega-church in Houston, Texas. Kirbyjon is a charismatic African American preacher who was later to offer the benediction at the inauguration of George W. Bush in 2001. Caldwell is a political independent. He clearly likes George W. Bush personally, but when we played golf together at a country club which had only just allowed in its first African American member, he was scathing of the widespread racism that some upper-class white Americans simply did not see at the heart of their mythic America. Throughout our conversation it was difficult to believe that allowing one black member into the country club was regarded as a historic breakthrough in the home state of George W. Bush in the 1990s. It sounded like the 1890s. George Dubya's 'origin of specious' story of his childhood fails to mention or notice these 'ordinary' aspects of his supposedly ordinary upbringing. Others are not so reticent.

The Bushes' black maid Otha Taylor recalled that in the Midland, Texas, George Dubya so idealises, 'the blacks couldn't wear dress clothes going downtown, only overalls or a uniform'. (As quoted in *Vanity Fair,* October 2000.) When it came down to 'Who are we?' George W. Bush did not appear to notice that his definition of 'we' did not include African Americans for a very, very long time. However, the storytelling skills of George W. Bush are remarkable. Like Ronald Reagan, and Sarah Palin, his simplicity is misunderstood and underestimated, or as he would say, *mis*underestimated. Bush had a difficult origins story to tell. He was an extremely privileged young man. He enjoyed a preppie lifestyle, and had a history of drunkenness, underachievement and frat-boy escapades. His business success owed a great deal to family connections. At times he spoke the English language like a foreign tongue. And yet his storytelling connected with the people of Texas and voters across the United States.

One early Democratic Party opponent, Texas governor Ann Richards, had described Bush's father George H. W. Bush this way: 'Poor George! He was born with a silver foot in his mouth.' She turned her smart rhetorical flair on the younger Bush, but it simply did not work. George Dubya went on to beat the 'smarter' Richards in the gubernatorial election and take her place as governor of Texas. Bush also beat (at least according to the final version of the disputed election results) the supposedly much 'smarter' Al Gore for the presidency in 2000. He then utterly destroyed the equally 'smart' Senator John Kerry in the presidential election of 2004. In each case, Bush won as a result of the power of stories, which identified him more closely than his opponent with the 'Who are we?', the American people. His story was that of an ordinary guy who had made his way in the world and liked nothing more than clearing brush on his ranch or having a barbecue with friends. He had been a bit of a rapscallion in his youth ('just like us'), but repented, and was redeemed through God and sobriety.

The genius of Bush's adviser Karl Rove and others in the Bush team was to take the worst counter-story criticisms of Bush and use them against his opponents with all the confidence of a skilled judo fighter. It was breathtaking to watch. The Bush campaign and its surrogates repeatedly attacked his opponents as if *they* were the members of privileged elites, Washington insiders, out of touch with ordinary folks. During the 2004 campaign the Bush-supporting and Rupert Murdoch-owned Fox News network repeatedly ridiculed the fact that Senator John Kerry speaks French. On their morning show the hosts said good morning as usual to the viewers, and then added, 'or as John Kerry would say, *bon jour*'. In European countries, the fact that a leader speaks a foreign language is generally considered a positive part of his leadership story. Tony Blair's fluency in French, for example, was regarded as impressive. But not in the United States. It reminded me of the quote attributed (possibly erroneously) to the first woman Governor of Texas in the 1920s, Miriam 'Ma' Ferguson: 'If English was good enough for Jesus Christ, it ought to be good enough for the children of Texas.'

In any event, such crude ridicule over his linguistic fluency helped turn Kerry's positives into negatives. He was boxed into the counter-story image that most served the Bush campaign – that of an out-of-touch, elitist intellectual. After 9/11 and the Iraq war, which France's president Jacques Chirac opposed, the French nation had been caricatured on *The Simpsons* TV show as 'cheese-eating surrender monkeys'. Kerry's strengths – intelligence and understanding of other cultures – became linked in some way to France's supposed cowardice.

Bush's weaknesses, on the other hand – his apparent dim-bulb character – were portrayed as strengths. As Jay Heinrichs writes in *Winning Arguments* (2010, as quoted by Sam Leith in *You Talkin' to Me?*, 2011), Bush's clumsy language stems from his use of

> … emotive, ethos laden code-words without the distraction of logic. He speaks in short sentences, repeating code phrases in effective, if irrational order. So when Bush says 'Families is where our nation finds hope, where wings take dream,' … the fact that it's nonsense is less important than the fact that the audience hears 'families … nation … wings … dream'.

Throughout the Bush years the author Jacob Weisberg made fun of what he called 'Bushisms', but Weisberg understood Dubya's storytelling abilities. When Bush was asked about his counter-story reputation of being a dimwit, he 'chuckled and replied, "No, I'm glad, I like that, I play up to that."' Weisberg noted that 'the real danger was not to Bush himself, but rather to his Democratic detractors who … by attacking the imperfect language of an "ordinary guy" allowed themselves to be portrayed as distant intellectuals who were unrepresentative of the population as a whole and therefore unfit to lead it'. Weisberg noted that 'elitist condescension, however merited, helps cement Bush's bond to the masses'. (As quoted in *The New Psychology of Leadership*, above)

You do not win Homer Simpson's vote by speaking French. You win by telling the American people over and over again that 'Who am I?' as a leader is identical to 'Who are we?', as a great nation. George W. Bush, for all his many flaws, did that remarkably well. He was 'just like us', the ordinary people of America; while in the words of one Republican advertisement during the 2004 campaign, the Democrats were 'latte drinking, sushi eating, Volvo driving' and consequently unlike the ordinary voters.

A Bush White House aide once reflected on all this by telling me that Europeans thought of George Dubya as 'nice but dumb', and yet 'neither part of that phrase is true'. Bush was certainly not stupid, nor, as his campaigns have shown, was he especially nice. Tony Blair, whose own affection for Bush was to cost him dear with British public opinion, offers a more general point when he writes in *A Journey* of people struggling for a position of leadership:

> … if you aren't naturally a bloke people would like to have a beer with and you're running for office, it is a problem. It may be irrational, but it's true. I always used to say to people about George Bush: don't underestimate his appeal as a normal guy. You might not agree with him, but if you're a voter, you would never think you would be uncomfortable or feel inadequate if you met him socially; you would think he would be nice and easy with you. And you'd be right.

The Billionaire as Everyman

Leader D is another Texan, Ross Perot, the independent candidate for the presidency in 1992; the extract above is taken from Todd Mason's *Perot: An Unauthorized Biography* (1990). Perot ended up with a creditable 19 per cent of the vote in the 1992 election. When I first met him in the summer of that year, he was for a time actually ahead of Bill Clinton and President George H.W. Bush in the opinion polls. Perot's Norman Rockwell fascination with small-town America and its virtues is authentic, but yet again, the small-town myth was more potent in the leader's imagination than in reality. In 1992 Ross Perot was one of the richest men in the world. He could well afford his collection of Rockwells and Remington bronzes. He was worth an estimated $3 billion, probably more. I found him to be convivial, likeable, waspish, sarcastic and fun. He took me to lunch and drove us in his own car; there was no money wasted on a chauffeur. He took me not to one of Dallas's many expensive fine-dining restaurants, but to a barbecue joint. We stood in line with our trays, rather like in the BBC canteen, though the food was better – barbecued ribs, brisket, slaw and fries. With iced tea, it came to $9 each. Perot, the richest person I had ever met, let me pay. He proudly told me that his extremely short haircut cost him just a few dollars. His head looked like a hand-grenade with stubble. He also told me that American leaders were out of touch with ordinary people and the value of money. 'They need to stand in line sometimes,' Perot often said. 'Fly coach. Lose their luggage. Eat a bad meal. Drive themselves.' Perot proudly did all these things.

It takes a special kind of storytelling genius for a multi-billionaire who has never held any elected office to argue, convincingly, that he is more in touch with ordinary people than career politicians. Perot's origin story was not specious. He did come from a humble background, worked as a paperboy, joined the US Navy, went into business and soon found himself, through ingenuity and hard work, to be one of the richest businessmen in the world. He was also a passionate supporter of those who believed that US troops in Vietnam had been badly served by the double-dealing of politicians in Washington, and he once visited Hanoi to ask the Vietnamese government about MIAs – US soldiers missing in action who some, including Perot, believed had been betrayed as part of a Washington conspiracy. Perot proudly showed me souvenirs of that trip, including a bottle of Hanoi beer and a revolver. Every object in his study had a story behind it, and he was always happy to tell these stories as part of his constant definition of 'Who am I?', as a way of making him 'just like us'.

But Perot of course, was utterly different. His money bought him airtime and a national platform from which to run for the presidency of the United States, without any support from a political party apparatus. It could not quite buy Perot the presidency, but it could buy him the opportunity to deny the presidency to George H. W. Bush, whom Perot loathed with a passion that only one Texan can feel for another. If his money could not buy him the future, it did buy Perot the past. He purchased the humble family home that he remembered from his childhood, the house described in the extract I quoted above, and turned it into a museum, dedicated to himself. Unfortunately, there was a snag. After the Perot family had moved out, subsequent owners had changed the way the house looked, painting the red bricks with white paint. That irritated Perot, especially when he discovered that no amount of sand-blasting and scraping by builders could remove the offending colour without disfiguring the bricks. And so Ross Perot – the man who was 'just like you and me'– had the old family house taken apart carefully, brick by brick, with every original brick turned around 180 degrees so the offending white paint was hidden on the *inside* of the walls, ensuring that nowadays the Perot house-museum looks exactly as it did in his childhood. 'Pluck and vision' might, as Perot's unauthorised biography suggests, overcome wealth and privilege, but $3 billion of wealth and privilege came to represent a load of bricks that could be turned, quite literally, to Perot's advantage.

Perot's storytelling genius, therefore, was to demonstrate to aspirational Americans not that he was exactly like them, but that he understood their hopes and dreams. One footnote, however, shows how a leadership story can go completely wrong. Perot chose as his vice-presidential running mate Vice Admiral James Stockdale. Stockdale had many strengths, but no storytelling skills. When he was rolled out in the October 1992 televised vice-presidential debate, he greeted the American people with the words: 'Who am I? Why am I here?' Stockdale asked the right questions but never adequately answered them. His bumbling attempt at telling his own leadership story made him look like a fool. He wasn't. But he seemed like one. On television, it's the same thing.

We All Need Another Hero

Leader E is General Colin Powell, the former US secretary of state and former chairman of the joint chiefs of staff; the extract above is taken from *Colin Powell: A Soldier's Way* (2001). Powell is the man who most eloquently made the case for the Iraq war of 2003, based, as he now ruefully accepts, on faulty intelligence. In the 1990s he was often tipped as a possible president, though he declined to run. His leadership story tells of a loving childhood in New York, in terms almost interchangeable with the stories of Clinton, Palin, George W. Bush and Perot, and also of his immigrant background (the Powells came from Jamaica), his belonging to an aspirational family, and his recognition that the US military was a ladder to success.

A very senior British diplomat who became friends with Colin Powell once asked him what might have happened if his parents had come to Britain instead of the United States. Powell laughed and told him that in Britain he would have been lucky to rise to sergeant in a not very good infantry regiment, whereas in America he became chairman of the joint chiefs of staff, national security advisor and secretary of state. In Powell's inspirational storytelling, America is a nation of immigrants who can make it to the very top and succeed in the world, no matter where they come from. His answer to the question 'Who am I?' again perfectly fits into his version of 'Who are we?', as it does with every one of these leaders. The only real differences in these biographical stories come when the leader tries to define 'What is our common purpose?' The most powerful, most diverse and, we are led to believe, most sophisticated democracy on earth, 300 million people strong, is reduced in these leadership stories to the homogenised ideals of what the leaders think will sell in the political marketplace. Each leader begins with a story about the most innocent time of all – childhood – a time when we tend to assume 'spin' is neither necessary nor possible.

Managing an origin story is yet another example of the 'earwig' doing its work. As we have seen, Margaret Thatcher did it, with her refrain of being the 'grocer's daughter from Grantham'. King Abdullah II of Jordan did it by reminding us that his mother drove around with a Kalashnikov and a pistol in her car. And Apple's Steve Jobs did it in a famous address to students at Stanford University in 2005. He told them, 'Today, I want to tell you three stories from my life. That's it. No big deal. Just three stories.' He began with the fact that he was adopted, the son of an unmarried mother, and went on to relate how he became a college dropout, a man who had never before attended a college graduation – and yet he came to found the world's most successful and innovative company. Such origin stories or myths work not just for a person but also for an entire nation: for the Romans, it was the myth of Romulus and Remus, the founding fathers who had been suckled by a she-wolf; among Jews, the idea that they are 'the Chosen People'; and for Britons, the story of the 'island race' locked into the mysterious past of Arthurian legends and Camelot on a 'sceptr'd isle'.

But as we have seen with the American examples, what works most successfully is for a leader or potential leader to connect their 'Who am I?' personal origin story with the best values of the nation. Mohammad Ali Jinnah, the founder of Pakistan, knew he had to create an origin story for his entire country, as he carved Pakistan from the partition of British India after the Second World War. Jinnah, as *The New Psychology of Leadership* puts it:

… brought together the disparate peoples who made up Pakistan into a single entity through his dress … on August 4, 1947, Jinnah stepped out from his plane and onto the soil of an independent Pakistan for the very first time. On his head he wore the *karakuli*, the black sheepskin cap as worn by the Muslims of north India. On his back he wore the *sherwani* (a knee-length black coat as worn by the Muslims of Aligarh). On his legs he wore the *shalwar* (baggy trousers worn by Muslims in the west of the country). Altogether his attire thus constituted the national dress and helped create the nation itself, not just the meaning of Pakistan but the very reality of a Pakistan entity.

As we have seen, Nelson Mandela did something very similar in his use of Xhosa dress and the Springbok shirt at various stages of his political story. Mandela's autobiography *Long Walk to Freedom* at every stage identifies his personal biography with the values of the nation. He was a ward of the regent of the Thembu and engaged in what was, as *The New Psychology of Leadership* outlines, a 'life-long quest to recapture the *ubuntu* (roughly, the sense of community and solidarity) of the African kings'. Mandela was to 'own' being a 'black African' and later a 'South African' from the Rainbow Nation, just as Ronald Reagan and Hillary Clinton strived to 'own' American, and Jinnah 'owned' Pakistan. In every case, rooting these shared values in childhood makes them seem particularly authentic. As we will now discover, if you can fake authenticity, you've got it made.

Leadership Lesson: Every one of us has a fund of stories from our childhood. We remember family pets, the discipline of our elders, the crazy things we did, the hard lessons of successes and failures, and the rebellions of our teenage years. Leaders are no different. But they also know that such stories connect with our common humanity. This phenomenon, of a leader using shared experiences of childhood to identify with a nation or people, is worldwide. As we will see in Chapter 6, next, King Abdullah of Jordan does it in his autobiography; so does the Ruler of Sharjah in the United

Arab Emirates, Sultan bin Muhammad al-Qasimi, who tells us (among other things) that as a small boy he once rode his horse into the suq (market) where the animal misbehaved and ate vegetables from the stallholders, requiring compensation and an apology from the ruling family. He also mentions that as a child he was once seasick on the uniform of a grand foreign general (Lucius Clay of the US army.) Just as with the American tales, the childhood naughtiness and misfortunes of a small boy cleverly reminds us of the common humanity we share with the future leader.

Followership Lesson: Leadership stories are aspirational. They are rooted in success. They are also an attempt to convince us of the moral worth of the leader, his politics or business. The most ruthless leaders understand that if they can call into question the leadership story of a rival by separating 'Who am I?' from the values of 'Who are we?', they can fatally undermine their rival's leadership. Moreover, childhood stories allow a leader to admit to flaws of character or errors of judgement – as Barack Obama did with his drug abuse. We always forgive our children.

6   Authenticity and How to Fake It

'I think most people who have dealt with me think I'm a pretty
straight sort of guy, and I am.'
                        Prime Minister Tony Blair, 16 November 1997

'BLIAR!'
        Popular T-shirt following the invasion of Iraq in 2003 based
        on Blair's often stated belief that Iraq possessed Weapons of
        Mass Destruction. No WMD were found.

*The search for 'authenticity' is not new. Nor is faking it. And,
importantly, a leader practising a bit of fakery may not always be
bad. There are plenty of examples from history, and from diverse
cultures, of what Huckleberry Finn called 'stretchers': leaders
exaggerating or changing some part of a story for their own benefit
or that of their country or organisation. 'Faking it' may sometimes
be justifiable. It may even be essential. Judge for yourself. Here are
some recent and very different examples of stories that demonstrate
why 'authenticity' is necessary and useful, and why some degree of
'managing' factual truth, even to the point of lying, may at times
be important. One example is from Pakistan, one from Jordan, one
from Tony Blair's artful inauthenticity – which, curiously, seems
quite authentic – and one from the person most British people would
cite as the greatest leader we ever had, a familiar staple of leadership
books, Winston Churchill. In Churchill's case, we can agree that this
is an example of faked 'authenticity' in a good cause. 'Stretchers'
have their place. Leaders understand this better than anyone.*

In August 2010 I interviewed a man under severe pressure, the president of Pakistan, Asif Ali Zardari. The highly artificial set-up process for this interview is not unusual to those of us who work in the television industry. The degree of managed 'authenticity' I am about to describe is typical of hundreds of interviews I have taken part in over the years. It's worth recounting in some detail, since it gives an insider's view of how an efficient leader's staff will manipulate events for the leader's benefit. Media organisers have one objective: making sure the leader looks good. In Zardari's case, his advisers did the best they could to construct and manage what millions of television viewers around the world were to see and hear from the Pakistan president. I doubt if one viewer in a million really noticed how well they did their job.

First, some background. Asif Ali Zardari is the widower of the former Pakistan prime minister Benazir Bhutto. I met and interviewed Benazir many times when she lived in the UK, during her exile from Pakistan, and her own leadership story was compelling. Her father, Zulfikar Ali Bhutto, had been toppled in a military coup and executed in 1979 by Pakistan's then strongman General Zia ul-Haq. Benazir was an intelligent, well educated and principled woman who waited to seize her moment in the predominantly male – and often corrupt – world of Pakistani politics. She believed that only democracy could save Pakistan from the generals in the military, the Islamic extremists in the madrasas, and the money politics of the rich elite. In trying to realise Muhammad Ali Jinnah's dream of a truly independent and successfully democratic Pakistan, Benazir Bhutto was assassinated on December 2007 by a suicide bomber while campaigning for election, one of many courageous Pakistani politicians to fall victim to extremists. She was a great loss to her country and the region.

After her death, Benazir's husband, Asif Ali Zardari, appeared reluctant to enter politics. Eventually he did, succeeding her as leader of the Pakistan People's Party (PPP) at a moment of profound crisis for his country. There was the long war in neighbouring Afghanistan, the perpetual rivalry with India, the question of what to do about Kashmir, the constant fears of another military coup, separatist movements in Baluchistan and elsewhere, Sunni and Shia rivalry, and, most potently, the insurgency of the Pakistani Taliban, which had the characteristics of a future civil war. There was also the nagging question of the whereabouts of Osama Bin Laden. He was assumed by western intelligence agencies to be hiding somewhere in Pakistan, perhaps in the mountainous tribal areas. Bin Laden, as we discovered from the American special forces attack that killed him in 2011, was not, as supposed, living rough, but enjoying comfort and security in a large compound in the military garrison town of Abbottabad.

By 2010, some Western diplomats fretted that Pakistan was becoming a failed state. Since independence it had fallen far behind its strategic rival, India, in economic and political development. The Pakistani Taliban threatened to topple Zardari and destroy the already shaky democracy, which could put Pakistan's nuclear weapons under the control of religious zealots who supported al-Qaeda. The British prime minister David Cameron had, on a visit to India, accused Pakistan of facing 'both ways' on terrorism. On the eve of my interview with Zardari, the head of Pakistan's intelligence service, the ISI, was widely reported to have cancelled a visit to Britain as a result of this perceived insult. On top of the man-made difficulties, torrential rains and floods had left millions of Pakistan's people homeless. There were many in Pakistan and in Britain who thought Zardari should cancel his trip to manage the humanitarian emergency. Instead, Zardari persisted with his visit and agreed to a BBC interview to explain himself. Zardari and his advisers were aware of the counter-stories in the news that showed him staying with a large entourage in a plush hotel in central London, which cost hundreds of pounds a night per room, while homeless Pakistanis in the disaster area were queuing up for food, blankets and tents.

When I arrived at Zardari's hotel, there was already a great deal of nervous activity. The president's staff scurried around the suites set aside for Zardari's party, worrying over minor details. Tony Blair's autobiography *A Journey* is revealing on a staff's role in managing a leadership story. When Blair was lobbied by a visitor, journalist, dignitary, contact or even by one of his own Labour MPs requesting an in-depth face-to-face meeting, he would almost always say yes. But he would add that the arrangements would need to be confirmed by his staff, among whom the diary secretary is the gatekeeper of the leader's time. Such people are formidable and sometimes plain rude. I mean this as a compliment. 'Creating time for a leader is a near-sacred task,' Blair writes. 'The person in charge of it is one of the most important in the team, and they have to be completely ruthless in saying no. *The leader has always got to be the good guy*' (my italics). So while staff may appear officious and brusque, the leader is trying to tell a different story.

As Blair knew well, visitors are always looking for stories of 'niceness' or 'nastiness' in leaders, and such stories travel further and faster than policy papers on inflation or control of immigration. Stories of Prime Minister Gordon Brown's temper tantrums and of how he had thrown a telephone at a member of staff became legendary. When I interviewed President Jacques Chirac at the Élysée Palace, although I remember little of the content of the interview, I do remember that when we finished filming he made sure we drank champagne together. An Arab leader, whom I have come to know and respect, invited me after Friday prayers to share a lunch of roast camel, which, unforgettably, he served me by hand. Germany's Chancellor Angela Merkel discussed with me everything from her own background as the child of a Lutheran pastor to the future of the Eurozone and the manner in which modern Germany was still haunted by the Nazi past, but above all I remember the most minor detail, that she said she tended to drink tea rather than coffee at home, but she did not much like the tea available in the Chancellor's office. And Nicaragua's president Violeta Chamorro invited me to a party at her home in Managua, where she told tales of being oppressed by the Sandinistas, but her diary secretary called me the next day to say regrettably there was no chance of an interview. All these leaders, in other words, were being, in Blair's words, 'the good guy' (or woman), while any unpalatable news (in the case of Chamorro) or any tough discussions about the format of the interview, were always left to other people.

Dressing the Set

With Zardari, as with any modern leader, I expected that he, too, would be 'the good guy', and he was. The less pleasant aspects of the demands from his staff were negotiated before he arrived. A Zardari aide, for example, suggested that the cameraman move the Pakistan flag so that the camera could see the white star more clearly on the green background. Good idea. The cameraman agreed. It looked better. Then, five minutes before we were to begin, another aide brought in two photographs and placed them behind the president's chair. One was of Muhammad Ali Jinnah, the founder of Pakistan. The other was of Benazir Bhutto, President Zardari's assassinated wife. This is called 'dressing the set'. It is not primarily about aesthetics, although bunches of flowers and pleasant lighting can be important parts of any interview. For a politician, it is an important storytelling procedure. The cliché is correct. Every picture does tell a story. In the case of Angela Merkel, when I interviewed her it was with the dome of the Reichstag in the background, telling the story that she was the representative of the people of Germany to whom the Reichstag is dedicated. In Zardari's case, his pictures were also telling a leadership story. The Benazir Bhutto picture: personal suffering at the hands of terrorists (Who am I? *Someone who has suffered for the cause*). The Pakistan flag: patriotism (Who are we? *The people of Pakistan, a proudly independent country*). The

Jinnah picture: legitimacy and leadership (What is our common purpose? *Gaining the respect of the world for Pakistan*).

All of these minor manipulations were rooted in truth. Zardari is of course patriotic. He is the elected heir to Jinnah. And his family have indeed suffered at the hands of extremists. But *being true*, as we have seen, is less important than *being useful*. The set-dressing was an artificial construct. It always is. Random hotel rooms in London do not carry a stock of photographs of foreign leaders, their families and their flags. Placing these items behind the president seemed 'authentic', although it was just another storytelling device. In the case of Lyndon Baines Johnson, sworn in as President of the United States after the murder of John F. Kennedy, the 'item' necessary to make the emergency swearing-in ceremony seem 'authentic' was in fact JFK's widow, Jackie Kennedy. As Johnson's biographer Robert Caro revealed in an essay in the *New Yorker* magazine (March 2012) 'whether she (Jackie) agreed explicitly or not, there was an understanding that when Johnson took the oath she would be present.' LBJ knew that as someone who succeeded to the presidency only as a result of an assassin's bullet he needed to create a scene of immediate legitimacy. In the memorable photograph of the occasion, Jackie Kennedy was just as much a prop used to 'dress the set' as the picture of Benazir Bhutto would be for President Zardari more than fifty years later.

Yes You Did. Oh No I Didn't

The president of Pakistan arrived punctually and, as Tony Blair rightly suggests is customary on such occasions, he was affable and charming. While the cameramen checked the lighting and coordinated the sound, Zardari – in 'good guy' mode – talked with me about Pakistan's national sport, cricket. The Pakistan team were doing badly. In truth, I was not much interested in the cricket at that moment, and as our conversation progressed, I suspected this was something the president of Pakistan and I

might have in common. We then began the interview. When I
mentioned that Pakistan's intelligence chief had cancelled his visit
to Britain, Zardari denied it. It was never planned for him to come
to London, he said. A confident and barefaced denial can be very
disarming. An interviewer would have to be very sure of his facts
to challenge the president of Pakistan on the travel arrangements
for the head of Pakistan intelligence. I have had considerable
experience in the barefaced denial of facts from politicians. For
me, the worst case was President Thabo Mbeki of South Africa,
who denied in an off-the-cuff interview with me that he had ever
said there was no connection between HIV and AIDS. Oh yes
you did, I persisted, and that denial meant many South Africans
did not receive the best possible treatment for AIDS. No, I never
said that, Mbeki insisted, although when I returned to the BBC
studios we dug out a TV library clip of him saying precisely what
he denied he had said.

With President Zardari, I simply did not know the truth of
the matter concerning his ISI chief, and so I moved on. I offered
up the quote from David Cameron about Pakistan facing both
ways on terrorism. At this, President Zardari slipped into a
familiar storytelling gear. He had clearly rehearsed his answer,
at least in his head, although possibly with his advisers. Many
senior politicians 'game-play' interviews with their staff, which is
why every word can sound processed and false, especially if the
politician has limited acting skills.

Zardari is, in fact, an accomplished performer. He reminded
the TV audience of his dead wife and of other terrorist victims
within his political party. He mentioned friends of his, associates
of his family, including children, whom he had known for years
who had been murdered. How could someone who had suffered
so much be 'facing both ways'? How could anyone doubt Pakistan's
role in the fight against terror when his own country had been
blighted by it? How could I even think such a thing when more
Pakistani soldiers were dying in combat with the Taliban and

other insurgents than NATO soldiers next door in Afghanistan? It was a good performance from Zardari, but, as with all TV interviews, it was still a *performance*. The tone was calm, the manner reassuring, the scene 'presidential'. The president of Pakistan was at pains to show that he was human – 'just like us', in touch with the suffering of his people – but also better than us, and, as a result of his status, it was absolutely right for him to stay in one of London's most expensive hotels, where he was lobbying for more Western aid. The ancient Greeks, as I noted earlier, understood that their leaders could be both 'ordinary' citizens and also have, as *The New Psychology of Leadership* terms it, 'exceptional qualities that legitimised their personal privileges (*metrios*)', including, no doubt, hotel suites and rooms which cost a small fortune.

The pictures of Zardari told the casual viewer – and when it comes to TV interviews, most people are casual viewers – a simple story of a patriotic leader who had suffered personally and grievously, surrounded by symbols of his patriotism and his grief, while looking and sounding presidential. He was not entirely faking authenticity, but he was, in a stylised and rehearsed way, making sure we could not possibly miss his version of what was authentic. Nor could our viewers worldwide. The lessons honed and crafted by Ronald Reagan's adviser Michael Deaver – the use of even the most simple pictures to make an impression – are now commonplace among leaders worldwide. Fakery? If you like. But, nowadays, for a leader or his staff to do otherwise would be incompetent.

The Bulldog Breed

Ingrained in all boys of my generation, like a poem committed to memory, is Winston S. Churchill's speech after the evacuation of Dunkirk in June 1940. It has a particular resonance for me because my own father had been one of the few who escaped from Calais, further down the coast from Dunkirk. Most of his comrades in Calais were either killed or captured. As one of Churchill's first acts as prime minister, he decided to sacrifice Calais (and therefore all the soldiers, including my father) in the hope of delaying the German advance on Dunkirk and saving the routed British Expeditionary Force. Hitler, in one of the more mysterious moments of the war, issued the famous *Haltbestellung*. This 'Halt Order' meant Heinz Guderian and other commanders were told to hold back the panzer sweep to the coast for reasons which still remain unclear. Whatever Hitler's motives, the *Haltbestellung* gave the British breathing space to evacuate the remnants of the BEF including, thankfully, William John Esler. Churchill told the House of Commons on 4 June 1940: 'We must be very careful not to assign to this deliverance the attributes of a victory. Wars are not won by evacuations.'

After that wisdom came the bit every British schoolboy learned, and which my father held dear as the epitome of true leadership:

> We shall go on to the end. We shall fight in France, we shall fight in the seas and oceans, we shall fight with growing confidence and growing strength in the air; we shall defend our island whatever the cost may be. We shall fight on the beaches, we shall fight on the landing grounds, we shall fight in the fields and in the streets, we shall fight in the hills; we shall never surrender.

These sentences are for many leadership books a paradigm of 'authentic' leadership and the 'authentic' Churchill: optimistic, persevering, tough-minded, morally right and, above all, confident. But what did Churchill *really* think? Did he really believe that Britain could 'never surrender', when Nazis and fascists controlled all of Europe from Spain to the borders of the USSR? In Sam Leith's study of rhetoric, *You Talkin' to Me?* (2011), Leith quotes contemporaries of Churchill, including his aide Jock Colville, who suggested the 'fight them on the beaches' speech was 'blasted rhetoric', a criticism many of his contemporaries voiced privately about Churchill on other occasions. The Tory politician Charles Waterhouse said Churchill, when delivering his 'finest hour' speech, was far from confident in his delivery to the House of Commons. 'Not on his best form,' was Waterhouse's verdict. 'He was inclined to be hesitant to start and introduced some rather cheap jibes and jeers which seemed to me ill-suited to the gravity of the moment.'

Whatever version of Churchill's artfully constructed leadership story we believe nowadays, he was not 'authentically' a natural orator. He worked at it. Hard. 'Nervous to the point of nausea before addressing an audience,' Leith writes, 'Churchill consulted specialists as a young man in the hopes of ridding himself of his speech defects. He had both a stammer and a lisp ...' He rehearsed his House of Commons speeches endlessly before he delivered them, and throughout the war he subsequently recorded the speeches for transmission on BBC radio to boost public morale. Leith adds that after recording the 'fight them on the beaches' speech, Churchill continued: 'We'll throw bottles at the bastards. It's about all we've got left.' The ad lib was, of course, censored on transmission. What remained on the radio, Leith says, was 'that presidential style – all that gruffness and avuncularity, all those rumbling climaxes ... without being interrupted by rustling order papers and barracking Opposition MPs. He was pure voice.' Churchill once said, with typical humour: 'History will be kind to me, for I intend to write it.' He did of course do precisely that. Churchill wrote six volumes on World War Two, and achieved something all the leaders in this book aspire to: he defined his own legacy in his own terms and in his own words, largely swamping the negative counter-stories. Even so, Winston Churchill was as hard-working in creating his 'authentic' style as President Zardari was at his. Missing from Churchill's defiant promise of eternal British resistance is the different tone of a conversation he was said to have had with General Hastings 'Pug' Ismay, his chief of staff while the two men left France by British military plane, just as the French government was about to fall and German forces were breaking through. Ismay tried to cheer Churchill up, saying that things were perhaps not as bad as they seemed. Churchill retorted that Ismay was talking nonsense. The pair of them, Churchill suggested grimly, would both be dead within three months. Part of any leader's public storytelling method has to be the ability to project confidence and competence, whatever his private doubts. A degree of acting ability is necessary to deliver the message, and Churchill's use of the V-sign became a shorthand way of delivering that message without words, as well as helping mask whatever doubts he shared only with his closest confidants. In the play *Three Days in May*, (Faber and Faber 2011) the playwright Ben Brown examines the moment of indecision at the time of the collapse of the French army from the 26th to 28th May 1940. Lord Halifax, Churchill's rival for the leadership, suggested to the War Cabinet that they should use Mussolini as a go-between to sue for peace with Hitler. Churchill decided against. But in his own version of his leadership story he was to claim that such a question never even arose:

'Future generations may deem it noteworthy,' Churchill wrote, 'that the supreme question of whether we should fight on alone never found a place upon the War Cabinet agenda … we were much too busy to waste time on such unreal, academic issues.' (As quoted in *Three Days in May*.) *Three Days in May*, first performed in 2011, recounts more accurately that Churchill, secretly and temporarily, did have doubts about Britain's ability to fight on alone. He did consider the alternative options with the War Cabinet which included Neville Chamberlain, Lord Halifax and Labour's Arthur Greenwood and Clement Attlee. Churchill would have been a fool to have done otherwise. But he knew, as a story-teller, that never once showing or admitting to any doubts about the necessity of fighting on alone was a part of his great 'Who Am I?' leadership story. It was a story so powerful it has thoroughly infused our national 'Who Are We?' story as the people of Britain even today, and in 1940 it put the spine in 'Our Common Purpose,' to fight Hitler and win the war. Churchill famously stated that 'in war-time truth is so precious that she should always be attended by a bodyguard of lies'. All the combatants in the Second World War were, of course, engaged in acts of deception. In May 1942 Franklin Roosevelt said that he was 'perfectly willing to mislead and tell untruths if it will help win the war'. Churchill's private wobbles remained private, and the British people both wanted and needed to believe in the self-confidence of the leader. Things have become much more difficult in the twenty-first century.

For some time I have followed on Twitter @UKMILOPS. At the time of writing this is Major General Nick Pope of the British Army. He is the chief of the defence staff's strategic communications officer, and he tweets about the various conflicts involving British forces, including, for example, Libyan positions being engaged by UK forces using Hellfire missiles to help the rebels overthrow Colonel Gaddafi. This is a very different world from Pug Ismay and the buried secrets inside Winston Churchill's heart conveyed in a private conversation to a trusted aide, or the secret diaries of some of Churchill's critics in the worst days of the war. Churchill did not have to contemplate the globalisation of gossip, twenty-four-hour news culture, the Freedom of Information Act and his own military PR staff using Twitter to keep the British people informed.

Imagine, for example, if Winston Churchill's private conversation with Ismay, or his burst of humour about defending Britain by throwing bottles at the Nazis, had leaked through Twitter or on WikiLeaks, or if, as happened to Prime Minister Gordon Brown, a forgotten microphone captured a confidential aside and the story ended up on YouTube. What then might have been the consequences for British morale, Nazi aggression and American support? 'Authenticity' demands a degree of privacy, which is why faking it is so much more difficult in the world of twenty-first century globalised gossip.

Make Something Up, Your Majesty

Monarchs fake authenticity too. In his autobiography *Our Last Best Chance*, King Abdullah II of Jordan suggests that faking authenticity was at times part of his job description. For decades the leader of Jordan has had to play an almost impossible hand which at any moment could cost him his life. King Abdullah is the leader of an Arab country that has made peace with its neighbour Israel while bordering two nations, Syria and Iraq, which remain theoretically in a state of war with Israel. Jordan also contains a large, dispossessed and aggrieved Palestinian population. As King Abdullah puts it in the preface, 'I never intended to hold the position I am now entrusted with, and expected instead that I would spend my life in the army. Part of my story is about that military experience and what it taught me about Jordan and about leadership more generally.' One of the things that his military experience taught the young Abdullah was the necessity of faking authenticity. In a chapter entitled 'Lessons in Diplomacy', the King recounts a meeting with North Korea's 'Great Leader', the despotic Kim Il-sung, in November 1993. At a formal dinner a North Korean army officer demanded of King Abdullah, 'What gifts are you going to give the Great Leader?' King Abdullah takes up the story:

> I said, 'I have brought a clock, a traditional Jordanian dagger, and a gift box from my wedding.' The general nodded his approval. But later that night, sometime after midnight, a group of generals returned. They wanted an explanation of the significance of the gifts. I replied that they were gifts of friendship. He was not satisfied and pressed for more detail on each specific present. 'What is the meaning of the clock?' the general continued. I was stumped. But as it was nearly one in the morning and I was keen to get to bed, I remembered one of the basic rules of international diplomacy and started making stuff up. 'The clock,' I said, 'signifies the precious time my father

and the Great Leader spent together at Tito's funeral, and the time that has passed since then.' The generals nodded in unison and began scribbling furiously in their notebooks. Getting into the spirit, I continued, 'The dagger is a gift from one warrior to another.' The general asked, 'And the wedding box?' I said, 'I look on the Great Leader as a father, and so this is a gift from my recent wedding, from a grateful son.'

This leadership story, which King Abdullah tells with characteristic good humour, is – as with Churchill – a question of the interests of the state taking precedence over the private thoughts of the leader. The King of Jordan, like the British prime minister, did his duty, and his 'authentic' storytelling is a piece of entirely justified fakery. King Abdullah lifts the lid on the 'authentic' world of an Arab hereditary monarch who may have to deal with many obnoxious characters, despots and crazy people. Faking 'authenticity' is a way to survive.

A Pretty Straight Sort of Guy

Let's turn now to Tony Blair – *BLIAR!* to the T-shirt makers. Blair remains a controversial figure in the United Kingdom while continuing to be much admired elsewhere, especially in the United States. When I met Blair at a conference in Dubai, after he had left office in Downing Street, he was regarded by the conference organisers as an international superstar. He did not disappoint. His speech, on the importance of education, was a big hit with the audience and visiting dignitaries, several of whom commented to me that they were extremely pleased Blair had written a speech specially for the occasion, and specially for them. Maybe he had done, but as I have already mentioned, the *fact* of whether this was a new or recycled speech is irrelevant. What matters is that Tony Blair made it seem, even to a highly sophisticated audience which contained prime ministers, presidents, members of Arab royal families, cabinet ministers and CEOs of multinational corporations, that he had 'authentically' tailored his thoughts specially for them. Rather like book-buying fans queuing up for Sarah Palin or the topless model Jordan to sign copies of autobiographies 'just for us', we all – even world leaders – like to think we are receiving something uniquely crafted for us. Blair then took part in a panel discussion which I chaired, sitting alongside a number of leaders in politics, business and education, including the prime minister of Kenya and the former president of Sri Lanka.

In Britain, and even within his own Labour Party, however, Tony Blair has often been criticised for believing in nothing very much, and characterised as 'an actor' delivering lines with a phoney kind of sincerity or authenticity. There are plenty of valid criticisms of the Blair years, but to see him only as 'an actor' is particularly dim-witted, especially when we have just considered the example of Winston Churchill. Blair, like John F. Kennedy, Ronald Reagan, Franklin Roosevelt, Abraham Lincoln, Bill Clinton, David Cameron, all the successful rulers in Machiavelli's *The Prince* and more or less every successful leader you can think of, does indeed have a degree of acting and storytelling ability. It is the indispensable, core leadership skill. John F. Kennedy not only worked on his phrasing and debating techniques, he even recycled his lines. Kennedy took Cicero's great 'Who am I?' phrase – 'Civis Romanus sum', 'I am a Roman citizen' – and on 4 May 1962 told an audience in New Orleans: 'Two thousand years ago the proudest boast was to say I am a citizen of Rome. Today, I believe, the proudest boast is to say I am a citizen of the United States.' A year later, in West Germany, on the front line of the Cold War, Kennedy reworked his lines for a German audience. This time it was: 'Two thousand years ago the proudest boast was "Civis Romanus sum". Today, in the world of freedom, the proudest boast is "Ich bin ein Berliner".' Had he avoided assassination, Kennedy no doubt would have continued to recycle the phrase, perhaps in his ancestral home in Ireland, 'I am a Dubliner.' Making a

2,000-year-old rhetorical flourish seem fresh for a new audience is indeed an acting skill. It is also leadership storytelling of the most memorable kind, Cicero's 'earwig' for two millennia.

Kennedy seemed to have inherited the technique. In his 2003 biography *John F. Kennedy: An Unfinished Life 1917–63*, Robert Dallek suggests Kennedy was confused about the origins of his great-grandmother because his grandfather, who was mayor of Boston, 'used to claim his mother came from whichever Irish county had the most votes in the audience he was addressing at that particular time'. Richard Nixon, Kennedy's opponent in 1960, was said to have an aunt in every state of the union because he usually referred to some relative as having originated in every place he campaigned. All these distinguished leaders understood that the 'Who am I?' leadership story could be shaped and even faked a little so long as it seemed – as it did with 'Ich bin ein Berliner' – an authentic statement of who the leader claimed to be.

Yet, as noted above, although Tony Blair seemed at times to be a master of leadership storytelling, with every word he uttered in public calibrated to appeal to his target voters, towards the end of his premiership, and especially after the debacle of the Iraq invasion, his 'authenticity' was openly questioned. Critics in the press, within the Conservative Party and, damagingly, also within Blair's own Labour Party, began to look back over the Blair years and the Blair vocabulary with all the scepticism of those who had criticised Newt Gingrich for hollowness and cynical manipulation. They began to level at Blair the most destructive charge facing any modern politician: that he was inauthentic. He was lampooned as 'Phoney Tony' and 'Bliar!' – 'earwigs' of the most damaging kind. The critics began to reconsider Blair's most memorable sound bites. They recalled that Blair (ably assisted by Alastair Campbell) had promised to be 'tough on crime and tough on the causes of crime'; that he had three priorities: 'Education, education, education.' He claimed to have 'scars on my back' for his attempts to reform public services. He had paid tribute to Princess Diana as 'the People's Princess'. Every one of these quotes touched accurately on what was then the public mood. But one 'earwig' summed up both Blair's genius for phrase-making and what some saw as the 'Phoney Tony' lack of authenticity, eroding trust in his leadership and seriously damaging Blair's reputation.

It came during one of Blair's great successes, the Northern Ireland peace deal, which began as the Good Friday Agreement. Blair was ready to supervise the signing on 8 April 1998 at Stormont Castle on the outskirts of Belfast. The participants – Unionists, Nationalists and Republicans – exhausted by decades of murder and sectarian hatred, genuinely wanted peace, but remained suspicious of each other and wary of being accused of 'selling out' their people. Nevertheless, they agreed the deal. Blair said to the waiting cameras, 'A day like today is not a day for sound bites, really. But I feel the hand of history upon our shoulders. I really do.'

Blair, that most sharp-minded of political phrase makers, had crafted the perfect sound bite for a day that he claimed was not for sound bites. It was such an obvious contradiction that Blair recounts in *A Journey*, 'in the corner of my eye, I could see Jonathan [Powell, chief of staff] and Alastair [Campbell] cracking up'.

Like Zardari's staff carefully arranging the photographs they had brought with them for our interview, or Churchill repeating for the radio his Commons speeches to rally the war effort, Tony Blair was very self-aware and self-conscious about what he was doing – he was telling a story. And this *was* the authentic Tony Blair, a brilliant story-teller, being advised by a communications genius, Alastair Campbell. Blair was artlessly artful, clever enough to spin us a line about it not being the time to spin us a line, and yet still knowing that the sound bite would be so powerful it would be on every news bulletin around the world. Then he shared a private joke with his advisers about what he had done, a nod and a wink to those in the know. This slight awkwardness was part of Blair's genius, and, although he always had his critics, for the majority of the British people, he largely got away with it at the time. It was only subsequently, after the Iraq invasion of 2003, that Blair was re-evaluated and the 'Phoney Tony' nickname began to gain traction. Nowadays the sections of Blair's autobiography on the faking of authenticity – storytelling – are among the most revealing. For years, and three landslide election victories, he connected to voters – 'Who are we?' – not by living 'just like us', but by being conscious and aware of how the rest of us live. It was an act which he worked upon and developed.

Here's a potent example in some detail. In *A Journey*, he writes:

> With an election in the offing, it had been decided that I should do a regional tour to 'reconnect with the people'. There is always something a trifle dubious about the 'connecting with the people' business. In modern politics you have to pretend to be living the life the ordinary person leads, when of course you can't, and don't, do the shopping in the supermarket, fill up the car, go down the pub for a few beers, the quiz night and a bit of banter. But everyone nowadays has to go through the elaborate pretence that the prime minister could and should do all that, otherwise he or she is 'out of touch', the worst criticism that can ever be made. I can't tell you how many cafes, fish and chip shops and shopping malls I would go into ... all in the interests of showing that I was a 'regular bloke'. One of the main reasons it's total rubbish is that prior to going in, the place is staked out by armed detectives, the shopkeeper is quizzed for security and politics, there are around twenty cameramen and film crews ....

Blair then recounts one particular piece of staged authenticity when his rows with his chancellor Gordon Brown threatened to upset Labour's re-election bid in 2005.

'Go and buy ice cream from that van there, one for you, one for Gordon, to show togetherness and being normal,' Blair was instructed by an aide, Kate Garvey, who pointed him in the direction of Mr Whippy.

'No,' Blair protested. 'It's absurd … we're two guys in suits, one is the prime minister, the other is the Chancellor of the Exchequer. What's normal about it?'

'Just do it,' Kate Garvey said menacingly.

Blair, of course, did as instructed. He is scathing about the 'elaborate pretence', but understood it was necessary and useful. And in the further pursuit of 'authenticity', before every general election, fearing being tripped up by some smart TV interviewer or voter, Blair's advisers would insist that he learn a price list of daily essentials for 'normal' people in the supermarket.

> I would have to go through a list of the price of everyday things like a pint of milk, a pound of butter, a shoulder of lamb. Bread used to produce lengthy debate about which type of loaf, white or brown, nothing too wholemeal, nothing too unhealthy, all of it done in the belief that if I knew such a fact, it would mean I might be going down to the shop near Downing Street (not that there was one) and collecting the groceries, which of course I wasn't. But people have great faith in the power of such trips to 'connect' with the public, and who's to say they're wrong.

If you doubt Blair's wisdom in this, then fast forward to March 2012 when the Conservative government of David Cameron and Chancellor of the Exchequer George Osborne were pummelled daily in the popular press for being 'out of touch' with working people for introducing a tax on hot fast food which became known as the 'Pasty Tax.' In the ensuing brouhaha David Cameron insisted he really liked Cornish pasties and tried to remember when he last ate one. Unfortunately he got the details wrong. Blair, in other words, may be right to be scathing about the story-telling nonsense, the 'elaborate pretence,' involved in modern democratic politics, but the perils of not doing it properly, as David Cameron and George Osborne demonstrated, can be severe. Finally, Blair accurately sums up twenty-first century leadership, and the power of stories: 'It's about temperament, character and attitude. It's also about being authentic.'

Blair's carefully crafted 'authentic' sound bites were repeated over and over again on TV and radio, and quoted in the newspapers. His staged 'authenticity' in sharing a Mr Whippy ice cream with Gordon Brown was often shown by TV news programmes. At first the pictures were used to suggest that the Blair–Brown problems had been exaggerated, and then later, as the breach between the two men became a gulf, these same pictures were used to suggest precisely the opposite: to confirm the public hypocrisy of two top politicians who, at times, could not stand the sight of each other. Blair was quoted in the subsequent autobiography of his Cabinet colleague Alistair Darling as saying that dealing with Gordon Brown was often 'like having dental treatment with no anaesthetic'. The same 'fact' – the ice-cream eating – could therefore be used both to back up the Blair leadership story, 'a pretty straight sort of guy', and also, when it fell apart, to demonstrate the core of the counter-story, fakery and artifice.

Authenticity, therefore, whether truly authentic or consummately faked, whether in a presidential candidate's autobiography or in the choice of pictures a leader wishes us to see on television, is the mother lode, the Holy Grail of twenty-first century power. Authenticity helps to connect leaders to followers, customers and voters, because it means the leadership story seems to be *true*, although it might not be factually accurate. A leader can get away with factual inaccuracies. He can even get away with blatant lies, as we will see when we come to Bill Clinton and the Monica Lewinsky scandal. But a leader cannot survive if his followers come to see him and his stories as inauthentic. Tony Blair, for all his political genius, was eventually seen that way. His reputation so far has still not recovered from the 'Phoney Tony' and 'Bliar!' gibes, and it may never do so.

Leadership Lesson: Leadership stories aspire to 'authenticity', but authenticity can be faked. Sometimes it should be faked. Churchill's optimism in the Second World War, or Jordan's King Abdullah II making up an 'authentic' story for Kim Il-sung were reasonable and justifiable examples of fakery. Authenticity is different from truth, and even stories which the audience suspects may not entirely be true can serve the leader's purpose as long as they sound 'authentic'.

Followership Lesson: Effective leadership demands not just 'authenticity' but a degree of privacy. How much do we want to know? If we really had known about Churchill's doubts of survival, would Britain have fought so hard against Hitler in 1940? All stories are shaped and edited by the storyteller. Even if there is nothing deceptive about pictures or flags placed carefully behind the leader on TV, they are not there by accident. Followers must understand that such devices are part of a leader's storytelling technique.

7 A STAR Moment: From Osama Bin Laden to the London Olympics

In his opening remarks to the NHS conference I mentioned in Chapter 3, Alastair Campbell did something quite surprising which immediately caught the attention of everyone present. He said he was pleased I had introduced him as Tony Blair's former spokesman because not all introductions had been so kind. Campbell joked that at a previous speaking engagement he had been introduced instead as the 'most evil man' in Britain. The audience laughed. They also paid close attention to everything Campbell said from that moment on. Telling a counter-story about himself was a very clever technique. It caught the audience's imagination because it was not what we expected. The American presentation expert, Nancy Duarte calls this technique a 'STAR' moment because it gives the audience 'Something They Always Remember'. Some psychologists suggest that effective storytelling offers a 'violation of expectations'. We need to be surprised, otherwise the story loses its power. In this chapter we will consider examples of the STAR technique from leaders including Chile's president Michelle Bachelet, Peru's president Ollanta Humala, Margaret Thatcher and Osama Bin Laden. The chapter ends with one of the most potent examples of the power of stories: the successful London bid to bring the 2012 Olympics to Britain. As we will see, telling a better story can often be the difference between losing and winning.

Alastair Campbell is one of the shrewdest communicators in recent British public life. So why would he tell a conference that he had been described as the 'most evil man' in Britain? Why would anyone make public the most damning counter-story criticism against himself? Campbell has told similar stories on other occasions. A friend – who had a very dim view of Campbell – spoke to me glowingly of a tale Campbell told to a highly suspicious business audience. Campbell related how while jogging in a London park he came across someone who was partially unconscious lying on the ground. He came to the man's aid. As the man began to recover, he seemed to recognise him. Campbell introduced himself as Tony Blair's press secretary.

'I knew it!' said the man on the ground. 'Alastair Campbell! I effing hate you!'

My friend, who is himself a skilled public speaker, was full of admiration for the way Campbell had opened with this story. He said: 'It had the audience in stitches and totally disarmed. Alastair was now a "good guy" and proceeded with his presentation. It was a fantastic use of a story.' Campbell's technique of telling jokes at his own expense demonstrates an important political virtue in Britain: being able to laugh at oneself. It also reminded the audience of Campbell's significance at the heart of power, and his supposed ruthlessness when managing the communications surrounding great events. He was someone capable, in the slang of the day, of 'monstering' those who disagreed with him.

Peter Guber, in his book directed at business leaders, *Tell to Win* (2011), puts tactics like Campbell's into perspective:

> Anybody who's ever read a novel or watched a movie knows that a story that fails to deliver surprise is dead on arrival. The same rule holds for stories told in person to business audiences. The shock value may be as subtle as a shrug or a pang of regret. Not every story needs thrills and chills, but without *some* surprise, you'll lose your listener's attention.

Guber quotes neuroscientists and cognitive psychologists who claim that good storytelling:

… emerges from violations to expectations … You have
expectations in your head; I have expectations in my head.
We sit down to breakfast. I tell you, I got up this morning, I
went into the bathroom and picked up my toothbrush and
put toothpaste on it, blah, blah, blah. Our expectations are
totally in sync. There's no violation of them. It's boring. It's not
memorable. It's not surprising, it's not a story!

In *This Is Your Brain on Music* (2006) the neuroscientist
and former music producer Daniel Levitin points out that the
'violation of expectations' is a technique also used by the greatest
songwriters and musicians. 'Magicians set up expectations
and then defy them,' Levitin writes, 'all without you knowing
exactly how or when they're going to do it. Composers do the
same thing.' He lists popular songs from the Beatles, the Kinks,
Steely Dan, Aretha Franklin and the Carpenters to scores by
classical composers like Beethoven as examples of music where
expectations are set up and then violated, to entrance us. 'When
cognitive scientists talk about expectations and violating them,' he
says, 'we mean an event whose occurrence is at odds with what
might have been reasonably predicted.'

The American writer and graphic designer Nancy Duarte
worked with Al Gore on his storytelling technique in the
movie *An Inconvenient Truth* (2006). Duarte calls rhetorical
tricks like Campbell's jokes a STAR moment, 'Something They
Always Remember', and when I talked to members of the
audience afterwards, they certainly did remember Campbell's
anecdote about being 'evil'. It was a twenty-word master-class in
communications. Duarte's STAR moment is not the same as what
I have called an 'earwig', except in the sense that both are supposed
to be memorable. When Bill Clinton described himself as 'the boy
From Hope' or Mrs Thatcher's aides presented her as 'the Iron
Lady', they wanted us to remember the phrase, and to ensure we
understood it as a core part of the leader's own story, a headline

to remind us who the leader is and what they are like. Campbell describing himself as 'evil' is not, of course, how he wishes us to think of him. But it is a surprising revelation about his character, which he hopes we will remember, including his ability to laugh at himself.

All The Sins Together

Effective leaders grasp this technique very easily. Chile's first female president, Michelle Bachelet, certainly understood the need to 'violate expectations'. I met President Bachelet in April 2008 in the middle of her four-year term, and was curious how a left-of-centre woman had risen to the top in Chile's notoriously conservative and macho political culture. Bachelet explained to me that she was helped by having served as Chile's defence minister, where she had used the 'violation of expectations' technique to her advantage. Chile had gone through years of turmoil. In 1973 the country's right-wing military led by Augusto Pinochet and supported by the CIA staged a bloody coup. They toppled the democratically elected president, Salvador Allende. The Pinochet regime killed many Chileans, including Bachelet's own father, who was on the moderate left. Bachelet told me she felt great anger and pain at that loss. When she entered politics in democratic Chile she knew that becoming defence minister, controlling and dealing with the generals, the successors to those who had murdered her father, could be a problem. At their first formal meeting she astonished the military leaders by the way she introduced herself: 'I am a woman, a socialist, divorced and agnostic,' she said. 'All the sins together. But we will work together very well.'

Michelle Bachelet made clear where she stood personally and politically in her leadership story. She also displayed a sense of humour that not even a Chilean general could find threatening. It was a STAR moment in which, like Campbell, Bachelet addressed the worst that the generals were probably saying about her in private, and by summing up the counter-story, she neutralised it. Bachelet told me that one of the achievements of governments all over the world in the early twenty-first century – from Turkey to Brazil, from Greece, Spain and Portugal to Indonesia and El Salvador – had been to ensure that the military was now out of power, where once the army had been the default setting for troubled developing countries. By 2008, civilian control was evident throughout Latin America. It was a profound change, and one which Bachelet helped to complete. She told me that from that tricky start, as president she now 'had a wonderful relationship' with Chile's military commanders and was therefore able to bring 'the feminine side' to politics in her drive for social justice and equity. Bachelet's election to the presidency was, in itself, a 'violation of expectations' for her country. She certainly understood that women leaders and their leadership stories are judged by different standards to men, quoting to me newspapers in Chile which had covered her 2008 visit to the UK by reflecting on the way she had dressed when she met the Queen, something they would never have done with a male leader. 'It's a matter of time' she said, of the singular failure of so many newspapers and broadcasters to 'violate expectations' when it comes to women in power.

When Bachelet left office in 2010 after a four-year non-renewable term she had 84 per cent approval ratings. She would easily have been re-elected if such a thing were permissible under Chile's constitution. In her supposedly macho conservative nation she appointed a cabinet in which women constituted half of the ministers. She tripled the number of free childcare places for low-income mothers and pushed through a pension overhaul which also helped women. She went on to become the head of UN Women, to try to bring about gender equality worldwide. Bachelet's leadership story is compelling because she surprised people and told them a different narrative from the one they were expecting. Unlike some women leaders – Sarah Palin with her hunting stories, and Margaret Thatcher with the myth of the 'Iron Lady' – Bachelet never played up the supposedly 'masculine' characteristics of leadership. 'She was our anti-Thatcher, not adopting the all male-dominated codes of power but transforming them,' one commentator, Paula Escobar Chavarría of the Chilean daily *El Mercurio* said of the changes Bachelet initiated (*International Herald Tribune*, 30 March 2011). 'In this small land at the bottom of the world's maps, little girls now want to be president and no one wonders if it's possible.' Expectations continue to be violated, in what proved to be a historic lesson from the top in how to tell stories.

Checkmate

The Peruvian president Ollanta Humala adopted a similar technique to that of Bachelet, but in reverse. Humala is a former army lieutenant colonel with a strong base among the poor indigenous people of Peru. Humala also sensed that the tide had turned against military governments and army hard men in Latin America, and so when he ran for the presidency he violated expectations by adopting left-of-centre populist policies more associated with civilian politicians like Bachelet than traditionally right-of-centre military officers. But Humala was also careful to groom his image through storytelling. When he heard I was making a BBC film on his first presidential election campaign he made sure that late at night after one of his rallies in Cuzco, in the high Andes, he and I could meet and be filmed playing chess. Humala, the military man of action, wanted to be seen as thoughtful and intellectual, and the chess game was the perfect photo-opportunity. I interviewed him while we played. He won. He promised a re-match in the presidential palace. Like Michael Deaver managing Ronald Reagan, Ollanta Humala perfectly understood the power of pictures to create a STAR moment. The quiet contemplation of his chess game was utterly different from the stereotype of a Latin American military officer. It was precisely the message he wanted the world to see.

A former BBC colleague David Lomax had a similar experience with the Palestinian president Yasser Arafat in Beirut. Many in the West regarded Arafat as a 'terrorist', but his deliberate chess-playing with Lomax was a violation of expectations. For men of action like Humala and Arafat, chess is a useful device. Relatively sedentary leaders like Tony Blair, George W. Bush, his father George H. W. Bush, and David Cameron, violate expectations in the opposite direction. They like to be seen playing football, tennis or golf, cycling and fishing or, in the case of Bush Junior, clearing brush on his Texas ranch. The solutions are different, but the need to violate expectations is the common currency in lessons from the top.

Uniters and Dividers

Margaret Thatcher had a very different problem. As we will see in Chapter 9, Mrs Thatcher had to overcome the familiar sexist complaints about women leaders – that they are shrill and hectoring or indecisive and vacillating. Hillary Clinton suffered from the former counter-story, Angela Merkel from the latter. Mrs Thatcher dealt with both complaints. She took voice-coaching lessons, softened her hairstyle and dress sense, while simultaneously and relentlessly working on building the myth of inflexibility, which was to become the core element of her leadership story.

But even the 'Iron Lady' and her advisers occasionally saw the benefit of violating expectations and providing us with a STAR moment in the opposite direction. She did it with breathtaking clarity on the day she entered Downing Street for the first time as prime minister. Her advisers, while emphasising her 'Who am I?' firmness of purpose, were also concerned that she had a reputation as a 'divider' not a 'uniter', which in the troubled times of 1979 could have wrecked her ability to lead. Like President George W. Bush a generation later, Mrs Thatcher simply denied what was, in fact, clearly the case, that she was a divisive figure.

On Friday, 4 May 1979, Margaret Thatcher presented Britain with a magnificent STAR moment. She lowered her voice as she had been trained to do, and as she stood in Downing Street she softly said,'I know full well the responsibilities that await me as I enter the door of No. 10 and I'll strive unceasingly to try to fulfil the trust and confidence that the British people have placed in me and the things in which I believe. And I would just like to remember some words of St Francis of Assisi which I think are really just particularly apt at the moment: "Where there is discord, may we bring harmony. Where there is error, may we bring truth. Where there is doubt, may we bring faith. And where there is despair, may we bring hope."'

If you expected the strident and bossy Mrs T, she violated those expectations by using words that depicted her very differently. Like Alastair Campbell and the suggestion of 'evil', or Michelle Bachelet referring to her personality as bringing 'all the sins together', Margaret Thatcher could not possibly have thought that she really was in the mould of St Francis. She was after all a woman who relished battles, demolished her enemies, saw aspiration as one of mankind's most noble achievements and appeared to claim there was no such thing as society. St Francis of Assisi was a thirteenth-century noble Italian who gave up the luxuries of life to sit with the beggars in St Peter's in Rome, and created the Franciscan and the 'Poor Clares' orders, known for poverty, chastity, obedience and humility – words which few would use to characterise the leadership of the Thatcher years. Expectations were not so much violated as annihilated, but nevertheless it was indeed a STAR moment, at least for TV producers, echoed, of course, in Meryl Streep's Hollywood portrayal of the Iron Lady in 2011.

The 'violation of expectations' technique was used privately by Mrs Thatcher as well as publicly. Bernard (now Sir Bernard) Ingham told me with great amusement how he was present when Prime Minister Thatcher first met Mikhail Gorbachev in December 1984. Andrei Chernenko was president of the USSR, but Gorbachev was regarded as his heir apparent. Here is the official view of the meeting, as told by Mrs Thatcher herself to the BBC's political editor John Cole:

> I am cautiously optimistic. I like Mr Gorbachev. We can do business together. We both believe in our own political systems. He firmly believes in his; I firmly believe in mine. We are never going to change one another. So that is not in doubt, but we have two great interests in common: that we should both do everything we can to see that war never starts again, and therefore we go into the disarmament talks determined to make them succeed. And secondly, I think we both believe that they are the more likely to succeed if we can build up confidence in one another and trust in one another about each other's approach, and therefore, we believe in cooperating on trade matters, on cultural matters, on quite a lot of contacts between politicians from the two sides of the divide … He was very ready to enter into full, detailed discussion; not to stick to prepared statements. So we had a genuine discussion.

Sir Bernard Ingham's account of the 'genuine discussion' is more colourful. In the version he told to me, and which he has related elsewhere, Sir Bernard explained that if Mr Gorbachev expected the usual diplomatic niceties, he was in for a shock. Mrs Thatcher opened the conversation by saying that she thought communism was a disaster for the USSR, the Russian people and the world. It sapped initiative and creativity. It held individuals and nations back. It enslaved the mind. She said that the Soviet system was quite dreadful and that Marxist-Leninism had been a catastrophe. While Gorbachev was still reeling in shock from this Something They Always Remember tirade, Mrs Thatcher apparently changed gear and assured him that despite her honestly held and clearly expressed criticisms, the Soviet Union had the right to exist and to do so behind secure and safe borders. The UK and USSR were two countries which could and should work together for peace in

Europe. A relieved Mr Gorbachev – like many other leaders from around the world – had been 'handbagged', by Mrs Thatcher's combination of charm, femininity and strongly held opinions. He never forgot this STAR moment. Neither did Bernard Ingham. Gorbachev and Thatcher did indeed do business together. That in itself was a violation of some people's expectations.

Kalashnikovs and Humour

Perhaps the most surprising practitioner of this type of leadership storytelling is Osama Bin Laden. Until his death at the hands of US Special Forces in 2011, Bin Laden offered a very different leadership story from all the others in this book – he was, of course, the man behind the attacks on the World Trade Center and the spiritual godfather of al-Qaeda, and his ambitions often seemed to lie in the next world rather than this one – however, his methods are similar to many of the other leaders we have considered. If American presidential candidates feel the need to tell us they came from a humble family, grew up in a log cabin or its equivalent, and represent the ordinary American people, Bin Laden's story turned that type of origin myth on its head. In his leadership storytelling, Bin Laden's entire life was a violation of expectations.

He was the child of one of the Arab world's richest, most powerful and influential families. He could have enjoyed the sybaritic life of some of his Saudi contemporaries and family members. Instead the story spun by Bin Laden and his acolytes was of an ascetic holy man who lived in a cave and sacrificed everything, including his life, for Islam. In the account propagated by his disciples, Bin Laden struggled first against the godless armies of the Soviet Union, then against the regime in his own country, Saudi Arabia, for tolerating American bases in the land of Mecca, and finally with the United States and its allies. Bin Laden carefully released videos and statements to massage an image as artfully crafted as anything from Michael Deaver, Alastair Campbell or Lady Gaga.

There were pictures of Bin Laden in flowing robes, sometimes perched on a beautiful white Arab steed with flowing mane, a masterful storytelling image that reminded Arabs that Bin Laden was the twenty-first century's Saladin, fighting the evil crusaders. Other pictures showed him sitting simply on the bare earth, rather like a religious hermit, except for the Kalashnikov rifle carefully resting on his knee. In other shots his advisers would 'dress the set' by propping AK-47s against the cave wall. Every image, every statement, every utterance, every tape, was created to tell the story of an 'authentic' Muslim leader struggling on behalf of his oppressed people to fight the 'crusader' nations and their dupes and allies in the Muslim world.

The facts of Bin Laden's life proved to be quite different. He was hiding out, as we now know, not in a cave but in a massive fortified compound in the Pakistan city of Abbottabad, near a major military base, enjoying the presence of his wives and almost certainly the protection of some people within Pakistani intelligence. He used modern communications technology to spread his message, and despite being a world away from Hollywood, Bin Laden was just as adept as the scriptwriter Robert McKee in shaping a good story. For guidance on how he did so I turned to the Palestinian journalist Abdel Bari Atwan. Atwan is editor-in-chief of the Arabic newspaper *Al-Quds Al-Arabi,* and he met Bin Laden in the autumn of 1996, five years before 9/11, at a time when Bin Laden was burnishing his image. Atwan spent three days with the al-Qaeda leader at his hideout in the caves of Tora Bora. At the time, Bin Laden actually had an office in London's Oxford Street, the busiest shopping area in the city; the UK branch of Osama Bin Laden's 'Reform and Advice Committee' lasted from 1994 until 1998 in central London and was managed by Khaled al-Fawwaz. In 1998 things came to an end when al-Fawwaz was extradited to the United States for his alleged part in planning the al-Qaeda bombings of the US embassies in Kenya and Tanzania.

Through contacts provided by al-Fawwaz in 1996, Abdel Bari Atwan travelled to Pakistan and then over the border into Afghanistan to meet Bin Laden. The description Atwan gives in his book *The Secret History of Al Qa'ida* (2006), and which he has also told to me personally, forms part of Bin Laden's carefully crafted leadership myth. It is worth recounting in detail as it is full of carefully constructed STAR moments and repeated 'violations of expectations'.

As Atwan tells it, Bin Laden is 'humble' throughout their meeting in the caves of Tora Bora, as are his aides. The al-Qaeda leader speaks in a low, soft voice in beautiful Arabic. Like Colonel Gaddafi with his books and Yasser Arafat or Ollanta Humala playing chess, Bin Laden is careful to groom his image as a thoughtful intellectual, not some barbarous, bigoted and unschooled fighter. He is a man, Atwan recounts, who appreciates intelligent conversation and dialogue. There is a library of books in his cave, which he is keen for his visitors to notice.

Atwan first met Bin Laden's 'envoy' in Jalalabad, an Egyptian called Abu Hafs al-Misri, who, Atwan found out later, was chief of al-Qaeda's military operations at the time. 'He [al-Misri] was a very striking looking person,' Atwan writes, '... bearded, full of youth and vigour. He was modest, extremely radical and exceptionally polite. I respected his sincerity, humility and profound faith ...'. Atwan was picked up by car and taken into the mountains. What follows reads like a religious pilgrimage to a holy shrine, the modern terrorist version of Chaucer's *Canterbury Tales*, the Jihadist's Tale:

> The road was unpaved and passed through mountain valley villages connected by terrifying rock-strewn spiralling roads. It was my bad luck that we had to tackle this road after nightfall and in pitch darkness. I felt as if we were hurtling into the unknown ... I was not blindfolded as we approached Tora Bora ... I had spent much of my trip in a state of near-terror, but ... I

never once felt that there was anything to fear from Bin Laden or his men ... I met Osama Bin Laden just before midnight on 23 November. He was sitting cross-legged on the carpet, a Kalashnikov in his lap ... Bin Laden placed his rifle on the ground and got up. He came towards me with a warm smile that turned into barely repressed laughter as he took in the way I was dressed.

Atwan was wearing Pashtun tribal clothes. After some twenty-five years living in London, his normal business attire is a smart, sober, dark blue suit, crisp shirt and elegant tie. Bin Laden immediately understood Atwan's awkwardness in tribal clothes, and made fun of it, an obvious violation of expectations for those who expected the leader of a fanatical religious movement to have no sense of humour. Atwan's account continues:

> [Bin Laden] embraced me warmly and asked about my trip. I felt like an honoured guest and was treated with the greatest respect ... Bin Laden made every effort to put me at ease and he somehow seemed very familiar to me – perhaps that is the essence of charisma ... I was surprised to find Osama Bin Laden, the son of one of the wealthiest Arab families and used to the utmost luxury, in this freezing, humble cave ... But Bin Laden told me he despised money, and had never sought a life of comfort and ease; unlike his brothers he had always lived modestly.

Bin Laden emerges from Atwan's account as a biblical or Quranic holy man, a hermit or monk in his austere cell, and yet with the 'essence of charisma' that you might find in Bill Clinton, Queen Elizabeth II or George W. Bush, the skill of being able to put people immediately at their ease. Here is Atwan's account of what he saw as one of Bin Laden's STAR moments:

> The cave was approximately 6 metres by 4 metres. The main feature of the room was an extensive library full of books on

Islamic heritage and *tafsir* [Quranic commentary]. Kalashnikov assault rifles decorated the remaining walls of the cave, hanging from nails here and there. Osama Bin Laden is tall and slender, and was without any apparent physical weakness. He had allowed his beard to grow ... Bin Laden's manner is one of extreme humility, and I discovered ... that he can be very pleasant to be with. His voice is soft, but clear. He is constantly smiling in a reassuring manner *that shortens the distance between him and his guest* ... Bin Laden has a lively sense of humour and often makes jokes at the least expected moments ... [my italics].

Atwan was to learn later when he published his account of their meeting that Bin Laden was particularly amused by his stories of the awful food in the cave, and especially by the fact that some of it made Atwan vomit under a pine tree: '... Bin Laden read it [Atwan's account] four times. Each time he got to the bit about how awful the food was, he laughed heartily ...'

Significantly, Atwan reveals that Bin Laden had a 'media adviser', and very carefully controlled his own leadership story. He was extremely savvy about journalists and refused to have the interview conversations taped in case he might make some 'grammatical or theological mistakes which, if recorded, could be used against him'. Bin Laden was as careful about the use of words as Michael Deaver or Newt Gingrich. He also understood very clearly his own talent for myth-making and storytelling, as well as the hunger among his followers or potential followers to see him as a great Arab and Muslim leader. Humble, humorous, hospitable, self-deprecating, interested in books, Osama Bin Laden was a perfect portrait of violated expectations. At one moment he could discuss the moral guidance of Islam, a religion of peace, compassion and submission, the next he would tell his visitors that the 'favourite' Kalashnikov in his collection had been captured from a Soviet officer many years before. Whether factually true or not, like much of the Bin Laden storytelling this anecdote is certainly 'authentic'. It is shaped to tell us what to think of Bin Laden in a coherent way, and to remind us of his years of struggle for his version of Islam. The Kalashnikov weaves Bin Laden's struggle against the 'invader' United States into the previous struggle against the 'invader' USSR and sets it in the context of Saladin's struggle against the Christian invaders during the Crusades. At every stage of Bin Laden's leadership storytelling, Muslim people are the victims of aggression from unbelievers. This narrative, as we know only too well, is compelling enough to radicalise a new generation of young Muslims by connecting them to the principles of Holy War at the foundations of their religion, and placing Bin Laden himself at the centre of that struggle. Like Ronald Reagan trying to 'own' American, or Mandela 'owning' the idea of being African, Bin Laden's storytelling tries to 'own' the idea of defender of his faith. It is all the more chilling because of his sophistication in violating our expectations.

How London Won the 2012 Olympics

I want to end this chapter with a completely different type of violation of expectations, because it shows how storytelling can work for a business or in an act of salesmanship. In this case it led to London winning the right to host the 2012 Olympic Games against the expectations of many of London's own residents. It is a lesson from the top which points directly to the power of stories to overcome other disadvantages. The STAR moments and violation of expectations here refer not to a person but to a place, London itself. The London story brings together many of the lessons we have considered so far. David Magliano, the director of marketing for the London bid, kindly talked me through how, as he put it, the London team 'fabricated' a story to 'do the job of winning' over bids from Paris, New York and Madrid, which, he accepted, 'might have seemed better bids'.

'Did London lie?' I wondered.

'No,' Magliano said firmly. 'Our story was authentic, meaning that it was rooted in truth, but we searched for a story to tell.'

Stories, as Magliano indicates, do not occur in nature. They are made, constructed, shaped or, in Magliano's word, fabricated. The London bid team searched for a story to tell and also searched for the right combination of people to tell it. That combination included a member of the British royal family with long-standing sporting credentials, Princess Anne; a former Olympic athlete, Seb Coe; and someone who at the time of the bid, July 2005, was a worldwide political superstar, the then prime minister Tony Blair. The London team added an endorsement from a great international hero, Nelson Mandela. Detailed planning made sure that every word used was correct (à la Newt Gingrich); that the story was told beautifully in pictures (à la Michael Deaver); and that the bid was coherently shaped as a story, with eyes on the *objective* of winning the 2012 Games, on the *strategy* of winning over members of the International Olympic Committee, and on the *tactics* – the films, words and storytellers in the right combination (à la Alastair Campbell). Every lesson about storytelling we have examined so far in this book was employed to ensure that London looked and sounded unlike any of its rivals.

The key presentation for the 2012 Games took place on 6 July 2005 in Singapore. The five cities in the final round – Paris, Madrid, New York, Moscow and London – were competing for the 105 votes of the International Olympic Committee (IOC). Each city had a maximum of forty-five minutes to make their final presentation. In practice the three likeliest candidates were Paris, Madrid and London. David Magliano and the London team knew that London had a number of major disadvantages, weaknesses or counter-stories: the city had hosted the Games twice before, most recently in 1948; there was a lack of existing top-quality sports facilities; and London's transport system was officially described by the IOC as 'good' – something Magliano admitted to me was polite Olympic-speak for 'rubbish'. Nothing, in the courteous world of the IOC is ever 'worse than good', is how he put it. So how could London win?

Hard work helped. The presentation script was reworked thirty-four times. Magliano spent hours considering one word in particular: 'we'. The 'Who am I?' part of the story was easy: London itself. But 'Who are we?' in the context of an Olympic bid could mean many things: London and Londoners, or Britain and the British, or athletes and Olympians. This was where a bit of storytelling genius came in. Throughout the presentation, when Seb Coe used the word 'we', he was referring to his audience in the entire Olympic movement. He suggested, as no other bid did, that London and the IOC voting panel were all together in a common enterprise to sell the idea of sport itself. As Magliano explained it to me, 'We told the IOC, you've got a big problem, and we're the guys to help you.'

The 'big problem' was getting young people worldwide interested in competitive Olympic sport. The IOC were very worried by the appeal of professional soccer, basketball, baseball and American football. They were also concerned that all over the world young people would rather surf the internet than spend hours running on the track or in the swimming pool. The London bid team ruthlessly exploited this concern, repeating in their presentation that to create one Olympic champion requires eight Olympic finalists, more than 200 national champions, thousands of athletes and millions of children 'to be inspired'. The genius of the London story, in other words, was that it was not about London at all. It was about the world's children. And who could resist such an appeal?

To build the ambitious story of claiming to speak for the world's children, Magliano and his team spent hours looking over every successful and unsuccessful Olympic bid in recent years. They were depressingly the same. They did not violate expectations, but instead tended to parade clichés. The films used by Paris, Madrid, New York and Moscow were all nicely shot, using pretty pictures, aerial photography, pleasant local music, and voices from ordinary people reminding us what a great place the city in question really was. The Moscow bid featured a Russian bear; Madrid had a flamenco dancer; Paris, romantic French music; New York, multi-ethnic New Yorkers. In this sea of stereotypes, the British bid violated every expectation. Instead of ducking the fact that London had already hosted the Games twice, Seb Coe reminded the IOC audience of the great successes of the Games in London in 1908 and 1948, also both times of difficulty for the IOC.

'London's vision is to reach young people all around the world,' Coe said, 'so that they are inspired to choose sport.'

Instead of the host city travelogue seen in all the other bids, London's bid featured African kids in some shanty town messing around in the streets, throwing stones. A police car goes by. The policeman frowns. The audience thinks that these kids might be up to no good. Then the kids see a TV clip of an Olympic hero from Nigeria winning a race. In another clip a Latin American boy sees a cycling race and jumps on his own bike. A Russian girl is transfixed by the swimming she sees on TV and decides to start training. A Chinese girl watches gymnastics, then we see her in the gym. In the film presentation all these children metamorphose into the athletes they are watching on TV. The moral is that inside every child there is a potential Olympic hero, and that sport transforms the world. The genius of the London storytelling was barely to mention London at all, except as an inspiration to the young.

'Amber is an emerging basketball player,' the presentation said. A British schoolgirl came on to the stage. Some thirty of her contemporaries were in the audience. The audience could see her dreams of Olympic glory written on her face, and could share them. 'We were looking for the STAR moment,' Magliano told me. 'And we found it.'

Magliano compared this storytelling to the notorious O. J. Simpson trial in the United States in the 1990s, when Simpson's lawyer gave the jury a STAR moment. He said repeatedly of the blood-soaked glove allegedly used by Simpson to murder his estranged wife: 'If it don't fit – you must acquit.' Magliano also cited the moment when Microsoft's founder Bill Gates persuaded a group of potential donors to support his anti-malaria campaign by opening a jar filled with mosquitoes, releasing them towards his audience and saying 'There's no reason only poor people should have the experience', i.e. of being bitten and contracting malaria. The mosquitoes were of course not carrying the malaria parasite, but that really was a STAR moment no one in the audience would ever forget.

The London bid was designed, Magliano told me, so that no one who saw it would ever forget the moment when aspiring young athletes took to the stage and reminded the world why the Olympics was important. But surely, I suggested, Paris or New York were also magnets for young people? If the IOC has a problem, any of the competing cities could also be the solution? Magliano laughed.

'We were not the only ones who *could* tell the story of how the Games could inspire young people to choose sport,' he replied, 'but we were the only ones who *did* tell that story … My theory is that if at the top level the argument is a little weak, you can compensate for that in a presentation if your evidence for each point is strong.' That meant reminding the IOC how many young people come to London to study, how enthusiastic Londoners were for the Games, and that the legacy of London 2012 would be a generation of young people enthused about sport worldwide.

Two other storytelling techniques helped to seal the bid. One was the use of the British prime minister Tony Blair to violate expectations in a most striking way. All the cities involved had rolled out their biggest names. Paris counted on the French president Jacques Chirac, who also attended the Singapore event. He stayed longer than Blair and 'worked the room' of IOC delegates at a cocktail party. Blair used a different strategy.

The British decided that there was a problem with working a room of delegates at a cocktail party. Only maybe a dozen members of the IOC were truly swing voters and worth lobbying. To get to them Chirac also had to spend a lot of time and charm talking to those who were already behind the Paris bid. Blair did not bother. He came into the Singapore cocktail party for just a few moments to show his face, and then left to go to a private room nearby. The London bid team then selected the very few key delegates they wanted to impress and asked them in turn if they would like a 'private' audience with Tony Blair. They were flattered and delighted, especially when Blair asked them humbly for their 'advice' on how best to secure the London bid. Blair violated expectations. Instead of working the room, he made sure that the room worked for him. In his filmed presentation Blair again violated expectations. He began by talking at length in French, not English – another STAR moment, especially for the Francophone guests, and impressive to everyone in the room. He followed up by quoting one of the few genuine world heroes, Nelson Mandela, who said that he couldn't think of a better place than London for the shared Olympic mission of inspiring young people and ensuring what he called 'our vision … to see millions more young people participating in sport'. Mandela's use of the word 'our', like the word 'we', was of course extremely powerful.

The final London storytelling trick was to make the political into the personal. Seb Coe, the former Olympic athlete, told his own 'Who am I?' story and concluded, 'On behalf of the youth of today, the athletes of tomorrow and the Olympians of the future, we humbly submit the bid of London 2012.' Paris's closing statement, on the other hand, was, 'Paris wants the Games. Paris needs the Games. Paris loves the Games.'

The London bid told a story of a shared vision, a universal story, full of violated expectations and STAR moments, even if it was clearly presumptuous to claim to speak for the world. Paris talked about Paris. London won by 54 votes to 50. Magliano and the others proved the power of stories and brought together all the rules and advice we have seen so far in this book. They defined 'Who am I?' – London itself – in glowing terms. They then defined 'Who are we?' as the Olympic committee, with its mission to bring sport to the world, to identify London with the people whose votes really counted. And they defined their collective mission as inspiring young people everywhere. Objective, strategy and tactics were clear. Expectations were violated. The film was not a cliché but a challenge. It was storytelling at its best. And it worked.

Leadership Lesson: To make an effective leadership story you need to engage your audience by violating their expectations, surprising them in some way. You can do this by being self-deprecating, humorous and humble, or, as with the London Olympics bid, by breathtaking presumption.

Followership Lesson: The storytelling techniques which work for politicians like Michelle Bachelet or the London Olympics can be used by all of us, in job applications or presentations. Humour is good. Kalashnikovs, for most of us, are probably best avoided. But think of a STAR moment, something which your listeners will always remember and associate with you, even if it is a story told against yourself.

8   The Shock of the New

'What time is it?' the Democratic Party vice presidential nominee Senator Al Gore roared at the crowd. 'It's time for a change,' they called back. It was Madison Square Garden, New York City, a hot and sticky evening in the summer of 1992. We had heard Aretha Franklin sing the US national anthem so beautifully that half the audience was in tears. Now it was time to feed red meat to the Democratic Party faithful. Their fervour was obvious. So was their desperation. The Democrats had not won a presidential election since 1976. Ronald Reagan had made them seem unelectable, through his extraordinary appeal to what became known as 'Reagan Democrats', people who were traditional Democrats and yet who crossed over to vote for a conservative Republican president. Reagan's vice president, George H. W. Bush, promised to continue what some called the Reagan Revolution. The Democratic Party seemed doomed for a generation. To win, they needed to change. But how does a political party or business change successfully, without scaring away existing supporters or customers? One way is to appeal selectively to past traditions while finding a new story and a new storyteller. The Democrats found Bill Clinton. He was to be the shock of the new.

Revolutionary leaders have always recognised the power of new. The French Revolutionaries implemented a new calendar, renaming the months of the year, changing the system of measurements, bringing in the new system of metrication. Kemal

Ataturk renewed Turkey's ancient civilisation by banning old items of dress like the fez and hijab, and switching to the new alphabet used by most of Europe. The most extreme example of the shock of the new in recent years was Pol Pot in Cambodia. When his Khmer Rouge seized power he declared it was 'Year Zero'. Everything started from scratch. What followed was a programme of murder, re-education and resettlement. But once a leader has declared that *everything* is new, then every *bad* thing as well as every good thing must, by definition, be his responsibility. Pol Pot's 'newness' could never last.

More successful leaders promise constant renewal, often with the proviso that they remain in power to supervise all this newness. In Libya, Colonel Gaddafi claimed in his *Green Book* to have discovered the secrets of bringing about continuous and beneficial change, although the biggest moment of newness had to wait until he was overthrown after forty-two years in 2011. Gaddafi had his own 'earwigs', designed to stick in the mind, calling himself, among other things, 'Brother Leader' and the 'King of Kings'. He introduced Libyans to his 'new' ideology of the 'Third International Theory' and the ideas in his *Green Book* were made compulsory subjects for Libyan schoolchildren. These ideas included the belief that boxing would eventually disappear because it is uncivilised, and this commentary on women's rights: 'It is an undisputed fact that both men and women are human beings.' When he was overthrown, the TV network Al Jazeera quoted one critic, Massaoud al-Kanuni, as saying that under Colonel Gaddafi, Libya had 10 universities and 120 prisons, but that was not the kind of newness Libyans desired.

Chairman Mao also sought a process of continuous change in China, beginning with the communist revolution, then the Great Leap Forward and finally the Cultural Revolution. But the real renewal of China and its emergence as a superpower for the twenty-first century had to wait until Mao died and he was replaced by Deng Xiao Ping. Deng provides a truly useful model for any political leader trying to bring in new ideas without frightening the conservative forces which exist in any society and any political system. I reported on Deng's renewal of China in the late 1980s, and it was clear that a Chinese economic miracle was in the making. On Hainan Island I observed the new, capitalist Chinese economy, right down to the spivs and chancers who frequented the restaurants and nightclubs. Near Chengdu, in Deng's home province of Sichuan, I talked with peasants tending their own crops who said that they had never been so wealthy, and exuded optimism for the future. But Deng's 'newness' – as we will see with Bill Clinton and others – depended on carefully balancing the past, present and future. Deng loyally quoted Mao's thoughts, like any acolyte, including the slogans from Mao's *Little Red Book*, while simultaneously abandoning Mao's disastrous policies, of which there had been many.

'Seek truth from facts,' Deng would say, quoting Mao, the 'Great Helmsman'. Then Deng would carefully point out that the 'facts' of the Cultural Revolution and Great Leap Forward had failed. People were starving. The population growth encouraged by Mao in China was unsustainable. In 1982 Deng was to offer a model for being 'new' while appealing to legitimacy from the past. He talked of 'socialism with Chinese characteristics'.

This clever new slogan was Deng's 'earwig', used repeatedly to justify a major change of course. He combined the ideologically necessary word 'socialism' with the patriotically useful word 'Chinese' in such a way that any reform Deng chose to implement could easily be covered by that umbrella. Deng, who had survived many purges and periods of disgrace, recognised that the key storytelling device necessary for any leader abandoning the past is first to embrace it and then to control it. He told stories which made people feel comfortable with change, including an old proverb from his native Sichuan: 'It does not matter whether the cat is black or white, so long as it catches the rat.' China's ideology was still called 'communism', but Deng changed it to pragmatism and, in effect, capitalism. He eventually offered a new slogan which is about as far away from one of Chairman Mao's as it is possible to be: 'To get rich is glorious'.

The Deng Xiao Ping method of seeking legitimacy from past great leaders while offering big changes is not confined to authoritarian states and dictators or even politics. Football and rugby managers taking over teams in trouble constantly speak of a new beginning, while paying tribute to their predecessors and the 'great traditions' of the club. The genius of the brand Burberry in recent years has been to retain its traditional Britishness, while marketing its products as new to a new generation, including various celebrities. George H. W. Bush, who followed Ronald Reagan into the White House, moved out from Reagan's shadow by using a storytelling device very similar to that of Deng Xiao Ping. While embracing the legacy of his predecessor, Bush promised a 'kinder, gentler America' and 'a thousand points of light'. It was Reaganism with Bush characteristics.

Two master storytellers will serve in this chapter as models for many others: Bill Clinton and his 'New' Democrats, based on Franklin D. Roosevelt's New Deal and John F. Kennedy's New Frontier; and Tony Blair and 'New' Labour, which built on the Clinton example. But one surprising example sticks in my mind. It is of an American president who is rarely given credit for any kind of skill, George W. Bush. Bush ran successfully for the presidency in 2000 when his Republican Party was in deep trouble and many commentators assumed that the Democrat vice president Al Gore was more likely to win. I was in the audience when 'Dubya' spoke at the Republican Party convention in Philadelphia, and his slickly written acceptance speech resounded with one key phrase. He did not use the word 'new', but he spoke of his 'compassionate conservatism'. I was puzzled as to what Bush might mean, and turned to an old friend standing beside me in the convention hall, someone who had an intimate knowledge of the workings of the Republican Party and who had worked in the White House.

'Compassionate conservatism,' my friend said, 'is Bush's way to broaden his support by claiming to be "new" while touching on the popular traditions of the Republican Party.'

' But what does it actually mean?' I persisted.

My friend laughed. 'Compassionate conservatism means if there is anything about us that you did not like – anything at all – well, we're not that any more. We're something different. But if there's anything about us that you've always liked, well, hey, we are still that.'

Compassionate conservatism worked for an American electorate just as 'socialism with Chinese characteristics' worked for Deng Xiao Ping. The leadership storytelling trick is to offer people a mirror of newness into which they will see anything that pleases them, while gently moving away from the past. Deng Xiao Ping and George W. Bush did it. Bill Clinton and Tony Blair did it masterfully.

A New Deal for the Democrats

I first met Bill Clinton in the old mill town of Manchester, New Hampshire, in 1991. I was waiting in the lobby of the Holiday Inn at around 7.30 in the morning, when a large, red-faced man entered through the glass doors, panting and sweating. He was wearing unattractive blue and grey Lycra running gear for his early morning run. He walked purposefully towards me, catching his breath. 'Governor Bill Clinton,' he said, thrusting out a hand with a warm smile. 'How're ya doin'?'

Presidential politics in New Hampshire is very intimate. It is sometimes called 'retail' politics – like buying something from a corner shop – to distinguish it from the 'wholesale' politics when a presidential campaign goes national and you only ever see leaders on TV. At the time the BBC was part of what Clinton's team called 'the No Votes Media'. We did not then broadcast TV programmes to the United States, and had no direct influence with US voters. Nevertheless Clinton understood that contact with the foreign media added to his leadership story. It made him seem internationally credible.

He was not then formally running for the presidency, but he was already working on his leadership story. He talked to me optimistically of being 'from Hope', and said that his mission was to rejuvenate the Democratic Party and his country. He talked to me of 'change' and a '*new* New Deal' for America, pushed forward by his 'New Democrats' who would move us away from 'the brain-dead politics of the past'. Even in those first few minutes Clinton lit up the hotel lobby and made me feel as if he had jogged a thousand miles from Arkansas for the great pleasure of making my acquaintance. His charm was infectious. The British foreign secretary Douglas Hurd, a seasoned former Foreign Office diplomat and the calmest of men in a crisis, told me that he found Clinton's charm utterly disarming, and he too experienced the illusion that Clinton acted as if he had travelled the globe just to meet him. Even Newt Gingrich, Clinton's great rival, once admitted to me that when he was engaged in a political life-or-death struggle with Clinton over the government shutdown in 1995, he still could not actually dislike Clinton personally. The British ambassador to Washington Christopher Meyer observed that Clinton's intimacy generally involved strong physical contact. At a first meeting he would shake hands. On parting he would shake hands and rub the palm of his left hand on your arm, and sometimes even offer a kind of bear hug. During the Lewinsky scandal Ambassador Meyer jokingly mentioned this extraordinary technique to a member of Clinton's staff. The staff member responded wryly that perhaps Clinton was just 'wiping his hands'.

There is one description which is as close as I can get to the Clinton charm:

> He smiled understandingly – much more than understandingly. It was one of those rare smiles with a quality of reassurance

that you may come across four or five times in a life. It faced
– or seemed to face – the whole eternal world for an instant,
and then concentrated on you with an irresistible prejudice
in your favour. It understood you just as far as you wanted to
be understood, believed in you as you would like to believe in
yourself, and assured you that it had precisely the impression
of you that, at your best, you hoped to convey. Precisely at
that point, it vanished – and I was looking at an elegant young
roughneck …

The description is of Jay Gatsby from *The Great Gatsby* (1925).
F. Scott Fitzgerald's words capture the Clinton enigma, but his
political problems could not be solved by charm alone. The
Democratic Party had to face a negative counter-story which
was so potent in 1991 that many commentators thought they had
become unelectable.

Polls showed that Americans considered Democrats to be
too left wing, tax-and-spend liberals, out of touch with ordinary
people, soft on crime and weak on defence, a disastrous cocktail.
Political parties and leaders run *on* their record, when things are
going well, and they run *away* from their record when things
are going badly. The old management cliché says that 'you
never get a second chance to make a first impression'. Clinton
had to prove that cliché wrong. He needed to make a new first
impression for himself – 'Who am I?' and for his party – 'Who
are we?' as Democrats. Part of his political genius was that he had
the storytelling skills to make a new impression so often during
his political career that he could call himself, accurately, 'the
Comeback Kid'.

Bimbo Eruptions

Before Clinton could change his party, he had to deal with his
own reputation. There was a damaging 'pre-story', a series of
rumours which swirled around him like a bad smell. A 'pre-story'

is something akin to a prejudice, a story journalists have in their heads before they meet someone. It may or may not be true, but either way it is especially dangerous because the laziest journalists seek facts to fit their preconceptions. In Clinton's case, the pre-story could have destroyed him. I heard it first in Iowa, months before meeting the man himself.

Early in 1991 I persuaded the BBC to make a documentary about the 1992 US presidential election campaign and the difficult position of the Democrats. The Republican president, George H. W. Bush, had 91 per cent approval ratings in the opinion polls after winning the Gulf War and handling the collapse of communism and the dismantling of the Berlin Wall. Prominent Democrats refused to face him, and even Clinton himself at first saw 1992 as a lost cause, merely a springboard to winning in 1996. The first declared Democrat to challenge Bush was an obscure former senator from Massachusetts, Paul Tsongas. I spent several days with him campaigning in small towns in Iowa. We walked together in the July the Fourth parade in rural Madison County, the place made famous in the Clint Eastwood film *The Bridges of Madison County* (1995). Tsongas had had a brush with cancer and tried to negate this counter-story by encouraging TV crews to film him swimming laps in local pools. It was a distant American echo of Mao Tse Tung's story-telling technique to emphasise his vigour by swimming in the River Yangtze. One night I sat in a bar in Davenport, Iowa, and drank beer with a few disconsolate Democratic Party operatives.

'Just what the Democrats need,' someone said sarcastically of Tsongas. 'A candidate who looks like a professor, talks like a professor, walks like a professor.'

'Because he *is* a professor,' someone said.

'Not ready for prime time,' another agreed.

'What about Harkin?' someone wondered. Tom Harkin was the local Iowa senator. Harkin's leadership story was that he listened to the Heartbeat of America and was an 'ordinary' fellow, plugged into the farming interests of the Midwest. When I went to see Harkin in his Senate office, an aide told me it would be easy to find.

'Just follow your nose,' the aide said.

Harkin had installed a popcorn machine in his front office. The smell of freshly popped corn really did fill the corridors of power, an effective story-shaping device, playing on the myth of small-town America which Americans adore but rarely live in.

'Harkin's too liberal,' someone said, meaning he could not reinvent the Democratic Party and would lose.

'So Tsongas can't do it,' one of the political journalists butted in. 'And Harkin can't do it. But Clinton might.'

'Clinton?' the Democratic Party workers grinned. 'You mean Governor Zipper Problem?'

The bar erupted with laughter at Clinton's 'pre-story' of sexual indiscretions. It became public in early 1992. Gennifer Flowers, a night-club singer, claimed in a 'froth of life' magazine to have been Clinton's lover for twelve years. There followed a string of what the Clinton staff privately called 'Bimbo Eruptions'. The Clinton team were faced with a profound leadership dilemma. Should he drop out? Colorado's Gary Hart had done so in 1988 over a sex scandal, and destroyed his career. If Clinton dropped out in 1992, he could never come back in 1996. No presidential candidate in recent memory had ever survived a credible adultery counter-story.

Clinton decided it was time to take an enormous gamble and tell a completely new kind of leadership story unlike any ever heard from a presidential candidate in the television age. It was aimed at a new generation who understood divorce, sexual affairs and marital problems, often from first-hand experience. The era of globalised gossip was to save him. One of those who understood this best is the pornographer Larry Flynt. In his book *One Nation Under Sex* Flynt writes:

Clinton used the confessional interview. Thanks to Phil Donahue, Oprah Winfrey and Larry King, Americans had become accustomed to watching famous people rehabilitate their reputations by confessing their sins on national television. The Clinton campaign scheduled both Bill and Hillary to appear on *60 Minutes*. 'We wanted them together, sitting next to each other,' recalled political advisor James Carville.

This was a piece of elaborate set-dressing to show the Clintons as a couple. The Clinton story, even before they spoke, was clear: whatever has gone on in our marriage, it's our problem, not yours. We are handling it, like millions of married couples across America. The interview was scheduled immediately after CBS's Super Bowl broadcast, the most watched TV show in the United States. The *60 Minutes* producer Don Hewitt assured Clinton, 'It will be great television … The last time I did something like this, Bill, it was the Kennedy–Nixon debates and it produced a president. This will produce a president too.'

But the difference between the television appearances of Clinton–Clinton in 1992 and Kennedy–Nixon at the height of the Cold War in 1960 goes to the heart of what has changed in how leaders tell stories. Even if Kennedy's charm on television won through, he did engage in a real policy debate with Nixon on the 'missile gap' and other vital issues. The 1992 Clinton broadcast was pure globalised gossip, a husband and wife discussing sex and infidelity on national TV and asking for understanding and sympathy, just as numerous other couples had done with Oprah, Jerry, Phil and in *Hello!* magazine. There was no content beyond human interest, no policy discussion. Bill Clinton was contrite, but, as ever, vague on the details.

'I have acknowledged wrongdoing. I have acknowledged causing pain in my marriage,' he told us. 'I have said things to you tonight that no American politician ever has. I think most Americans who are watching this tonight, they'll know what we're saying. They'll get it. They'll feel we've been more than candid. And I think what the press has got to decide is – are we going to engage in a game of "gotcha"?' He added, 'You're looking at two people who love each other. This is not an arrangement or an understanding. This is a marriage.'

Hillary said, 'You know, I'm not sitting here, some little woman standing by my man like Tammy Wynette. I'm sitting here because I love him, I respect him … and you know, if that's not enough for people, then, heck, don't vote for him.'

Every one of us who watched it knew immediately that it was an astounding performance. But it was a *performance*. When Bill said, 'I have said things to you tonight that no American politician ever has,' he staked his claim to be 'new'. He used his notoriety to introduce himself to the American public as a man, a husband, a father, facing problems millions of others faced. The Clintons won the Super Bowl of politics, even if his rival Newt Gingrich was to claim that the Clinton Democrats represented the sex, drugs and rock-and-roll counter-culture of the 1960s and were in some way 'the enemy of normal Americans'. Gingrich's statement was totally out of touch. To millions of TV viewers, the Clintons, with all their flaws, were absolutely 'normal Americans'.

Throughout 1992 Clinton revelled in what made him new, but only up to a point. He admitted 'wrongdoing' but never said the word 'adultery'. He told us he had smoked marijuana but 'didn't inhale'. He played saxophone on late-night TV shows wearing sunglasses and looking like one of the Blues Brothers, but he also went to church and carried a big Bible. The Clinton adviser James Carville was delighted at how the Gennifer Flowers scandal worked for the campaign: 'Our name recognition skyrocketed,' he said.

President Bush's political adviser Mary Matalin was worried. 'The way they ju-jitsued the Flowers fiasco gave us the heebie jeebies,' she said. No one had ever seen anything like it before. To the alarm of the Republican Right, Clinton began to own the words 'normal American', as Ronald Reagan had done twelve years earlier. But the task of bringing 'new' to the Democratic Party was far from complete. The incumbent President George H. W. Bush himself had tried to harness the power of 'new' by talking of America leading a 'New World Order'. Clinton spoke of the 'New' Democrats, but the Democrat brand was so contaminated he had to do far more than change the label on the box. In 1992 he picked battles with his own side, especially the old Left, including, memorably, the Reverend Jesse Jackson. He angered Jackson by attacking comments from an African American musician called Sister Souljah. The details are irrelevant, but Clinton knew that picking on the 'Old Democrats' embodied by Jackson boosted his own claim to be a 'New' Democrat from the centre, the place where the votes were to be found. Clinton drilled home a constant vocabulary of 'change', of being 'different', of the 'future', and, always, his determination to escape 'the brain-dead politics of the past'.

But he also drew on that past to suggest that he was consistent with the core values of his party. He told me at our first meeting that when his grandfather died he thought he would meet Franklin D. Roosevelt at God's right hand in Heaven. Clinton explained that FDR was not hidebound by ideology. He was a Democratic president from a Republican family who cared only about 'what works.' Like Deng Xiao Ping, Clinton, too, didn't care whether the cat was black or white so long as it caught the rat. But when I suggested that a Big Government programme like FDR's New Deal would not be acceptable to US voters in 1992, Clinton responded that it would have to be adapted. He called it 'a *new* New Deal', from his '*New* Democrats'. By the end of these encounters, Clinton and his allies had drilled the word 'new' into my brain. The 'earwig' was doing its work. We also had a title for our documentary: 'A New Deal for the Democrats'. That damn earwig.

Losers to Winners

Despite Clinton's energy, if you had asked a cross-section of Americans to describe the Democrats in early 1992, or British voters to describe the Labour Party that year, you would have heard a familiar refrain. Losers. Big Government parties. Profligate. Too left wing, too liberal, unrealistic, and not hard-headed enough to meet the challenges of modern government. Put an American face on that critique and you get Vice President Walter 'Fritz' Mondale, who lost to Ronald Reagan in 1984, Carter who lost in 1980, or Michael Dukakis who could not beat George H. W. Bush in 1988. The British face of failure would be the Labour leader Michael Foot. Foot, Dukakis, Carter and Mondale were swamped by counter-stories that they, and their parties, were stuck in the past. In 1984, Mondale announced that he would raise taxes. It was political suicide. Foot believed in unilateral disarmament, an issue which was irrelevant to the concerns of the majority of British people in the 1980s. By that time in Britain and the United States, it was the right-of-centre parties, the Conservatives of Margaret Thatcher and the Republicans of Ronald Reagan, who were the shock of the new, breaking the old post-war consensus on economic policy and the role of the trade unions, and suggesting that communism should not be contained but rolled back. Voters of that period never troubled Labour or the Democrats with a second look.

Until Clinton.

He moved his 'New' Democrats as close to conservative Republican policies as he dared. During the election campaign he pointedly returned to Arkansas to sign the death warrant of a convicted murderer. The more protests there were on the left, the better Clinton liked it. Instead of Mondale's tax rises, Clinton promised a middle-class tax cut. He told Americans that as a Southerner he was innately more conservative than Northerners like Dukakis and Mondale. In the magnificent Arkansas state legislature in Little Rock an old ally, an FOB (Friend of Bill), explained to me the secret of Clinton's success. The FOB held his left and right hands in front of him, straight out from his waist.

'This is the Democrats,' he said, waving his left hand. 'And this,' he shook the right hand, 'is the Republicans. And in between, all these votes are up for the taking. But now look here.'

Keeping his right arm in place, Clinton's Arkansas ally moved his left arm as far as he could to the right until the two arms nearly touched.

'This is Clinton. He moves so close to the other feller that he takes all the votes in between. That's how he wins. Works every time.'

This was the leadership story of the Clinton years. He changed the tone and language used by his 'New' Democrats, moving them to the centre, picking fights with opponents on the left and stealing policies from the right. He reformed welfare in a way that pleased conservatives. He co-opted what could have been a Republican slogan in 1995, claiming that the 'era of Big Government is over'. He bore down hard on the budget deficit. Clinton's on-off political adviser Dick Morris was among those to call the Clinton leadership story 'triangulation', by which Morris meant Clinton's natural tendency to split the difference between left and right, refusing to be defined by those traditional categories. Like Reagan and Thatcher, he not only captured the centre ground, but he redefined it, just as he redefined 'normal Americans'.

In November 1992 William Jefferson Clinton and his 'New' Democrats, aided by Ross Perot (who also demanded 'new' political thinking and took 19 per cent of the votes), scraped into the White House with the endorsement of just 43 per cent of the American people. He had passed the first two hurdles – 'Who am I? *A new type of candidate.* Who are we? *Americans, in the only surviving superpower, looking for change after the Cold War.*' That meant he now had to articulate a new story: 'What is our common purpose?'

And this was where he ran into big trouble.

Did I Really Promise a Tax Cut?

The first real change came even before Clinton was sworn in as president in January 1993. He abandoned his promised middle-class tax cut. It had voter appeal and distanced him from the 'old' tax-raising Democrats of the past, but Clinton was forced to change his mind. He did so in the way that Machiavelli recommends in *The Prince*, right at the start of his honeymoon period, quickly and ruthlessly.

On 7 January 1993, around ten days before his inauguration in Washington, Clinton called together his economics team in the Governor's Mansion in Little Rock. The team included Leon Panetta, who was to become Clinton's budget director and chief of staff, and more recently Barack Obama's director of Central Intelligence and defence secretary; Alan Blinder, a professor of economics from Princeton; and Bob Rubin, a Wall Street multimillionaire who was later to become Treasury secretary. Clinton was late for the meeting. His reputation for tardiness would soon become a damaging part of his leadership story, coupled with disorganisation, indiscipline and slowness to make decisions.

The economics discussion, when it eventually started, was about the budget deficit left by the Reagan–Bush years, which at the time was around $290 billion a year. Alan Blinder delivered an economics lecture of the sort that Clinton had already received from the Federal Reserve Board chairman Alan Greenspan the previous month. Both men argued that Clinton's middle-class tax cut would unsettle the markets. The bond market would react badly. That would cause interest rates to rise. That would, in turn, take money out of the pockets of the middle classes, because they would pay more for their mortgages and credit cards. Abandoning the middle-class tax cut and instead bearing down on the deficit would settle the bond markets. Interest rates would drop. Government borrowing costs would drop. Mortgage payments and credit-card bills would go down. Witnesses say that Clinton's face turned beetroot with fury.

'You mean to tell me that the success of the programme and my re-election hinges on the Federal Reserve and a bunch of fucking bond traders?' is one account. Yes, Mr President-elect.

In his book *The Agenda: Inside the Clinton White House* (1994) the journalist Bob Woodward reported Clinton as saying, 'Where are all the Democrats? I hope you are aware we're all Eisenhower Republicans ... and we are fighting the Reagan Republicans. We stand for lower deficits and free trade and the bond market. Isn't that great?'

This was the pivotal moment for Clinton's leadership story. He was a new kind of leader, for a new media age, and his 'New' Democrats occupied the centre ground politically, although at the expense of adopting policies which had previously been Republican. Clinton's decision was to abandon the tax cut and steady the bond market. It led to more than a decade of economic expansion. With Bob Dylan and Wynton Marsalis playing on the Mall at his inauguration, talk of a new Camelot filled with the best and the brightest, inauguration balls full of youth and glamour, and the bond market suitably tickled, as long as the economy improved most people did not seem to care about the reversal of policy which brought it about. Some even spoke hubristically of a 'New Paradigm' of constant growth and an end to boom and bust. They were to be proved wrong, of course, in the return of an old-fashioned crash in the twenty-first century, but for the moment Bill Clinton represented the triumph of the new, which was an inspiration to left-of-centre parties across the world, including, most clearly to Tony Blair and Labour.

Across the Pond

When I had met Clinton in 1991 in New Hampshire I noticed one other British observer who found the Arkansas governor politically interesting. Jonathan Powell was a diplomat in the British embassy in Washington. Powell became so close to the Clinton team from 1991 onwards that during the 1992 election he was allowed remarkable access to their campaign offices in Little Rock. He was to go on to become chief of staff to Tony Blair, helping Blair to adapt Clinton's leadership story and make it his own.

Blair also told a simple story. He was a 'new' kind of Labour leader, not in thrall to the old labour unions, not in any sense a traditional socialist. Blair spoke of 'New Labour' and copied Clinton in moving to the right on a series of key policies. As Dick Morris advised Clinton, Blair also 'triangulated' his opponents and occupied the middle ground. In his autobiography Blair writes of his personal leadership story in words which could equally have come from Clinton himself: 'I was and remain first and foremost not so much a politician of traditional left and right, but a moderniser. I wanted to modernise the Labour party so it was capable, not intermittently, but continuously, of offering a progressive alternative to Conservative rule.'

In his 1998 book *The Third Way* Anthony Giddens summed up the impact of the 'new' wave of Clinton and Blair, which inspired politicians from Africa and Europe to Australia and Latin America. Giddens writes of 'the debate now going on in many countries about the future of democratic politics', after the Cold War. He notes that 'political ideas today seem to have lost their capacity to inspire and political leaders their ability to lead'. Then he quotes the German cultural critic Hans Magnus Enzensberger, whose words seemed to apply to Western Europe, the USA and beyond:

> The politicians are insulted that people are less and less interested in them … (but) innovations and decisions on the future have not originated from the political class for some time now … Germany can afford an incompetent government because ultimately the people who bore us in the daily news really do not matter.

Giddens quoted research findings showing that in 1964 76

per cent of Americans trusted their government most or all of the time to do the right thing. By 1994, five years after the end of the Cold War, that figure had collapsed to just 25 per cent. Enzensberger's view that people are 'less and less interested' in politicians is not, in my judgement, correct. Tony Blair is more accurate in understanding that people were less interested in political parties and *policies* at the end of the Cold War, but they remained interested in politicians as *people*, especially those who seemed fresh and 'new' in the stories they had to tell, like Blair and Clinton. At every opportunity Blair stressed that his was no longer the tax-and-spend, weak-on-the-economy, soft-on-crime, wobbly-on-defence Labour Party which had lost every election since 1979. He said he was 'tough on crime, tough on the causes of crime', a slogan which, with the word 'grime' substituted for 'crime', could easily be adapted to market a new washing powder. Rather than 'tax and spend', Blair said he would stick to the Conservative Party's spending plans. His finance minister, Gordon Brown, promised 'prudence'. And despite the long anti-militarist tradition in parts of the Labour Party, epitomised by Michael Foot, Blair was to lead the United Kingdom into wars or significant military conflicts on three continents – Europe, Africa and Asia – with fighting in Yugoslavia, Sierra Leone, Iraq and Afghanistan.

The wisdom of Blair's policies is a matter of debate. The efficacy of Blair changing Labour's leadership story to 'New Labour' is not debatable. He was elected in three landslides and further rewarded by imitation. David Cameron was elected leader of the Conservative Party in 2005 and came as close as he dared to aping Blair's techniques, the 'Heir to Blair'. Cameron could hardly speak of the 'New Conservatives', which would sound too contradictory, but in coalition with the Liberal Democrats, both parties talk of a 'New Politics'. The latest Labour leader, Ed Miliband, now speaks of a 'new generation' of Labour leaders and a new bargain with the people of Britain. A year after he was elected leader of Labour in September 2011, Miliband addressed his party conference and used the word 'new' more than twenty times in his speech. As leaders soon realise, the old trick, 'newness', is forever young.

The King Is Dead. Long Live the (New) King

I want to end this chapter with some surprising examples of newness from one of Britain's oldest institutions, the monarchy, which boasts traditions stretching back a thousand years but survives because it manages, with great skill, to renew itself through storytelling. When I have met top advisers at Buckingham Palace it is clear that they understand the hierarchy of objective, strategy and tactics. Their objective is to ensure the survival of the monarchy as the guardian of stability and domestic tranquillity. Their strategy is to make sure there is something within the monarchy to appeal to everyone, always. And their tactics include the invention of new 'traditions', together with the very English habit of revelling in a reputation for being amateurish and bumbling, while in fact being adept, efficient and even ruthless. The genius of the British monarchy has been to suggest that while change is inevitable, the really important parts of the monarchy remain constant and unchanging. They share this ability with two other well-known institutions, the Roman Catholic Church and the BBC. All three institutions try, as one Buckingham Palace courtier once put it to me, 'to offer something for everyone, something for almost every taste, something for every generation'. They survive by moving forward inventively while appealing to a natural human instinct to venerate tradition, something we have seen in diverse cultures, from Deng to Clinton, or President Zardari telling a story of legitimacy by making sure that Jinnah's portrait was behind him. Royal advisers invent, adopt or embellish traditions as a way of telling stories to the British people. The storytelling depends upon ceremonial set pieces including coronations, weddings and other events.

Here's the official account of the investiture of Prince Charles as Prince of Wales in 1969, taken from the Prince of Wales's website:

The investiture of The Prince of Wales, during which the 20-year-old Prince received the insignia as the 21st Prince of Wales from The Queen, took place on 1st July 1969, at Caernarfon Castle in front of 4,000 guests inside the medieval walls. Thousands more were in the dry moat and outside the castle, and millions around the world watched on television. The Queen had created her eldest son Prince of Wales when he was nine years old. The Queen later let it be known that the Investiture would be held when The Prince was old enough to understand fully its significance. In a ceremony with many historic echoes, directed largely by the Constable of the Castle, Lord Snowdon, The Queen invested The Prince with the Insignia of his Principality and Earldom of Chester: a sword, coronet, mantle, gold ring and gold rod.

Note the storytelling. It was 'a ceremony with many historic echoes'. That means it was 'authentic'. It was indeed 'directed' by Lord Snowdon because it was a theatrical production, a high-class entertainment. Charles was already Prince of Wales at the time of the ceremony. What we witnessed was simply a magnificent storytelling event for the 'millions' watching on television around the world. It was not a necessary part of any constitutional process. Prince Charles accepted the title with words which sound as if they were taken from Shakespeare: 'I, Charles, Prince of Wales, do become your liege man of life and limb and of earthly worship and faith and truth I will bear unto you to live and die against all manner of folks.' Or, as Bill Clinton put it in New Hampshire, I will be with you 'until the last dog dies'.

In an essay in *The Invention of Tradition* (1983) the historian David Cannadine writes of how from 1932 onwards the new radio broadcasts by the monarch on the BBC immediately became 'traditional'. Cannadine calls them 'audible pageants', which rapidly became 'visible pageants' as television became more popular. Cannadine also spots a paradox. In the modern, complicated and technologically advanced world of the twentieth and twenty-first centuries, such pageants actually became more popular because the stories they told seemed so 'traditional'. 'In the world of the aeroplane, the tank and the atomic bomb,' Cannadine writes, 'the anachronistic grandeur of horses, carriages, swords and plumed hats was further enhanced.'

By the time of the coronation of Queen Elizabeth II the demand for combining tradition and the newness of the new post-war queen was so great that there simply were not sufficient horse-drawn carriages for the ceremony. As a result, as Cannadine writes, 'it proved necessary to borrow seven extra carriages from a film company'. Of course. Where else would storytellers look for material, than from the professionals of a film company? The resulting pictures of the coronation, or more recently of the royal wedding of Prince William and Kate Middleton, seem utterly 'authentic' and 'traditional', but it takes a lot of work to make the story of authenticity and tradition renew itself for each generation. The British assume that we are in some way 'good' at these kinds of shows, but as Cannadine demonstrates, this competence at tradition is in itself an invented tradition, another piece of storytelling. He quotes a nineteenth-century observer who says that in the mid-Victorian period there was no talent for pageants or royal celebrations – quite the reverse: 'Some malignant spell broods over our ceremonials, and inserts into them some feature which makes them all ridiculous.' Cannadine also quotes the *Illustrated London News* of 1852, which observes that the English 'are said to be a people who do not understand shows and celebrations, or the proper mode of conducting them.'

When I have commentated live on important state occasions, including Armistice Day at the Cenotaph or the 70th anniversary of the Battle of Britain, every moment is timed and choreographed. While the words I utter are my own, there is a script detailing with brilliant precision who stands where, who talks when, which piece of music is played and how long – more or less to the second

– each part of the parade or celebration will take. At the Prince of Wales's investiture in 1969, for example, the canopy above the dais was deliberately made transparent so TV cameras could see through it and relay around the world pictures of the new prince in the 'ceremony with many historic echoes'. Rather like a bottle of German beer which boasts that it is fresh and new, but also brewed according to the German purity laws of the sixteenth century, the monarchy in Britain contrives to offer the same great taste of tradition, but a sparkling fresh flavour for every generation.

The royal wedding of Prince William to Kate Middleton in April 2011 demonstrated Buckingham Palace's attention to detail in storytelling and managing the shock of the new. In the month or so before the wedding there was a daily titbit of news to remind the British people of what was to come, a series of *hors d'oeuvres* before the main meal. One day, the coat of arms of the Middleton family was revealed. Then there was constant speculation about the dress. There were stories about the flowers, and their significance, together with news about the music in the service, the revelation that Kate would not 'obey' her husband in the marriage vows; the news that the Middletons had ancestors who were 'working class', and so on and on. The photogenic couple were 'just like us', except of course that one day they will be King and Queen. As Hamlet said of another royal court, 'there's Providence in the fall of a sparrow'. At Buckingham Palace, the sparrow's fall is carefully rehearsed, timed for maximum impact, crafted to combine traditions, real or otherwise, with newness, and then diced into bite-size morsels to be fed to the ever-hungry news media. This is storytelling so effective that most people do not even know that a story is being told. Appearing to be new while simultaneously appealing to the past is one of the greatest storytelling skills of real leaders. As an article in the *Guardian* newspaper (12 April 2012) put it: 'Once they (the royal family) were seen as irrelevant, stuffy and surrounded by "ghastly rah-rahs". Now they hang out with sports stars, watch Danish crime dramas and thriftily share clothes. Is the campaign to make the royal family seem "normal" the PR coup of the century?' Possibly, yes.

Leadership Lesson: Truly successful leaders change their own leadership stories and bring people with them. Bill Clinton was deeply flawed but a political genius. He changed his personal story, he changed his own party, he changed his country. Policies really did change too, but they were part of Clinton's tactics to reinforce a strategy of seeming 'new' with the objective of holding on to power. The lessons were learned by Tony Blair and many other leaders. It is important, however, to manage the shock of being 'new'. One way of doing that is to make people understand you are also rooted in tradition. We can all adopt the same patterns for our businesses, professions or other areas of our lives. To be new, effectively, a leader must not be like Pol Pot, destroying the past and starting again. Like Clinton and Deng and the House of Windsor, or the fashion house Burberry, the past has to be built on, not destroyed.

Followership Lesson: As followers we must beware of those who market themselves as 'new'. They may indeed have something 'new' to offer, but it is also the oldest storytelling device any leader can use. That's because it works.

9 Story Wars and Reputation Management: How to Counter the Counter-Story

Jesus was the most successful storyteller in history. His leadership story connects with followers worldwide through homely parables which still touch us two thousand years later. Jesus, like Moses, did not merely lecture us on how to behave. He told stories, from the Good Samaritan to the wise and the foolish virgins, that were designed to connect us emotionally to a code of moral behaviour. The New Testament essentially follows the three-step storytelling technique we have seen all leaders use: Who am I? Who are we? What is our common purpose? (I am the Son of God; we are followers of Christ; our purpose is to save the souls of sinners.) But Jesus was not immune from counter-stories, the stories enemies tell to undermine and discredit a leader. This chapter begins to explore some of the techniques leaders use to handle such negative stories successfully. Nowadays we call these techniques 'reputation management'. Successful politicians create 'instant response units' to rebut claims made by opponents within that day's news cycle. Celebrities, or their staff, monitor blogs and Twitter feeds as well as newspapers and TV for signs of negative stories, and rapidly craft a response. Businesses are on twenty-four-hour alert, knowing that, like the oil company BP, they may be just one accident away from billions being wiped off their share price and long-term damage to their corporate reputation.

Imagine an obituary of Jesus. It's being written by two of Britain's highly partisan newspapers. One newspaper, the *Daily Christian*, supports Jesus. The other, the *Roman*, doesn't think much of him and focuses mainly on the negative counter-stories. The positive newspaper obituary would tell us of the great loss to mankind of the Son of God, focusing on what this means to you and me.

'World mourns Saviour,' the *Daily Christian* might say, characterising Jesus as all-too-human in his suffering, 'just like us'. He was 'Our' Redeemer, the human face of the deity, a man with wounds inflicted by the Roman colonisers to appease the mob in Jerusalem. This leadership-story obituary would speak of his 'Who am I?' origins as the son of an itinerant carpenter from Nazareth. It would tell how the family was so humble – again, 'just like us' – that this great man was actually born in a stable in Bethlehem. It would go on to recount the many achievements and miracles he had performed during his short life, quoting at length from the Sermon on the Mount and the Beatitudes. It would be more or less the leadership story narrative told by the Apostles through the Gospels, which is the core of Christian faith.

Now imagine a hostile British newspaper obituary, the counter-story as told in the *Roman*. We would read of the death not of one of 'Us', but of 'Them', of a dangerous subversive, a zealot crucified in the company of thieves, a religious fanatic who tried to undermine Roman civilisation, an eccentric man who had peculiar friendships, including with a prostitute.

'A Nazareth man was executed after claiming to be the King of the Jews,' the *Roman*'s report might say, recounting how Jesus had an altercation with merchants going about their lawful business changing money in the temple. 'He undermined the banking system, showed scant respect for property rights and flouted the law. He claimed to accept the rule of Caesar while at every stage subverting it. Such was his unpopularity that his fellow citizens asked that another man be spared execution rather than this troublemaker.'

The counter-story tells us that throughout his life Jesus, a rootless man who suffered delusions to the point of appearing to be mentally unstable, even claimed to have had a conversation with Satan in the wilderness. He encouraged simple fishermen to abandon their nets and told one follower he could leave the dead unburied. In the twenty-first century this counter-story would probably end with the hostile newspaper obituary quoting anonymous experts who would claim Jesus's activities resulted in a slump in house prices.

This war between leadership stories and counter-stories, the stories a leader tells about himself and the hostile accounts of his enemies, is clearly as old as history itself. In fact one definition of history is the story told by the victors, the leadership story of those, like Jesus, who triumphed over the numerous counter-stories told against them. No one in a leadership position is immune from such counter-stories, including, obviously, Jesus himself, other religious leaders, and everyone from the British royal family to rock stars and business leaders.

Britain's Lord (Chris) Patten, formerly a Conservative MP and now chairman of the BBC Trust, is one of Pope Benedict's most eloquent defenders. He characterised the Pope to me as 'one of the world's leading public intellectuals', pointing to a leadership story of scholarship and engagement with the great moral and theological issues of our time. The counter-story from the Pope's detractors, however, who sometimes call him by his former title of Cardinal Ratzinger, is that he is devious and callous, a former member of the Hitler Youth, a man who cares only about the superficial integrity of the Church, and who was prepared to suppress or ignore cases of child abuse. Those attacking Pope Benedict undermine not just his sense of common purpose in the Church, nor merely his 'Who are we?' definition of what it means to be a Roman Catholic. They attack the very core of his personal 'Who am I?' story, to the point of not even using his title as Pope, attempting to delegitimise his pontificate. This is a pattern we will see repeated in the most damaging counter-stories, right down to the use of a negative 'earwig' – Ratzinger – to boost the counter-story's power. With Richard Nixon the negative earwig was 'Tricky Dicky'. With Bill Clinton it was 'Slick Willie'. With Zimbabwe's president Robert Mugabe it was 'Uncle Bob'. In each case a refusal to use the correct title is part of the counter-story technique used by opponents to deny the leader some of his supposed legitimacy.

A similar de-legitimising technique is used against Barack Obama. Unlike the 'Origin of Specious' sanitised and pasteurised accounts of American politicians we saw in Chapter 5, Obama's story comes, quite literally, from a different place. Here he is writing about his own childhood in *Dreams from My Father*:

> I had learned not to care. I blew a few smoke rings,
> remembering those years. Pot had helped, and booze; maybe a
> little blow when you could afford it. Not smack though ...

Obama's 'Who am I?' story is extraordinary for a modern political leader. He is the product of a broken home, a mixed-race family and an often itinerant childhood. He is the USA's first African American president, and the first to admit to cocaine use. As mentioned in Chapter 4, by publishing *Dreams from My Father* thirteen years before he would run for the presidency of the United States, Obama got his retaliation in first. He wrote about his drug abuse, and therefore denied any rival or media organisation the ability to cry 'Gotcha' at a future date. Admitting to wrongdoing before anyone else notices or cares is one of the most potent ways to counter a counter-story because it suggests the leader is being honest, and has changed or in some way redeemed himself. Even Obama's most visceral critics have been unable to damage him by referring to this teenage drug abuse, but the attacks on the forty-fourth president have nevertheless been particularly personal. Obama's most strident opponents not only dispute his policies on the economy or health care ('What is our common purpose?'), they also dispute his legitimacy as president and as an American ('Who am I?') by casting doubts on his personal history.

Obama, they claim, was not born in the United States. He is not a Christian, they say, but a Muslim. Bizarrely, these same critics frequently cite Obama's association with the extreme views of his former Christian pastor the Reverend Jeremiah Wright, without noting the obvious contradiction with his supposed 'Muslim' heritage. In this counter-story Obama is also some kind of stuck-up Ivy League intellectual rather than someone who overcame great personal and political difficulties. Obama has dealt with these counter-stories in ways that are perfectly suited to the demands of the modern media. He appeared with his family on a sympathetic Christmas special programme in December 2009 hosted by the queen of 'froth of life' journalism, Oprah Winfrey. He has explained his complicated past eloquently in print and in interviews. But this was never enough for his critics. Facing re-election and under pressure as some elected politicians began to join what became known as the 'birthers' in questioning the story of his birth, on 27 April 2011 Obama finally made public his birth certificate. It shows he was born in Hawaii. But beyond the facts, Obama's other weapon to counter the counter-stories has been humour.

At a black-tie White House Correspondents' dinner on 30 April 2011, where the multimillionaire Donald Trump was present, Obama confronted head-on the allegations that he had not been born in the United States. Trump was considering running as a Republican presidential candidate and had joined the 'birthers' in questioning Obama's birthright to run for the presidency. Obama stunned his audience by saying that he was going to go beyond releasing his birth certificate and show the audience his birth video. The room felt a shiver of puzzlement. A birth video? At a black-tie dinner? The lights dimmed. The screen behind the president lit up with the birth video of Simba in *The Lion King*. The clip subsequently appeared on YouTube for the world to see, as the White House communications team knew it would. Donald Trump was not exactly cast as the envious rival Scar, but for some reason he decided not to run for the presidency of the United States.

The 'birther' movement, except for a few late-night radio talk shows, was a counter-story which died, but Obama's use of humour continues to be a potent weapon. When bad feeling with the Republican leader in the House of Representatives, Speaker John Boehner, became a significant political problem, Obama addressed a Washington dinner where Boehner was present. Speaker Boehner is a middle-aged Caucasian with a slightly orange complexion. Talk-show hosts and newspaper columnists suggest he might use make-up, spray tan or a sun-ray lamp. Obama, at the dinner, praised Boehner, saying that he felt they had so much in common. There were again puzzled expressions all around the room. The two men are poles apart politically and the Republican Congress has been proud to delay or derail Obama's presidential initiatives, leaving government in gridlock. Obama cheerfully explained that despite the bitter partisan differences, he and John Boehner were both 'people of colour', though in Boehner's case not any colour naturally occurring in the environment. The room erupted in prolonged laughter, at Boehner's expense. This clip was also available for the world to see on YouTube. Humour not only makes a leader sound witty and clever, it is a way of countering a counter-story without appearing to take it too seriously.

Charlie, Whaur's Yer Troosers?

Members of the British royal family face similar challenges in trying to counter the counter-stories told against them. Being humorous or writing an autobiography are not strategies open to the royals, but they do have an arsenal of storytelling techniques. The most damaging anti-royal counter-stories, as with 'Ratzinger' and the supposedly 'not-American' American president Obama, are the ones that hit at the very legitimacy of the monarch and her immediate family. In these counter-stories the royals cost too much. They symbolise the class system. They have too many 'hangers on'. They are greedy, lazy and an anachronism in twenty-first century meritocratic and democratic Britain. In Scotland, Wales and Northern Ireland they are sometimes characterised as the 'English' royal family, a similar technique to the attempts to de-legitimise Obama. This Englishness was once symbolised by the Queen's title, Elizabeth II. There never was an Elizabeth I of Scotland or the United Kingdom, only of England. Some minor royals, or ex-royals like Sarah Ferguson, provide perfect fodder for some of these counter-stories. Their sexual affairs, divorces, business dealings, dim-witted behaviour and even fashion sense or lack thereof feature prominently in British and other newspapers.

Since the revelations surrounding the divorce and subsequent death of Diana, Princess of Wales, one further counter-story has been that the Windsors are the world's most famous dysfunctional family, emotionally cold and referring to themselves as 'the Firm', as if they are in the royal family business. Stephen Frears's film *The Queen* (2006), set at the time of the death of Diana, captured the dysfunctional elements of the royals, but also their survival instincts, and the shrewd advice given to them at this moment of great crisis. One point of contention was whether the Queen should return from Balmoral, in Scotland, to Buckingham Palace, in London, after Diana's death. The Queen eventually did return to London, but according to royal courtiers I spoke to at the time, she was well aware that since Scotland is also part of her realm, to return to London might fall into the damaging counter-story trap by suggesting that one part of the United Kingdom, Scotland, was less important than England. It was one of the rare occasions when the palace misjudged the public mood. In avoiding one counter-story – that the Queen is 'English' – they fell into another – that the Queen and the royals are emotionless and dysfunctional as a family. The popular newspapers were full of criticism and robust advice to the Queen. When she eventually did return to London, the Queen made sure she was seen looking at the hundreds of thousands of floral tributes to Diana placed outside Buckingham Palace.

It was a return to the familiar royal leadership story of connection to the emotions and views of her subjects, that central desire of many leaders to be seen as the embodiment of their nation. And the embodiment-of-the-nation mission means sensitivity on the part of the royal family to every kind of counter-story, no matter how trivial, and relentless, but quiet reputation management.

Officials at Buckingham Palace are usually drawn from some of the best minds in the Foreign Office and the upper ranks of the British military. These are people who often become ambassadors and generals. Pretending to be amateurish is part of their own rather cunning leadership story. Like US Secret Service agents, who are famously trained to 'take a bullet' for the president of the United States, royal courtiers are often prepared to take the negative press counter-story 'bullets' for the Queen and her family. The royal storytelling technique is that Her Majesty the Queen never gets things wrong; her advisers sometimes do. These advisers – caricatured as anonymous, faceless bureaucrats, chinless wonders – of course took the blame for not countering the counter-story after Diana's death. But as Frears's film suggested, it was probably the Queen herself who at first misread the public mood. Nevertheless, the overwhelming popularity of the monarchy in Britain demonstrates that such mistakes in telling the royal leadership story are rare. Support for Republicanism is currently very low. A quiet attention to detail means that royal advisers are among the shrewdest reputation managers anywhere, especially in their mission to root the royals in every part of the United Kingdom. The Prince of *Wales* and the Duke of *Edinburgh* are titles which give a clue to a simple kind of brand management, along with the Duke of York, the Duchy of Cornwall, the Duke of Rothesay and so on. Princess Anne has a long association with the Scotland rugby team. Her daughter married England's rugby captain Mike Tindall.

A few years ago I followed Prince Charles to various events

in Aberdeenshire and had a short, private discussion with him about the importance of the idea of 'Britishness'. While I cannot report the content of the private conversation, I can say that at every event Prince Charles wore a kilt, and that at every event Prince Charles was the only male wearing a kilt. With echoes of Jinnah in his multifaceted Pakistani dress, or Nelson Mandela in Xhosa traditional finery, the Prince of Wales acknowledged his connection to Scotland without words in this leadership story.

Grief Is the Price We Pay for Love

This attention to details and symbols was clear on a much bigger scale in the aftermath of September 11, 2001. The Queen – at least, we were told it was the Queen – ordered that the guards' band at Buckingham Palace play the US national anthem. It was a sight which made a hard-bitten New York journalist friend of mine cry, and brought a lump to the throat of many of my American friends. The pictures were transmitted around the world. Those few minutes of music probably did more for the supposed US–UK special relationship than the campaigns of warfare in Iraq and Afghanistan. The Queen consoled the people of the United States by saying that 'grief is the price we pay for love', a tribute memorialised in the park outside the US embassy in Grosvenor Square. Later I attended a social event at Buckingham Palace at which someone asked a senior royal aide if Her Majesty the Queen had come up with that resonant phrase herself.

'Of course,' he said with a wink to me. 'She always comes up with the best phrases herself.'

Of course she does. Just as she ordered the band to play 'The Star-Spangled Banner'. It's a royal *tradition* that everything good which happens within the royal family is the responsibility of the monarch, and anything bad, well, it's those inept and amateurish courtiers. A senior royal aide once summed up for me what he called the paradox at the heart of the British affection for the royal family. The courtier told me, 'The monarchy is something which does not work in theory. Fortunately it does appear to work in practice.' He said that the same was also true for the Roman Catholic Church. I would add that it is also true for the BBC. That courtier explained that he saw his job as one in which he constantly had to remind us of the 'good' royal story, the 'practice' of the monarchy – weddings and jubilees, state visits and state openings of parliament – while avoiding the 'theory', the counter-story of class resentments in a meritocratic and democratic modern Britain. He added that the genius of the British monarchy was to offer 'something for everyone', managing change while offering continuity. If you do not like one bit of the royal leadership story, the royal aide told me, you almost certainly will like another. Prince Charles: traditional architecture, organic farming, the environment. Prince William: military service, glamorous mother, youth. Princess Anne: no-nonsense sporting achievement. And so on. Countering the counter-stories ad infinitum, or so one suspects.

Margaret Thatcher: Squashing and Squaring

Winston Churchill was among those leaders said to have adopted the attitude of any great political fixer towards counter-stories: 'What we can't squash, we square; what we can't square we squash.' Margaret Thatcher used similar techniques in the modern era. She tackled some counter-stories head-on and squashed them, and sometimes squashed those who told the stories against her too. Other counter-stories she 'squared' by annexing the negative story and treating it as if it were a compliment, or simply by using her influence with Conservative-supporting newspapers and their proprietors.

She learned the hard way. After the 1970 general election the then prime minister Edward Heath appointed her Secretary of State for Education and Science. Heath needed to cut public spending, and Mrs Thatcher decided to end free school milk for children aged seven to eleven within the state education system.

It was a presentational disaster. Newspaper headlines told a counter-story of meanness which was to cling to Mrs Thatcher for years. Students and young mothers protested together, chanting the memorable rhyme 'Mrs Thatcher – Milk Snatcher'. It was the kind of devastating 'earwig' that she was never allowed to forget, the equivalent of Pope Benedict being called 'Ratzinger' or Nixon 'Tricky Dicky'. Reflecting on the fact that this counter-story could have destroyed her, Mrs Thatcher wrote in her autobiography that she 'had incurred the maximum of political odium for the minimum of political benefit'. The lesson she learned was to be willing to incur political odium but only if it was for the *maximum* political benefit. She understood that she would never be universally liked. All her energies were devoted to making sure that at least she would generally be respected.

When she became the first woman to lead a major British political party, Margaret Thatcher was told by her advisers that her image was going down badly with voters, including many Conservatives. She was seen as shrill and hectoring. Opinion polls repeatedly showed that voters preferred the personality of Labour's then prime minister 'Sunny Jim' Callaghan to 'Milk Snatcher' Thatcher. When I discussed this and his own political career with Jim Callaghan, he admitted to me (with a smile) that of course he could be ruthless, when he felt it necessary. In public 'Sunny Jim' was usually optimistic and charming. But by the time of the 1979 general election, voters were tired of Labour, tired of industrial discontent, tired of unions who seemed out of control, tired of the post-war consensus and compromise, desperate for change. Mrs Thatcher rode the wave of being 'new' – a new face, a woman leader, making new arguments about the role of government, the state and the trade unions, and overturning the post-war consensus.

A large part of Mrs Thatcher's success over eleven years in Downing Street and three election victories, was as a storyteller about herself, about Britain ('Who are we?') and about 'our common purpose' as a nation. She effectively turned the title 'Milk Snatcher' and other counter-stories to her advantage, substituting a compelling and carefully crafted new leadership story about herself and her party as agents for change. Mrs Thatcher surrounded herself with her own apostles, some of the brightest reputation managers in the growing communications industry, people who generally adored her. These included ad-men like Tim Bell, the Saatchi brothers and the journalist and TV producer Gordon Reece. Reece and the others helped Thatcher sharpen her answer to the first and most important leadership story question 'Who am I?' with the reply 'a grocer's daughter from Grantham', a perfect 'earwig', loaded with storytelling energy. It defined Thatcher partly by what she was *not*: she was not the typical Conservative leader, not schooled at Eton, she didn't have an aristocratic background, totally unlike her predecessors, Sir Alec Douglas-Home or Harold Macmillan. Nor was she a 'milk snatcher', this story went, but merely a grocer's daughter from a small provincial town who was prudent and cost-conscious, who understood the price of milk – 'just like us'. Reece suggested Mrs Thatcher allow herself to be filmed doing the washing-up, presenting herself as a housewife who knew how to balance the family budget around the kitchen table, and by extension the country's budget around the Cabinet table. It is difficult to imagine Macmillan or Douglas-Home having even a passing acquaintance with washing the teacups. This was a clear 'violation of expectations', that most powerful of storytelling devices. Such surprises countered some of the counter-stories and forced people to take a second look at the Conservative Party and its 'new' leader.

The Thatcher myth-making has proved so enduring that in the Hollywood film *The Iron Lady* (2011), Meryl Streep's Mrs Thatcher complains to her husband Denis (or his ghost) about the price of milk having risen to 49p a bottle, thrifty and full of common sense even in her dotage.

But there was one big problem, however, which Mrs Thatcher's counter-story experts found particularly tricky since it was rooted in who she was. She spoke in the constrained tones of the English upper middle classes. At times she sounded posher than the Queen. When she was put under pressure, as prime minister, she was shrill. Gordon Reece hired a National Theatre voice coach to teach her to lower her voice. She was told to get rid of her hats, which made her look old-fashioned. She avoided the possibility of a televised debate with James Callaghan in 1979. This was not because Reece and the others doubted her ability in verbal combat. It was because they understood that Mrs Thatcher's stridency in debate, while a great leadership quality, could alienate voters on television by playing into the 'Milk Snatcher' meanness counter-story. 'Sunny Jim' Callaghan could get by on a few smiles and avuncular nods to the camera.

The Iron Lady

Above all, Reece and her other advisers helped the new prime minister create one of the most successful leadership storytelling myths of the past thirty years, that Margaret Thatcher was unbending, unyielding and intractable. In part this was to address the sexist counter-story we have touched on earlier, that women leaders are indecisive or vacillating. Throughout the Eurozone crisis from 2010 onwards, Germany's chancellor Angela Merkel has been particularly vulnerable on this score. In the consensus-building atmosphere of post-war German and European politics, it has never been possible for any German leader to develop a leadership story of principled unwillingness to negotiate. Too many dangerous echoes of Hitler and the war.

But for Mrs Thatcher, precisely the opposite was the case. The legend of decisiveness and inflexibility was carefully crafted to echo the positive associations with Winston Churchill and the bulldog breed. When members of her own party wanted her to change tack on matters of policy, Mrs Thatcher showed her genius for undermining them publicly with a counter-story 'earwig' of her own. She characterised Conservatives who did not support her as 'Wets'. In England being 'wet' means to be limp and uninspiring. By defining her opponents in one word, Mrs Thatcher was also defining herself as the opposite. Those who expected her to make a U-turn on policy early in her premiership in 1980 were lectured otherwise: 'You turn if you want to … (*pause*) The lady's not for turning.'

These words are a reworking of the title of the 1948 Christopher Fry play *The Lady's Not for Burning*. It was funny, memorable and in character for Mrs Thatcher. It was also phoney. The magnificent 'earwig' – that the lady is not for turning – was part of a crafted storytelling illusion. Mrs Thatcher had not seen the Christopher Fry play, nor even heard of it or him. Nor did she understand the joke until it was explained to her. The 'earwig' phrase was the creation of her excellent speechwriter, the playwright Ronald Millar. It was to become the core of the self-created Thatcher leadership story, of resolution and stubbornness, strangling the sexist counter-story at birth. Angela Merkel could never get away with such a trick. Margaret Thatcher did. She created the legend of her own constancy and firmness of purpose. Like Julius Caesar, she spoke of herself in the third person, as 'the lady', with echoes of the famous operatic aria *La donna è mobile* ('*The Woman is fickle*'). This 'lady' was trying to convince us that far from being '*mobile*' she was a fixed star in the political firmament. Behind the scenes the truth was more complicated and more interesting. Mrs Thatcher was indeed often tough and unrelenting, but she did listen to, and value, private criticism from trusted advisers. She did at times 'turn' or change her mind, although rarely in public.

Her advisers learned from Ronald Reagan's Republican Party how to structure events and photo-opportunities to show her off at her best. She was the first British leader to use a tele-prompter to read her speeches without appearing to refer to notes. During election campaigns she would be told that she should hold a calf on a farm visit, or walk a dog with her husband Denis (she did not own a dog), or climb into a battle-tank. Her advisers knew the pictures would be on every news bulletin and every front page the next day, and of course they were. As with the attention to detail we have seen in the House of Windsor, nothing about managing the Thatcher leadership story, or destroying the counter-stories, was left to chance. For Reece and the others, getting the story right came down to the precise shades of blue as a backdrop to Mrs Thatcher's appearances or to the beautifully lit and orchestrated speeches at party rallies, or to the provision of placards for adoring Conservative delegates to wave with the message of the day.

Privately, however, Mrs Thatcher was open to ideas and debate and sometimes did change her mind on issues of profound importance – for example, on proposed radical reforms to the National Health Service. She dropped her ideas of forcing the BBC to take advertisements. She altered course on some aspects of economic policy. She wobbled on the question of the pound shadowing the Deutschmark, vacillated between the views of her Chancellor of the Exchequer and her unofficial advisers, and dropped the much-hated poll tax after it produced street riots. When British Cabinet papers were declassified under the thirty-year rule in 2011, we learned that during the July 1981 IRA Hunger Strike, while publicly refusing any kind of mediation or negotiation with terrorists, she twice authorised contacts with the IRA to outline what she would concede in any deal. It was the IRA, in need of martyrs for the cause, who proved not for turning.

Astonishingly, the declassified papers reveal she even allowed the Cabinet to discuss British withdrawal from Northern Ireland. Given her military defence of the Falkland Islands as British territory after the Argentine invasion of 1982, a failure to retain Northern Ireland would have signalled one of the most remarkable U-turns in recent history. If knowledge of such discussions had leaked, it might have split the Conservative Party. All this came from the lady who was not for turning. Or so her stories were designed to tell us.

Love Thine Enemy

As often happens when dealing with counter-stories, Mrs Thatcher was also helped by her enemies. A Soviet newspaper called her 'the Iron Lady'. This was a storytelling gift beyond price, a headline the world could understand, and one that even her British political opponents had to concede was rooted in fact. The Russians created a more powerful Thatcher 'earwig' than even Saatchi and Saatchi, a resonant phrase that everyone remembers. At home, the trade unions also helped with the Thatcher myth-making by agreeing with her own self-assessment that the lady was not for turning in the miners' strike or in limiting certain kinds of strike action. The core of Mrs Thatcher's leadership story, therefore, was conceded by her enemies in the Soviet Union and her opponents in the Labour movement and on the Left. No prime minister could ask for more.

As we have seen with Barack Obama and Pope Benedict, and will explore in more detail with Gordon Brown and Bill Clinton, the counter-stories that are truly damaging are not those about policies, but those that undermine the leader's character, attacking the basic leadership question 'Who am I?' Mrs Thatcher was helped immeasurably in dealing with counter-stories by the simple fact that both friends and enemies, from the Tory right wing to the Soviet Union, agreed on the essence of her character. She was, as the Meryl Streep film rightly said, always thought of as 'the Iron Lady', even in the minds of those who hated her. It meant that her enemies usually focused on the third and least damaging part of storytelling, 'What is our common purpose?', suggesting that her policies were wrong-headed or harmful. No political opponent at any stage ever managed convincingly to tell a *personal* counter-story about Mrs Thatcher which she could not easily fit into her own leadership story of constancy, thrift and toughness. There was one exception, the French president François Mitterrand. He quipped that she had 'the lips of Marilyn Monroe and the eyes of Caligula', in other words a femininity and an attractiveness to men of a certain age, combined with a devastating certainty that she was right, plus a degree of cruelty. She was routinely described by Conservatives as 'the best man among us', an observation which famously led one satirical TV programme, *Spitting Image,* to show her smoking cigars, wearing a man's pinstripe suit and urinating while standing up. How she must have loved the compliment. *Spitting Image* also showed her dining with her Cabinet colleagues and ordering steak for dinner. The waiter asked, 'What about the vegetables?' She looked at her dreary colleagues and replied, 'They'll have the same.' From satirists to the Soviets, from miners to Mitterrand, they all conceded the one point of character which made Mrs Thatcher so formidable.

At European summits in Brussels, I often tackled Mrs Thatcher's spokesman and trusted adviser Bernard Ingham about why, time after time, Britain was out of step with all the other members of the European Union.

'The prime minister believes they are out of step with us,' Ingham would say, partly reflecting his own brand of Yorkshire humour, and partly Mrs Thatcher's own sense of rectitude. If eleven European nations voted one way and Mrs Thatcher voted the other, Bernard would quip that Mrs Thatcher worried that the eleven others were 'isolated'. In Houston, Texas, after a G7 economic summit, I spoke to Mrs Thatcher in one of a series of interviews she gave on the world economy, and I saw her humour, and bossiness, first hand. On such occasions the leader is on a storytelling production line, attempting to explain why the summit has been a success. (Summits, diplomats will tell you wryly, are generally 'condemned' to be 'successes'.) Typically two 'pool' cameras are set up, one pointing at the leader and one focused on a chair occupied in succession by several interviewers from different networks who amicably share costs and facilities. On this occasion, I was second in line. The first interviewer was from a rival network, Sky News, and he conducted his five minutes with the British prime minister and then, nervous in the presence of 'the Iron Lady', had walked the wrong way. Instead of leaving with his valuable news-tape, he walked into a dead end in a corner of the interview room and could not get out without walking past the cameras and into the shot either behind the prime minister or behind me – a terrible, terrible faux pas in the television world.

I began my interview with Mrs Thatcher almost immediately, and could sense the Sky reporter's increasing anxiety that, trapped as he was, I would get my tape on air before he could. I could see that Mrs Thatcher was perfectly aware of the humour of the situation too, although we both carried on our televised conversation as if nothing was amiss. Eventually my rival, now sweating with anxiety, decided that the only way he could get out of the room was to get down on his hands and knees and crawl out behind the prime minister, under the eye-line of the cameras. He began to do so, padding like a rather large dog in a suit. I had asked the prime minister about the dangers she saw in a world developing into three great trading blocs based on three powerful currencies, the Japanese yen, the dollar and the Deutschmark, with Britain and the pound sterling on the outside of all of them. Mrs Thatcher condemned what she called 'Bloc-ism' and came to the end of her sentence. Then, without missing a beat, she turned in her seat towards the man from Sky and said, 'For goodness sake, you stupid boy! Do get up off the floor!' He did as he was told. This was the authentic Thatcher who Gordon Reece had helped turn into one of Britain's most extraordinary leaders – bossy, in control, quick witted, no-nonsense, 'not for turning' (or crawling, as it happened) and, as those of us privileged to get up close always knew, often very funny as she projected power at every opportunity and refused to suffer fools gladly.

On another occasion, an acquaintance of mine was once invited by Mrs Thatcher for a late evening drink. It was the time reserved for those, like Bernard Ingham, whom she most trusted. This person asked for a gin and tonic.

'Gin and tonic?' Mrs Thatcher said to my informant, incredulous. 'You'd be better with a whisky.'

'But I don't like whisky, Prime Minister.'

'Well, there's no nourishment in gin,' replied Mrs Thatcher, though she eventually relented and poured a G&T anyway.

Years later, during her retirement, when a bronze statue was unveiled on 21 February 2007 in Westminster, Mrs Thatcher referred yet again to her crafted story of inflexibility when she admired the artwork and then quipped, 'I might have preferred iron – but bronze will do … It won't rust.'

She was, among other things, one of the most successful prime-ministerial storytellers of recent times, gifted at squashing or squaring those who told stories against her. She got there by hard work, listening to criticism and where necessary changing course, while maintaining that of course she never did so.

Leadership Lesson: Leaders have to deal with negative counter-stories or, as we will see in a moment, they can easily be destroyed by them. Counter-stories are most damaging when, they question the very basis of the leader's character, his or her personal story, 'Who am I?'They are less damaging when they focus on policies – the 'collective mission'. There are various strategies for dealing with counter-stories. Humour works, especially for someone who is a natural raconteur like President Obama, or for that matter the London Mayor Boris Johnson. But the most important point for a leader is to recognise which counter-stories are particularly important and to deal with them relentlessly, every single day. Margaret Thatcher's team and the British monarchy's advisers have been among the great experts at doing so.

Followership Lesson: Followers will hear a great deal of stories and counter-stories about those they follow, because this is the key battleground of leadership. Leaders who control that battleground are extremely powerful. Any leader who can get away with telling jokes about potentially detrimental situations, like Barack Obama, or who, like Mrs Thatcher, can accept criticism of her policies while maintaining consent about her character, is likely to succeed in maintaining the relationship of trust with followers which is at the heart of credibility.

10 The Hedgehog and the Fox: How to Handle Scandal

A scandal is simply the name we give to the worst counter-story a leader can confront. As a journalist, I covered two of the biggest Washington scandals of the twentieth century: the Monica Lewinsky affair and the Iran–Contra affair. The former could have brought down Bill Clinton. He was impeached but survived on a narrow vote in the US Senate. Iran–Contra is less well remembered now, but it could have brought down Ronald Reagan. The way those two great communicators, Reagan and Clinton, survived their respective scandals demonstrates the most astoundingly successful uses of a leadership story against two of the most powerful counter-stories that I have ever come across. In the next chapter we will learn What NOT to Do, and see how lesser men were brought down by lesser counter-stories. Here we will learn What to Do – how Reagan and Clinton handled their scandals and survived, using the power of their stories.

Ronald Reagan was the first American president I covered as a reporter. Along with Margaret Thatcher, Tony Blair and Bill Clinton, Reagan's leadership story is among the most controversial of my lifetime. He continues to be divisive long after his death. When I delivered the live commentary on Ronald Reagan's state funeral for BBC television in June 2004, I suggested – not very controversially, I thought, given that Reagan had been elected overwhelmingly to the presidency twice – that what Americans remembered was his constant optimism and the clear, simple way in which he delivered his political message. I was immediately criticised by one veteran left-wing British journalist as some kind of Reagan-lover for daring to suggest that Reagan might have had praiseworthy qualities which Americans found endearing. The European Left never understood Reagan's popularity, nor why he still connects with Americans today, more than thirty years after he was first elected to the White House.

Within his Republican Party, would-be presidential candidates try to compete for the Reagan mantle, partly because he won a war, the Cold War. He was the man who defined the Soviet Union as 'the Evil Empire' and then worked not to contain it but to destroy it. As that Evil Empire phrase suggests, the storytelling methods Reagan and his advisers used were very different from those of Bill Clinton a generation later when the USSR did indeed collapse. The differences between Reagan and Clinton are worth studying because they get to the heart of the very different characters of two men who shared one simple objective: survival. In each case, it was survival against the odds, beset by scandals which would have destroyed the careers, reputations and legacies of lesser storytellers.

The Hedgehog

An American friend once explained to me that the reason why the counter-story about Ronald Reagan was believed by many in Britain was because Europeans are habitually condescending towards Americans. We are secretly angry, he said, that 'a nation full of so many stupid, fat, ignorant, uncultured people could be so rich and successful, and far greater than their own'. Reagan was lean rather than fat, but in the minds of those who disliked him, he fitted most of the other parts of that counter-story. He was stupid, they said. Inattentive. A warmonger, a cowboy, a simple-minded actor who 'played' the role of president of the United States, while he was 'directed' by people in the shadows who manipulated his presidency for their own ends. In this caricature, Reagan was the Forrest Gump of the White House. Perhaps more accurately, Reagan was the spuriously profound Chauncey Gardiner played by Peter Sellers in the 1979 film *Being There*, a man who said dim-witted things which his followers took to be words of wisdom.

Ronald Reagan's version of his own leadership story was quite different. To friends and followers, Reagan was a 'hedgehog' rather than a 'fox'. The description comes from a 1953 essay by the British philosopher Sir Isaiah Berlin. In 'The Hedgehog and the Fox', Berlin categorised writers, thinkers and human beings in general according to the words of Archilochus, the ancient Greek poet: 'The fox knows many things, but the hedgehog knows one big thing.' Clinton was most certainly a fox. He was intellectually voracious, inquisitive, blessed with an extraordinary memory, a gift for debate and a love of being challenged intellectually. There was nothing – nothing – which on the face of it Bill Clinton would not find interesting, often staying awake until two in the morning to discuss the topic of the day. Reagan was very different. The 'big thing' that his supporters say 'the hedgehog' Reagan held on to was an idea of Good and Evil which Reagan's critics regarded not just as simple but as simplistic.

For Reagan, the hedgehog, it really *was* simple. The American system of democracy was Good. The Soviet Union system was Evil. (Foxes like Clinton find the word 'evil' difficult to use.) In Reagan's domestic policy this Manichean world view translated into a series of simple ideas reducible to political slogans: Big Government: Bad. Small Government: Good. High Taxes: Bad. Low Taxes: Good. Low Defence Spending: Bad. High Defence Spending: Good. Communist-leaning governments all round the world: Bad. Capitalist governments all round the world – even those run by unsavoury and oppressive dictators – Good, so long as they remain pro-American. And so on. All of this became the core of Reagan's leadership story. He said in virtually every campaign speech in 1980 that he wanted to 'get Big Government off the backs of the American people' and 'turn you loose', so that voters could do what they did best, create wealth for themselves, their families, their communities and their country. That, in the 1980s Reagan storytelling, was all that was necessary for the USA to reinvigorate itself.

Reagan really was the shock of the new. He promised 'new' thinking on the economy: 'supply side economics', which went back to the teachings of Friedrich Hayek, Milton Friedman and others. It meant deep cuts in public spending (except defence), cutting taxes, shrinking government, taking on the trade unions – beginning with the air traffic controllers' union PATCO, who were summarily dismissed when they went on strike. Reagan was also 'new' in rolling back the political consensus about what government was for in the United States, a consensus which had lasted for almost fifty years since 1933 until Reagan took power in 1981. Supporters called it the 'Reagan Revolution', but as we have seen with other leaders, to bring about change demanded an appeal to the past. In Reagan's case it was to the 'traditional' America of Theodore Roosevelt and 'rugged individualism', as well as to an idealised Norman Rockwell small-town America. It was the paperboy throwing the morning newspaper at the porch of an old-fashioned colonial house used in one of Reagan's famous campaign ads, the Mythland America in which fewer and fewer Americans actually lived. Rather like the British monarchy with their plumed hats and horse-drawn carriages bearing the Queen, Reagan's Mythland told a story about the United States – 'Who are we?' – which his fellow countrymen simply adored.

For the purposes of this book, the specific policies pursued by Ronald Reagan do not matter. What does matter is how he succeeded in driving those policies through a Democrat-controlled Congress, and how he appealed directly to the American people by telling stories and creating an extraordinary new phenomenon in American politics, the 'Reagan Democrats'. These were natural Democrat voters, often blue-collar or semi-skilled workers, who switched parties to vote for Ronald Reagan because his stories reflected a vision of America which made them feel at home. In their influential book *Nudge* (2008), the Chicago academics Richard Thaler and Cass Sunstein recount studies which show that one determined individual who sticks fast to his or her ideas can make others agree with them, a habit common to leaders as diverse as Reagan, Mao Tse Tung, Margaret Thatcher, Gandhi, the Reverend Ian Paisley and Nelson Mandela. Thaler and Sunstein write, 'The clear lesson here is that *consistent and unwavering people*, in the private or public sector, can move groups and practices in their preferred direction' (my italics).

Reagan started his presidency in January 1981 as one of those 'consistent and unwavering people' – a 'hedgehog'. Clark S. Judge, who was one of his speechwriters from 1986 to 1989, noted in an essay for the *Claremont Review of Books* (Spring 2011) that Reagan had two unusual political heroes. One was Calvin Coolidge, generally considered to be one of the architects of the Great Depression. Judge notes that while governor of California, Reagan provocatively 'admired Coolidge's tax-rate and budget cuts and the prosperity they produced. As president he held up Coolidge's economic policies as a model for his own' and he hung a portrait of Coolidge in the White House Cabinet Room. He did the same for another underrated president he admired, Dwight Eisenhower, saying that Ike 'halted dead in its tracks the advance of communism'. In Coolidge and Eisenhower Reagan sided with two unfashionable American leaders, but there may have been another reason for his admiration of Ike beyond his resistance to communism.

'As president,' Judge reports, '[Eisenhower] presented an avuncular, sometimes befuddled manner to the media. Yet behind the mask, he was sharp, exacting, driven, a precise speaker and close editor ...' Judge quotes studies that found:

> ... that the concept of linking a military build-up with the goal of bankrupting the Soviet Union appeared in Reagan's

statements reaching back several decades ... One Soviet official summed up Reagan's negotiating style saying: 'He takes you by the arm, leads you to the edge of the cliff, and then invites you to take a step forward for the good of humanity.'

His avuncular, sometimes bumbling manner concealed a ruthless ability to communicate even the most unpalatable messages to audiences in ways which seemed calm and unthreatening, even if, like the former Soviet official, his listeners were ideologically opposed to everything Reagan stood for. They knew they might be on the edge of the cliff, but Reagan's charm was reassuring and constant. His leadership story revolved around calmness and decency. Hedgehogs, after all, look cute and slightly befuddled, but they are prickly when threatened, and ruthless when it comes to their own survival. Some Americans always loved Reagan. Some always hated him. But many in the middle came to separate who Reagan *was* – a person they liked and respected – from what he *did*, policies which were often controversial, and to some Americans absolutely abhorrent. They liked the 'Who am I?' and 'Who are we?' parts of Reagan's narrative, even if they did not buy into his definition of 'What is our common purpose?' – a distinction Reagan's critics in the European Left largely never understood.

Reagan was so successful at separating himself from the unpalatable consequences of his policies that the veteran *Washington Post* columnist Mary McGrory, who was my guide to Washington in the 1980s, and a long-time Democrat, used to joke with me that Reagan's storytelling genius lay in 'running against the government which he himself leads'.

The Sorcerer's Apprentice

It took Ronald Reagan a very long time and a great deal of practice to hone his supposedly 'natural' or 'innate' storytelling skills. As his Hollywood acting career waned he found a role as corporate spokesman for General Electric, and on their behalf he would address up to ten audiences a day. Telling stories is like flying an aircraft. However much you know in theory, there is no substitute for actually doing it. You need to keep up your flying hours, or storytelling hours.

During his time at GE, Reagan found out which stories worked for a live audience and which did not. He made every speech seem as if it was tailored for his audience, even if it was a piece of boiler-plate rhetoric recycled a thousand times. In the 1984 campaign the White House press corps had fun mouthing along to the well-worn words of Reagan's repetitive stump speech, because every reporter had heard the same sound bites dozens of times. The 'earwig' was getting on our nerves. But at every campaign stop Reagan was able to make it sound fresh for the voters, sometimes for several audiences a day. As Michael Deaver told me, Reagan never forgot that a man or woman in the audience might only hear the president of the United States talk live in the flesh once in their lifetime, and he made sure that what he had to say sounded as if it was directed personally at them. Academic research shows that business people who want to ensure compliance with surveys or requests for assistance are far more likely to achieve their goals if they stick a yellow Post-it note with an informal but personalised appeal attached. The social scientist Randy Gardner who carried out the research concluded 'that the more personalised you make a request, the more likely you'll be to get someone to agree to it'. (As quoted in *YES! 50 Secrets from the Science of Persuasion*, see p. 172.) Those who heard Reagan speak, even to a large crowd or on television, often felt that he had crafted the words especially for them, a personal Post-it note from the president.

Clark Judge quotes one story about Reagan arriving at a campaign stop in California to meet a school class of blind children:

After reporters had left for their bus, Reagan stayed behind and asked the teacher if the children would like to feel his face. The teacher said they would be thrilled. So, for a few minutes, without publicity, the children got to 'see' him in the only way they could.

Judge's words 'without publicity' are accurate, and yet misleading. Stories of the 'authentic' Ronald Reagan getting up close and personal 'without publicity' are legion. They became part of the Reagan myth-making machine, and appear to offer an insight into his character. Stories 'without publicity' are particularly powerful, as the Reagan team knew, because the implication is that the leader is not doing something for personal or political gain. That's just what the leader is 'authentically' like. And then the story leaks out so everyone knows about it. Reagan was all hedgehog, all the time, and that was to save him from possible impeachment when in 1986 his administration teetered on the brink of self-destruction.

A 'Neat Idea'

The Iran–Contra scandal of the mid 1980s came about as a result of a bizarre plot orchestrated from a basement in the Old Executive Office Building next to the Reagan White House. The key player was a US marine, Colonel Oliver North. The plot was duplicitous, hugely complicated and in parts illegal. It involved the Reagan administration secretly dealing with terrorists in Lebanon, despite public assurances not to negotiate with terrorists; courting the mullahs in the Islamic Republic of Iran, despite officially regarding Iran as a pariah state and sponsor of terrorism; laundering money; and paying paramilitary thugs in Latin America against the express wishes of a law enacted by Congress. It was to lead to the indictment of Colonel North and others, plus a truly extraordinary series of congressional hearings which I sat through for several weeks in the summer of 1987. At these Iran-Contra hearings we heard how Colonel North wanted to secure the release of American and other hostages held in Lebanon by the paramilitary group Hezbollah. These captives included the Archbishop of Canterbury's aide Terry Waite and the British journalist John McCarthy. The conspirators had what North described as a 'neat idea'.

They would pay a ransom to Iran, and then Iran would secure the release of the hostages. The terrorist kidnappers would, in effect, be rewarded by the US government for their behaviour. Colonel North arranged to trade sophisticated military equipment with the Iranians, including TOW anti-tank missiles. The Iranians were so grateful they paid large sums in cash to the Americans, and the cash was then used by Colonel North to fund another top-secret project: Reagan administration support for right-wing 'Contra' guerrillas in Nicaragua. The *Contrarevolucionario*s were a bunch of thugs and killers attempting to overthrow the left-wing Sandinista government of Nicaragua led by Daniel Ortega.

The Iran–Contra plot was devastatingly damaging to the Reagan administration. It challenged the president's authenticity. It undermined everything Reagan publicly said he stood against: negotiating with terrorists, rewarding kidnappers and trading weapons to Iran, as well as sending money to the Contra guerrillas, in direct contravention of the Boland Amendment, a law which specifically forbade the US government supporting the Contras in that way. The Iran–Contra hearings gutted the Reagan administration and put those guts on display.

By 1987 Reagan was to claim no knowledge of what had been done. It was the lowest point of his presidency, an admission of incompetence, ignorance and detachment. Perhaps it really was, as Reagan had joked, a case of the 'right hand' not knowing what the 'far right hand' was doing. Reagan the hedgehog curled up into a protective ball, and for a time it looked as if the elderly president, showing what we now know to be the early signs of Alzheimer's, might even be impeached. Hillary Clinton was one of the lawyers working behind the scenes for the Democrats trying to figure out how to handle the scandal, but the more they considered their options, the less the appetite even among Reagan's strongest opponents to bring him down.

Part of the reason was raw politics. There had been too many failed presidencies. John F. Kennedy had been shot. Lyndon Johnson had quit as a result of failure in Vietnam. Richard Nixon destroyed himself in Watergate. Gerald Ford wasn't very bright and proved unelectable. Jimmy Carter's presidency ended in failure after just one term. Not since Reagan's hero Dwight Eisenhower was elected in 1952 had any American leader served out two successive terms. Through his leadership story, Reagan had changed the battleground of American politics and had come to embody 'American' in a different way from all the others. During the Carter presidency it was a commonplace of talk shows and newspaper opinion columns to suggest that the modern presidency might be too big a job for any one man. In the Reagan years, that argument died. Any attempt to impeach him in 1987 would, therefore, have torn America apart. For patriotic reasons, nobody – not even Reagan's political enemies – wanted another failed presidency, another White House scandal. On top of that, Reagan retained the personal affection of most Americans, which carried him through. They loved his stories.

The Teflon President

I once asked Reagan's former deputy chief of staff Michael Deaver how it was that the American public always forgave Reagan his mistakes, and liked him even if they disliked some of his policies. Deaver smiled and – as we saw in Chapter 3 – he agreed that Reagan was indeed the 'Teflon president' to whom bad things never stuck. Americans, Deaver said, and maybe most people in most countries, generally consider a good temperament more important than a high intellect. They will accept leadership from someone apparently trustworthy and likeable over that from some kind of intellectual genius. The retired Supreme Court justice Oliver Wendell Holmes famously remarked that Franklin Roosevelt had a 'second-rate intellect but a first-rate temperament'.

Reagan, Deaver repeated, really was a hedgehog. He told Americans the same simple story about their nation's essential goodness. In one speech he referred to America as a 'shining city on a hill', a beacon of freedom and virtue. Americans loved him for it. They did not turn to Ronald Reagan for the complex solutions and nuances offered by a fox. Instead it was for the simple truths of a hedgehog – good and evil – together with his warmth, sincerity, good humour and the supposedly consistent and unwavering way in which he pursued his policies. When Reagan was shown to be in the wrong in the Iran–Contra affair, inconsistent and suddenly very wobbly on issues of great importance, most Americans forgave him. The Reagan team persuaded the American people of Reagan's essentially good, patriotic motives. He had wanted to free American hostages, and that had meant his underlings making deals with unsavoury people. They had wanted to overthrow a 'dangerous' government in Nicaragua, and that had meant paying counter-revolutionaries. By 1987 the beleaguered Reagan administration fell back on the method used by Richard Nixon when he made his notorious 'Checkers' speech in 1952 and during the Watergate scandal in the 1970s. The Nixon method had three parts.

Part One: deny it.

Part Two: question the motives of accusers and adversaries.

Part Three: tell people how much the scandal or counter-stories have hurt the leader, his family and friends.

The Reagan team employed the Nixon method and because Reagan's personal authority and likeability was so immense, most Americans expressed feelings of disappointment rather than outrage. The simplicity of Reagan's storytelling charm, his 'hedgehog-ness', was obvious. He even appeared to share the disappointment of the American people at what had been done in his name. Throughout the Iran–Contra affair Americans questioned Reagan's judgement, his competence and his staff, but they never questioned his basic decency or supposedly good motives. The power of stories saved the Reagan presidency. It was to do the same in a very different way for Bill Clinton.

Enter the Fox

Clinton, on the face of it, could not be more different from Reagan – a different party, a different generation, a different ideology. He was, in Isaiah Berlin's terms, a fox. He knew many things. A Rhodes scholar, he loved Oxford, travelling, debate, finding out new things. He visited the Soviet Union while a student in Britain. From personal experience I can say he was as happy discussing the music of Kid Creole and the Coconuts as he was allied strategy in North Africa in 1942, the rise of China or the possible ways in which welfare could be reformed. Journalists called him a 'policy wonk'. While Ronald Reagan apparently liked to be briefed using six by four-inch note-cards, Clinton loved briefs full of details. When Clinton published proposals to reform health care in the early 1990s, the resulting bill, orchestrated by his wife Hillary, was fox heaven. It came to more than a thousand pages. I once asked Bob Dole, the Republican leader in the Senate who was to become Clinton's opponent in 1996, if he had read the Clinton bill. He laughed and told me, 'Read it? I couldn't even lift it.' But if Clinton was one for details and Reagan one for the broad statement, they were both the great communicators of their generations. Clinton used skills very similar to Reagan's to handle his scandal and survive against all the odds.

When I first heard that the president of the United States had had an affair with an intern at the White House and that there was a blue dress stained with what was coyly described as the president's DNA, I assumed that the Clinton presidency was over. This was an attitude shared for a time by some members of Clinton's own inner circle. The Monica Lewinsky scandal was by no means a repeat of the Gennifer Flowers scandal, an affair that had occurred long ago between an obscure Arkansas politician and a night-club singer. This was the most powerful man in the world having sex with an unpaid volunteer many years his junior.

'Whatever you do, you don't do the interns,' Bob Schieffer, a veteran White House correspondent from CBS, said. It was a line which inspired a similar utterance from the Ryan Gosling character in the 2011 George Clooney film *The Ides of March*: 'You can lie, you can cheat, you can start a war, you can bankrupt the country … but you can't fuck the intern.' The reason, of course, is that all the other sins – lying, cheating, starting a war or bankrupting the country – tend to refer to 'our common purpose', and therefore are matters of policy. Having sex with an intern hits directly at the president's own personal story and morality. Or lack of it. When the Lewinsky scandal broke it was, for the Clinton Haters, the answer to a prayer, in some cases quite literally. William Jefferson Clinton was to become the first president to be impeached for 'high crimes and misdemeanours' since the nineteenth century. Not even Richard Nixon had to endure that humiliation, since 'Tricky Dicky' resigned before the formal impeachment process over Watergate could begin. But – like Reagan – Clinton owed his survival to his ability to communicate with the American people. Storytelling saved his presidency. What makes it remarkable is that it also included a blatant lie.

Briefs or Boxers?

In 1992, when Clinton survived the Gennifer Flowers scandal, it was because he had mastered the confessional TV interview. He told us that he was answering questions by saying things that no top politician had ever said before. While the astounding TV performance turned Bill and Hillary Clinton into household names all across the United States, it also meant that Clinton became fair game for questions that no president had ever been asked before. I followed him on some of his presidential 'town meetings' to connect with ordinary voters. On one occasion a young woman asked him about his underpants: briefs or boxers? Clinton replied that it was boxers. His advisers winced, not just at the question but at Clinton's decision to answer it. Such 'town hall'-style meetings were immediately curtailed because they were beginning to make Clinton seem unpresidential. But to understand how Clinton survived impeachment, we need to understand not just his openness about what were normally considered private matters, including underpants, but also the facts about how the Lewinsky scandal came to light. Between November 1995 and March 1997, Clinton had a sexual relationship with Monica Lewinsky. She was twenty-two years old at the time the relationship began. Her family were Jewish, from California. They were well connected within the Democratic Party. To defend himself from the charges in the Lewinsky case, Clinton hired a private lawyer of Catholic Irish background. White House staff joked at the time that this must be a mistake.

'His mistress is Jewish? His lawyer is Catholic? Wrong way round. Catholic *mistress*, Jewish *lawyer*, right?'

Beyond the gallows humour, there was shock, hurt and anger in the Clinton team. They had defended him against so many attacks in the past, but this time it could be terminal. In the early 1990s there had been allegations of financial double-dealing, known as the 'Whitewater controversy', together with allegations that Clinton had sexually harassed a state employee in Arkansas called Paula Jones, and on some of the more lunatic radio talk shows allegations that Clinton had been involved in every kind of crime you can think of, including murder and drug dealing. The pornographic publisher Larry Flynt's commentary is, as always, perceptive:

> Jack Kennedy never had to contend with talk radio hosts who filled hours of airtime every day with random callers offering up rumours ... Only two radio stations had talk formats in

1960; by 1995 there were 1,130, and nearly 70 per cent of talk radio listeners were conservative. Rush Limbaugh alone had 20 million listeners and was broadcast on 659 radio stations ... in the year before the 1994 mid-term elections, the press ran more news stories about Whitewater than on Clinton's domestic agenda ... incoming House Speaker Newt Gingrich announced his plans to have 20 congressional committees simultaneously investigating the Clinton administration ...

These investigations at times had the appearance of the Salem witch trials. Some in Congress had already decided that Clinton should be burned at the stake and were perplexed that all their investigations failed to turn up any significant evidence of wrongdoing. Then came the Lewinsky affair. It burst into the open because Lewinsky had confided in a woman she thought was a friend, a former co-worker called Linda Tripp. Lewinsky told Tripp that she was having sexual relations with the president. From September 1997, Tripp secretly recorded their conversations. In January 1998 Tripp handed over the tapes to the special prosecutor investigating Clinton's supposed wrongdoing, Kenneth Starr. This gave the otherwise hopeless Starr inquiry something to investigate, although consenting adults having unwise sex was not contrary to any known law. The turning point came when the worst counter-story ever told about Clinton was leaked to Matt Drudge, who, as Flynt describes him, was 'a 31-year-old blogger who lived in a $600 a month apartment in Los Angeles'. The headline read: '23 year old former White House intern, sex relations with President'. In words which define the era of globalised gossip, Drudge was to tell the National Press Club in Washington that the American public 'has a hunger for unedited information. We have entered an era vibrating with the din of small voices. Every citizen can be a reporter. The Net gives as much voice to a computer geek like me as to a CEO or a Speaker of the House. We all become equal ... no middle man, no Big Brother.'

Under pressure to rebut the story, Clinton lied publicly. On 26 January 1998 he told an internationally televised news conference, 'I want to say one thing to the American people. I want you to listen to me. I'm going to say this again. I did not have sexual relations with that woman … Miss Lewinsky. I never told anybody to lie, not a single time, never. These accusations are false. And I need to get back to work for the American people.' Clinton said that 'there is not a sexual relationship, an improper sexual relationship or any other kind of improper relationship' with Ms Lewinsky. Clinton's lawyer in the Paula Jones sexual harassment case had also assured the judge that 'there is no sex of any kind, in any manner, shape or form' between Clinton and Lewinsky. Later, on 17 August 1998, Clinton defended these statements that there 'is' no sex between them by saying: 'it depends on what the meaning of the word "is" is.' He meant that the affair was over, and so the word 'was' would have been more accurate, but this was Clinton at his worst, not the commander-in-chief but the lawyer-in-chief. Like many in Washington, when I heard this hair-splitting nonsense I thought he was doomed. The Comeback Kid was to prove us all wrong one more time.

Hail to the Storyteller-in-Chief

The president was impeached by the House of Representatives, in the manner prescribed by the Constitution of the United States, on 19 December 1998. The charges were perjury, obstruction of justice and malfeasance in office. Those who impeached him claimed that in lying under oath about sex, Clinton's conduct amounted to 'high crimes and misdemeanours' as specified by the US Constitution. The only other similar proceedings in American history had been against President Andrew Johnson in 1868. In February 1999, Clinton was acquitted by the US Senate. The verdict was in line with American public opinion. Polls showed voters condemned his adultery and gave him extremely low *personal* approval ratings, yet continued to give Clinton high *job* approval ratings. Even a week after the Lewinsky story broke, Clinton's job approval was at an astonishing 67 per cent in a *Washington Post* poll. By March 1998 his job approval hit 70 per cent, whereas his chief tormentor, the independent counsel Ken Starr, had a job approval of 11 per cent. Nevertheless, Republicans, spurred on by Speaker Newt Gingrich, voted overwhelmingly to impeach and then convict. Only five Democratic House members voted to impeach, and no Democratic Senators voted to convict. Clinton was wounded, but not fatally. He went on to serve the rest of his term and leave office more popular than when he was elected in 1992, so popular that if the Constitution permitted it, he would easily have been re-elected in 2000 instead of George W. Bush.

Yet the big question remains: how did Clinton do it? How did one of the greatest verbal Houdinis of the twentieth century escape certain political death? He did it, of course, through the power of his stories. While his lawyers fought the legal battle, Clinton and his advisers fought the far more important political battle for public opinion. The White House spokesman Joe Lockhart, a man who radiates good humour, common sense and basic decency, admitted to me he was shocked by what the president had done. Like many in the staff, he felt personally betrayed. But he – and all the Clinton staff I met – were able to separate the stupid conduct of a flawed man from what they saw as a political coup by right-wing Republicans to throw out of office someone who had been elected twice to the presidency of the United States, and who, they believed, had performed well in that capacity.

Reagan, as we have seen, was always admired for his 'Who am I?' leadership story, even if he was often disliked for some of his policies, his 'What is our common purpose?'. For Clinton, what saved him was the reverse. Americans, in other words, were able to separate the two parts of Clinton's leadership story – the 'Who Am I?' *An adulterer* from 'What is our common purpose?' *To make America strong and prosperous.* In the latter endeavour Clinton and America seemed to be doing rather well. The

Clinton team rapidly realised that if he was to survive they had to emphasise that part of the storytelling, and explain once more who Clinton really was: a repentant sinner. At the White House we joked that there were really two Bill Clintons, Saturday Night Bill who played the saxophone, looked cool and had a certain weakness for the ladies, and Sunday Morning Bill, the southern Baptist who never stopped asking for forgiveness.

For the making of a BBC radio series called *The Clinton Years*, and on other occasions, I interviewed many of the key players in the Clinton storytelling team, including the political consultant Dick Morris. After his own sex scandal a few years earlier, Morris had been ejected from the Clinton inner circle, to the relief of almost the entire Clinton team, who generally despised him, often in language that is best not repeated. Morris was so disliked that when he called Clinton's private number, if a secretary answered, Morris always said it was 'Charlie' on the line, in an attempt to avoid the wrath of Clinton's official staff. Even Clinton himself had a love–hate relationship with this unofficial adviser. On one occasion, I was told, they actually came to blows until Hillary Clinton separated them. As soon as the Lewinsky scandal broke, Morris called Clinton.

'It occurred to me that I may be the only sex addict you know,' he said.

Morris took a snap private poll which showed a majority of Americans thought Clinton should be impeached if he had lied under oath. As many as a third thought he should go to jail. The results meant panic stations at the White House. Morris urged Clinton that his only option was to stonewall, to delay, to survive long enough for the public to get over their anger and surprise. He hoped that the political tide would turn. That was when Clinton lied about Ms Lewinsky, and that lie saved his presidency. It allowed the public anger to cool and opinions slowly to change. Rather like the mind-numbingly complicated details of the Iran–Contra scandal, the more we heard about Bill Clinton's sex life, the less interested most Americans became. The press secretary Joe Lockhart told me that he even came to welcome the daily feeding frenzy of the White House briefings, the ugliness of sessions with reporters. The smuttier the questions and the more disgusting the allegations, the more Lockhart believed that the majority of the American people would draw the line of privacy for themselves.

As the weeks went by and Clinton clung to power by his fingertips, Lockhart could sense the story was changing. The counter-story of sex with an intern and lies under oath slowly became the story the Clinton team had been telling for years: a right-wing witch-hunt against a successful and twice-elected president who was doing a good job. Tony Blair, speaking to me a few years later about the same period, told me he was absolutely astonished at Clinton's powers of concentration and compartmentalisation. While all around him swirled amid the seamiest public sex scandal ever to hit the White House, Clinton – Blair told me with great admiration – would focus on what to do about Kosovo, the bombing of Yugoslavia, the world economy, al-Qaeda and other matters. It was, Blair said, real leadership. The strategy of buying time also meant that the most determined of Clinton's enemies began to sound less like independent investigators and more like a bunch of dirty old men. Larry Flynt writes:

> Once the FBI had matched the semen on Lewinsky's dress with a blood sample from the president, Clinton had no choice but to finally come clean in testimony before Starr's grand jury. On August 17, 1998, the grand jury watched a closed circuit television feed of Clinton's deposition taken in the White House Map Room. In the same room where Franklin Roosevelt marked allied advances against the Axis powers, Clinton had to answer such questions as, 'If Monica Lewinsky says that you ejaculated into her mouth on two occasions in the Oval Office area, would she be lying?'

And so on, ad nauseam. On 11 September 1998 Ken Starr's office published a 452-page report which read like extracts from Larry Flynt's infamous *Hustler* magazine. Starr included details such as 'the president inserted a cigar into [Miss Lewinsky's] vagina, and then put the cigar in his mouth and said, "it tastes good."' More than sixty-five major US newspapers demanded Bill Clinton's resignation, including the formerly supportive *Los Angeles Times*, which said, 'The picture of Clinton that now emerges is of a middle-aged man with a pathetic inability to control his sexual fancies.'

But the immediate crisis was passing. Public anger was cooling. Those closest to Clinton, the staff members and friends who knew him best, forgave him. Remarkably, there were no resignations from Clinton's Cabinet or staff over the Lewinsky affair. Nor were there 'resignations' from his marriage or family. Hillary Clinton and their daughter Chelsea endured a terrible time, but they also understood the nature of the battle. As she had done in 1992 over Gennifer Flowers, Hillary Clinton prepared to stand by her man. This time it was in a solo appearance on the *Today Show* with Matt Lauer. Mrs Clinton made sure to tell the story that really mattered to her husband's survival: 'Look at the very people who are involved,' she said of Clinton's accusers who had dredged up such sexually intimate details. 'The great story here, for anybody who is willing to find it and write about it and explain it, is this vast right-wing conspiracy that has been conspiring against my husband since the day he announced for president.'

The Clintons used the same kind of strategy employed by the Reagan team in the previous decade, based on Richard Nixon's three-point way of handling a scandal: first, deny it; secondly, cast aspersions on the motives of your accusers; third, say how much all this hurts you and your family. The idea of a conspiracy by one's enemies is a very useful element in a leadership story, as scandal-hit leaders of all kinds have found. Among the most egregious, Silvio Berlusconi, adopting the Nixon–Reagan–Clinton method, frequently told Italians that all the seamy allegations against him were false; that they were part of a left-wing conspiracy involving journalists, magistrates and political opponents, and that he found them very hurtful. Ronald Reagan's supporters railed against the conspiracy of the 'liberal media elite', who they said 'blamed America first' instead of putting America first. Hillary Clinton's 'vast right-wing conspiracy' therefore was a brilliantly evocative piece of storytelling which helped turn the tide in Clinton's favour, along with her own loyalty to her husband.

The battle to counter the counter-story began in earnest. Democratic Congressman John Conyers called the special prosecutor Kenneth Starr 'a federally paid sex policeman'. The highly regarded lawyer Alan Dershowitz referred to the entire procedure as 'sexual McCarthyism'. Larry Flynt called the Starr report 'more depraved and scandalous' than anything Clinton did. Being called depraved by a pornographer may be a bit like being called ugly by a frog, but in a stroke of genius Flynt then offered a million-dollar reward for anyone who could supply 'documentary evidence of illicit sexual relations' involving members of Congress. It took less than a week before the first counter-scandal broke.

Hypocrites in the House

The Republican leader of the House of Representatives team fighting to impeach Clinton, Congressman Henry Hyde, a man who always seemed, when I interviewed him, to exude pious Midwestern values, was revealed as having conducted an extramarital affair. The Republican House Speaker Newt Gingrich – yes, Holy Newt himself, the man who promised to unleash a score of anti-Clinton ethics investigations – was revealed to be carrying on a secret extramarital affair with a 27-year-old congressional aide called Callista Biesek, while publicly calling for Clinton's impeachment and lecturing Republican audiences about 'family values'. You could not make it up. Instead of being what Gingrich described as the 'enemy of normal Americans', it dawned on 'normal Americans' once more that Bill Clinton was one of them: flawed, but fundamentally decent, with a mixed-up private life but demonstrating competence in the job he was hired to do.

Clinton's objective was to remain in the presidency. His strategy was to look 'presidential' and refuse to be deflected from the business of governing. His tactics meant he lied, delayed, obfuscated and fought against impeachment while others spun stories on his behalf, spoke of the conspiracy against him and said how much Hillary and Chelsea had been hurt by it all. Hillary Clinton's intervention was a game changer. She turned the story away from the dubious morals of her husband and towards the dubious politics of his opponents. When asked by opinion pollsters, Americans accepted that the Clinton years had been good ones, that Clinton had behaved badly but should not be thrown out of office. The Comeback Kid, to the dismay of his enemies, had come back once more.

Everybody Likes a Winner

In the November 1998 midterm elections Newt Gingrich's Republican revolutionaries hoped for an anti-Clinton backlash. Instead, the Democrats picked up seats, something quite astonishing for a president's party in the sixth year of office. The Republican losses were so shocking that Gingrich was forced to resign as House Speaker. Who could have predicted that he would lose his job while Clinton kept his? And there was even worse to come. As Larry Flynt writes in *One Nation Under Sex*, 'When Congressman Bob Livingston was announced to replace Newt Gingrich as Speaker of the House in December 1998 I reported that Livingston engaged in numerous affairs including one with a staff member.'

Larry Flynt had claimed yet another victim among the Republican leadership. On 19 December 1998 Bob Livingston resigned from Congress, the second Republican choice for

Speaker to bite the dust within a few days. It came on the very same day on which the US House of Representatives impeached Bill Clinton. The smell of hypocrisy from a Congress which contained numerous adulterers impeaching a president for lying about his sex life was rank in the nostrils of the American public. By the time it came to a vote in the Senate on 12 February 1999, Clinton was acquitted, even though, quite obviously, he had indeed perjured himself by lying under oath. The Senate majority leader, the Republican Trent Lott, was utterly bewildered:

> There are only a couple of political things in my career that I still have not been able to understand. One is the fact that the American people apparently continued to support Clinton through this whole thing, knowing what he did, knowing what he said, knowing how he had demeaned the office ... I still think history needs to try to explain why the American people thought that all that was okay.

Trent Lott simply could not comprehend the power of Clinton's storytelling for a generation of Americans used to a new kind of morality and a new kind of media, and infuriated more by the hypocrisy of politicians than by Clinton's dangerous liaisons. Since Larry Flynt had spotted the way this crisis would unravel with greater perspicacity than many members of Congress, I asked him for his analysis. Clinton's sex life, Flynt told me, was of public interest. When you become very successful, 'you give up the right to privacy ... that's the price you pay for fame. People who complain about that should just be ignored.' Clinton, therefore, was fair game for exposure. Politicians, Flynt told me, 'have an enormous ego and they feed that ego through sexual conquests'. But impeaching Clinton was wrong, Flynt said, because everyone lies about sex.

'Americans were no longer disgusted by talk of oral sex in the Oval Office,' is how Flynt puts it. 'They knew plenty of presidents had affairs, including some of the heroes of American history

... the impeachment of Bill Clinton failed because Americans thought their president was doing a good job.'

When Clinton left office in January 2001 his job approval ratings were as high as those for John F. Kennedy after his assassination. Larry Flynt argues that conservative Republicans did not realise they had lost the Culture Wars of the 1960s. He told me, 'Your reputation is what you come to town with. Your character is what you leave with. People lie about sex all the time. The lie that Bill Clinton told was simply self-preservation.'

If Ronald Reagan's character was one which the majority of Americans instinctively trusted during a scandal, Bill Clinton's character was one which the majority of Americans understood. Sunday Morning Bill saw out the rest of his presidency, doing what he had done so often before: admitting mistakes, being contrite and ashamed, and apologising endlessly. He apologised first to his wife and family. Hillary Clinton had become such a sympathetic figure during the scandal she was soon to be offered the vacant New York Senate seat by the Democrats and spoken of as a possible future president. Then Bill Clinton apologised to the White House staff, to his Cabinet and to the American people. He sought forgiveness from leading Christian ministers.

By May 2010, almost a decade after he left the presidency, Clinton was still so popular that he 'raffled' himself as a prize in a fund-raising effort to retire his wife's campaign debt from the time she did run for the presidency against Barack Obama in 2008. Contributors could pay $5 and the winner of the raffle would get a chance to spend a day with Clinton. There were plenty of takers.

Status of the Storyteller

The fox and the hedgehog used different storytelling techniques appropriate to different times and different types of scandal. Reagan saw the Cold War world in terms of Good and Evil, black and white. As the first president elected after the Cold War, Clinton could see, and be seen, in terms of moral relativity, in shades of grey. What they had in common was their ability to tell stories that connected with the American people, to accept blame for their mistakes and yet not be destroyed by them. Both were helped by the fact that the allegations against them became so complicated that it was never entirely clear who held the moral high ground. Both managed that great performance trick of a leader seeming 'just like us' – Reagan with his dogs, his frailty and yet optimistic good humour; Clinton with his bad-boy scrapes, 'aw, shucks' mannerisms and unbounded contrition. Above all, both men had used similar storytelling techniques.

The theatrical director Keith Johnstone, who worked for a time at the Royal Court Theatre in London, can help us to understand a little of the shared storytelling genius of Reagan and Clinton. Johnstone changed the way acting is taught by his emphasis on what he called 'status transactions'. Johnstone was fascinated by the ideas of submission and dominance which he found in books on zoology by the author Desmond Morris. He would therefore instruct his acting students to play parts on a scale from 1 to 10, with 1 being the most submissive and 10 being the most dominant. He would also advise students, 'Don't concentrate', 'Don't think', 'Be obvious' and 'Don't be clever'.

On this 1 to 10 scale, both Reagan and Clinton aimed at a 5. The British actor David Gillespie, who offers media training for leaders and potential leaders in business, gives the example of a 10 as a dominant Saddam Hussein standing on the podium at a military display firing a shotgun in the air, the unchallenged dictator at the height of his powers. A 1 would be the humiliated Saddam Hussein being dug out from an underground bunker, photographed in his underwear, having his mouth probed by a US doctor wearing rubber gloves. A 10 would be Margaret Thatcher shouting down the Opposition in parliament at Prime Minister's Questions. A 1 would be Mrs Thatcher leaving Downing Street as prime minister for the last time, in tears.

When it came to defining the perfect 'status' of a communicator

– a mid-scale 5 – Gillespie, and other actors with whom I have discussed political leaders, fixed on Bill Clinton: warm, affable and approachable, neither dominant nor submissive – exactly the same qualities we have seen in Ronald Reagan. What Keith Johnstone calls 'status' defines the relationship between a speaker and his audience. Reagan and Clinton, the hedgehog and the fox, the Republican and the Democrat, the right and left of American politics, have nothing much in common. But where it really counts, they had everything in common. As great storytellers, they knew how to handle a scandal.

Leadership Lesson: A scandal is the worst kind of counter-story imaginable. When it comes to managing a scandal, temperament is more important than intelligence. The objective is survival. The strategy and tactics will vary with different leaders, but the key is to engage the audience, or voters, with the leader's character and personality and to make the scandal seem either out of character (Reagan) or, if clearly in character (Clinton), irrelevant to the overall performance of the leader.

Followership Lesson: As followers we need to consider whether we are judging a leader on their actions, on their character or both. American voters knew that Ronald Reagan was not really too concerned with the details of his policies. It was therefore 'in character' that he knew nothing about the Iran–Contra scandal until it became public. Bill Clinton's interest in women, similarly, was no surprise to most Americans, even if the details were shocking. The key questions about any scandal are: were the actions wrong? If wrong, were the motives at least understandable? And if the actions were wrong, and the motives dubious, as in the case of Clinton, is it our business or a private matter for the leader and those closest to him?

11 Losers: What NOT to Do

The primary purpose of this book is to be positive. As we examine the lessons we can learn from the world's greatest storytellers, it is obvious they tend to be winners. This chapter is about losers. We can all learn from those who get things profoundly wrong, just as we can all learn how not to run a hotel from watching Basil Fawlty in Fawlty Towers. Tony Hayward of BP, Sir Fred Goodwin of the Royal Bank of Scotland and the former British prime minister Gordon Brown are among those whose leadership has failed. We will hear about them now in some detail, together with others including Senator John Kerry and Colonel Gaddafi. History, as we have observed, is the storytelling of the victors. The victors tend to follow many of the methods I have outlined for promoting their own stories and challenging the counter-stories of their opponents. As for the losers, well, they are considered guilty of all kinds of misjudgements, but sometimes, as we will see, things could have turned out very differently if they had simply been better storytellers. Ronald Reagan and Bill Clinton both made profound errors of judgement, and yet their ability to tell a convincing story about themselves helped them to leave office even more popular than when they took the presidency for the first time. The stories which follow are, in contrast, exemplars of What NOT to Do.

When I began meeting political, business, military and cultural leaders, I thought some of them had delusions of grandeur. Nowadays I tend to think they often have delusions of competence.

Politically active people all over the world are accustomed to thinking in terms of '-isms'. They categorise politics, politicians and other leaders according to words like capitalism, socialism, communism, fascism, conservatism, environmentalism, anarchism, and so on. But the politically active classes rarely discuss the one '-ism' which counts above all others: egotism.

A common mistake among leaders, one shared by Mrs Thatcher, Tony Blair, Chairman Mao, Robert Mugabe, Fidel Castro, Muammar Gaddafi, Saddam Hussein and legions of others, is to try to hold on to a leadership position for too long, coupled with an increasing sense of their own infallibility. Some of these leaders seem to share the belief that their country, business or great project would go to hell without them running it. One test of a leader is knowing when to quit. The first major politician I ever came across was Enoch Powell, who came to Northern Ireland in his declining years as an Ulster Unionist MP. He frequently lectured that 'all political careers end in failure', but like many egotists, Powell was making a general rule to apply to all humanity when he was actually thinking about himself. One of the great intellects of his time, Powell destroyed his career when he made a play for the leadership of the Conservative Party over the issue of immigration. He lost the gamble and ended his life as the relatively unloved Ulster Unionist MP for South Down.

In contrast, those leaders who are regarded with the greatest affection tend to be like great entertainers who leave the stage while the audience still wants more. In the case of John F. Kennedy, it is difficult to believe that had he survived to see out his presidency, history would have treated him as kindly as the Kennedy romanticism does nowadays. While he is routinely praised for his handling of the Cuban missile crisis, most people forget that his inept handling of the Soviet Union led the Russians to embark on a number of strategic gambles, including the construction of the Berlin Wall in August 1961 and putting missiles in Cuba in the first place. Nikita Khrushchev thought Kennedy weak and inexperienced. He was assassinated in Dallas whilst on a campaign trip in 1963 organised because his advisers thought he might lose the vital state of Texas – and the presidency – in 1964. Yet Kennedy retains a great deal of public affection because of the tragic end to his leadership story and our sense that he left office before his time.

Nelson Mandela is universally acclaimed as a great leader for also leaving office early. He brought down the apartheid regime, and set a model for black Africa in taking power and then voluntarily relinquishing it. Robert Mugabe has become a pariah for doing the opposite – taking power as a revolutionary hero in Zimbabwe and then refusing to go. He will be remembered as a despot while Mandela will for ever be a hero. Colonel Gaddafi was another leader who flirted with various ideologies – nationalism, socialism, pan-Arabism – but for whom egotism was the defining feature. He described himself, without irony, as 'Brother Leader' and 'the King of Kings'. The name 'Brother Leader', like George Orwell's Big Brother, has a touch of Gaddafi's genius about it, because it suggests someone just like us – a brother – but also better than us, 'big.' To the end, Gaddafi protested that he could not step down from power after more than forty years because in truth he did not have any real power, except by the will of the Libyan people. A Gaddafi, Mugabe, Saddam Hussein or Hosni Mubarak would do well to recall the lessons of the poet Shelley's sonnet 'Ozymandias' (1818):

> I met a traveller from an antique land
> Who said: 'Two vast and trunkless legs of stone
> Stand in the desert. Near them, on the sand,
> Half sunk, a shattered visage lies, whose frown,
> And wrinkled lip, and sneer of cold command,
> Tell that its sculptor well those passions read
> Which yet survive, stamped on these lifeless things,
> The hand that mocked them and the heart that fed.

And on the pedestal these words appear –
'My name is Ozymandias, king of kings:
Look on my works, ye Mighty, and despair!'
Nothing beside remains. Round the decay
Of that colossal wreck, boundless and bare
The lone and level sands stretch far away.'

The Ozymandias tendency of business leaders is described with great clarity by the *Financial Times* journalist Lucy Kellaway. In July 2011 Kellaway wrote about what business leaders had said when she had asked them to sum up their strengths and weaknesses. Kellaway discovered that they frequently chose as their 'weaknesses' failings which gave them an excuse to retell stories of their basic *strengths*, rather like the stand-up comedian's joke that his only fault is being too modest. Kellaway wrote that in the eighteen months from the beginning of 2010, the *FT* had asked sixty business leaders twenty questions. One key question was 'What are your three worst features?' She continues:

When it comes to describing their dark sides, 58 out of 60 leaders felt bound by the same rule – any weakness is perfectly admissible, so long as it is really a strength. They almost all cite impatience, perfectionism and being too demanding – all of which turn out to be things that it's rather good for a Chief Executive Officer to be. What is particularly interesting about this mass outpouring of faux weaknesses is that there is no difference between men and women, and no difference between Americans and Europeans. All are as bad as each other. In the past 15 years of studying them, I've drawn up a list of the seven most common deadly sins.

- They are control freaks.
- They are vain.
- They are ditherers.
- They don't listen.
- They are bullies.

- They are afraid of conflict.
- And they can't do small talk.

Given that most of the 60 interview candidates were probably guilty of at least one of the above, why did none of them own up? The first possibility is that they didn't dare. But I suspect the real problem is worse: they don't know what their faults are. A decade of psycho-babble, coaching and 360-degree feedback has made no difference. It has not changed the most basic truth – people never speak truth to power. This denial of flaws is a pity. *We like people better when they wear their blemishes openly. It makes them seem more human.* [my italics]

Such errors extend way beyond leaders in business, but when great business enterprises get into trouble the stench of decay soon surrounds the 'colossal wreck', because many of the underlings are too terrified to tell the king of kings what a hash he is making of things. BP and RBS are two obvious examples.

BP: Big Problem

From the moment of the explosion on the Deepwater Horizon rig and the leaks of oil into the Gulf of Mexico on 20 April 2010, the oil giant BP and its boss Tony Hayward were left floundering. At least some of Kellaway's seven deadly sins of business leaders were to be found in BP's handling of the spill, though the question of apportioning blame will continue for some years. Eleven men working on the platform were killed and seventeen others were injured in the largest accidental marine oil spill in the history of the petroleum industry. The wellhead was eventually capped and the leak declared stopped on 15 July 2010, after it had released almost 5 million barrels. By 19 September 2010 the US federal government declared the well effectively 'dead'.

Throughout those months, BP tried to cap the leak, stop the pollution, disperse the spilled oil and minimise the political and economic damage. But – to remind ourselves of Alastair

Campbell's Golden Rule – what was their core objective? A Washington lawyer once told me that when the law is against you, you argue the facts. When the facts are against you, you argue the law. And when everything is against you, you just argue. BP argued. They seemed unclear about their overall objective, blaming contractors and sub-contractors, and fatally trying to play down the scale of the disaster, claiming the impact would be 'very, very modest'. Hayward and others suggested that the spill was 'relatively tiny' while the ocean was vast. This was monumentally stupid storytelling: Mr Hayward appeared to think the world would believe his protestations rather than the evidence of their own eyes. As we saw in the last chaper, both Ronald Reagan and Bill Clinton rapidly faced up to the enormity of the scandals which engulfed them, admitted wrongdoing and asked for forgiveness. In their study *YES! 50 Secrets from the Science of Persuasion* (2007), the authors Noah Goldstein, Steve Martin and Robert Cialdini refer to the importance of admitting mistakes. They quote the Duc de la Rochefoucauld: 'We only confess our little faults to persuade people that we have no big ones.' The authors approve of the techniques used by Reagan in dealing with counter-stories, including, as we have seen, his age. Admitting to mistakes, the *Yes!* authors argue, can enhance a leader's reputation for candour and openness if handled correctly:

> Organisations that attribute failures to internal causes will come out ahead not only in public perception but also in terms of the profit line … blaming internal, apparently controllable failures makes the organisation appear as if it has greater control over its own resources and future … this research suggests that if you play the blame game – pointing your finger at external factors rather than yourself – both you and your organisation will likely end up as the losers.

What NOT to Do: do not attempt to minimise your own responsibility by blaming others.

For BP worse was to follow. On 12 May 2009 Tony Hayward had lectured postgraduates at Stanford Business School that 'our primary purpose in life is to create value for shareholders'. He qualified those words by saying 'in order to do that you have to take care of the world', but the damage was done. He chose to define BP's primary objective as money, using words which fell into the most powerful counter-story trap for any big corporation: greed; profits before people.

What NOT to Do: do not hand your enemies or opponents the most powerful counter-story to use against you.

And then, it got even worse. On 31 May 2010, more than a month after the spillage, Tony Hayward said that 'there's no one who wants this thing over more than I do. I'd like my life back.' He was quickly reminded that the families of the eleven dead workers would like their lives back too. It was a moment when the egotism of the leader – 'What about ME?' – reared up like the hubris of Ozymandias. A 'long line of PR gaffes' was one of the more polite public descriptions by Rahm Emanuel, Barack Obama's chief of staff, on Hayward's leadership.

What NOT to Do: do not put yourself and your needs at the centre of the story, especially if it is a disaster affecting millions of other people.

BP shareholders saw the value of their assets, in what had looked like one of the world's safest investments, fall off a cliff. The company's previous boss, Lord Browne, had for years been alarmed by the counter-story of uncaring, greedy, environmentally destructive Big Oil and had tried to cultivate a 'green' image, rebranding all BP petrol stations with green and gold sunflowers. He spoke of BP not as 'British Petroleum' but as 'Beyond Petroleum'. By June 2010 President Obama, referring to the PR gaffes, said that Hayward 'wouldn't be working for me after any of those statements'. It was an interesting turn of phrase. Obama did not say that he would fire Hayward for the spill, or for failing to cap it, or for poor engineering. Obama would fire the boss of BP for *those statements*, i.e. for his abject failure to tell a coherent story.

On 19 June 2010, Hayward turned up in Cowes on the Isle of Wight, watching a yacht he co-owned taking part in a race, while on the other side of the Atlantic beaches were closed, fishermen could not work and newspaper headlines suggested Hayward had become the most loathed man in America.

BP: Beyond Parody

A year or so after the BP debacle, I talked to one of the top executives of another giant US corporation whose business activities sometimes lead to serious accidents. This corporate executive said that he used Tony Hayward's failures as part of his own company's training of its most senior managers in order to show What NOT to Do.

'So, where did Tony Hayward go wrong?' I asked.

'Everywhere,' was the reply, 'every time he opened his mouth.'

This executive, in a company with a long history of interest in safety issues, (and a creditable safety record,) said it was actually difficult to fault BP's technical response to the oil spill. The problem was almost entirely one of presentation.

'So what should Hayward have done?' I asked.

'He should have stepped in immediately as CEO, said how much he regretted what had happened, showed that he cared, visited the site, been seen to be concerned, talked to people, not tried to minimise the scale of the problem, announced someone else would take day-to-day control, and then stepped back into the shadows.'

I wondered if anyone handled that kind of disaster well.

'Obama,' the executive said. He explained that he was a Republican and generally not much of a fan of President Obama, but that in this case the Obama team had quickly recognised the significance of the Gulf of Mexico oil spill for his presidency and reputation. They also knew that President George W. Bush's handling of the aftermath of Hurricane Katrina in the Gulf a few years previously had almost destroyed his presidency. Obama's advisers saw Bush as an example of What NOT to Do, and therefore did differently. Obama flew to the Gulf of Mexico, toured the region, spoke to the people most affected, and showed human sympathy. He became not just the commander-in-chief but also the comforter-in-chief, giving a great hug to the bereaved and those who had lost their livelihoods. Once the story of 'I care' had been told, Obama left it to others to manage the details. In purely technocratic terms he could have dealt with the spill just as effectively from Washington as from Louisiana, but his objective was to show Americans that he cared and was personally in charge. His strategy involved visits to the area, plus the coordination of US and state forces, and the delegation of day-to-day responsibility. And his tactics included meeting those who had suffered, as well as attacking BP and implying that it was a foreign – i.e. British – company. The latter, of course, was unfair. Many of BP's shareholders and employees are in fact American. But fairness, like facts, is not the central issue when it comes to storytelling, as Hayward was to discover. He appeared to think BP's objectives were to cap the leak, mitigate their legal responsibility and place the blame as far as possible on others. A better leader would have recognised that his core objective was the survival of BP as an internationally respected company.

Tony Hayward was eventually replaced by an American CEO whose soothing tones, acceptance of some responsibility and the capping of the leak brought matters to a close. BP's precise share of the blame will ultimately be judged by the courts. But in a world hungry for stories, the one told by Obama was an example of What to Do. The one told by Hayward and BP was What NOT to Do. He, and they, paid dearly for it.

Money Can't Buy Me Love

In the terms we have seen in John Kay's book *Obliquity*, a true leader understands that building a cathedral has the objective of glorifying God, while a lesser leader may see it as merely a matter of creating a building and a workman may think of it only as a question of cutting stones (see p. 35). Tony Hayward may have been a brilliant stonecutter and even competent in fitting the stones together, but he forgot his true objective. Kay quotes one of the most highly regarded business people of the past twenty years, Jack Welch of GE, a man who could be ruthless when he needed to be – his nickname was 'Neutron Jack' – and who considerably increased the wealth of GE shareholders. Welch derided those businessmen who claimed, like Hayward, that their objective was to 'maximise shareholder value'. As Welch put it, 'That's not a strategy that helps you know what to do when you come to work every day.' Worse, and especially as we endure the effects of the post-2007 worldwide recession, those who lecture us about shareholder value or crude money-making play into the damaging counter-story of greedy, unregulated capitalism, of business leaders who know the price of everything and the value of nothing.

Someone who has attracted this kind of disastrous counter-story is Sir Fred Goodwin, known as 'Fred the Shred' for his enthusiastic cost-cutting and ambitious acquisitions at the Royal Bank of Scotland in pursuit of 'shareholder value'. Perhaps he would have benefited from Shelley's 'Ozymandias' being pinned to his wall. Sir Fred Goodwin was an ambitious Scottish-born banker, driven to create what he hoped would be a world-beating bank. When I met him in 2007 before the banking crisis broke he was extremely proud of his achievements. He spoke warmly of his own leadership, his ambitious links with China, his hopes to expand in what he clearly thought was a Far East market filled with opportunity, and his belief that he was ahead of the game, whatever that game might be. Goodwin struck me as a man with many qualities, but humility was not one of them. Nor was self-doubt. He had invited me to dinner with an eclectic group of economists, scholars and thinkers, each of whom was encouraged to talk for a few minutes on an area of expertise ranging from the problems of inventiveness in China to the American political system. Goodwin himself talked at length about China and how the Chinese wanted to know every tiny detail about RBS's credit card system, down to the layout of the processing offices and who sat where. He admired their attention to detail.

My impression was that Fred Goodwin probably enjoyed his 'earwig', 'Fred the Shred'. He seemed to revel in both his power and his reputation for ruthlessness. His commercial mistakes can safely be left to other analyses, although his takeover of ABN Amro is now widely recognised as the wrong move for the wrong target at the wrong time. For my purposes, what is important is that Goodwin, like Tony Hayward, disastrously confused objective, strategy and tactics. He never told a leadership story which could cope with failure. His tactics were based on ruthlessly cutting costs. His strategy involved taking over other banks. His objective was to become a world player in banking. But somewhere along the line he failed to see that the true objective of any great bank is to be trusted, reliable and, of course, solvent. As the 'Sage of Omaha' Warren Buffett astringently pointed out, when the tide goes out you soon see who has been swimming naked. Fred Goodwin lost his shorts. And his job. And his bank. In 2008 RBS posted a record loss for the United Kingdom of £24.1 billion. Whereas Tony Hayward was once described as the most hated man in America, Goodwin was described by one commentator as 'The World's Worst Banker'.

In *Obliquity*, John Kay gives an interesting account of the pursuit of money in business. He notes that the founders of many great corporations personally became extremely wealthy. But for Kay the important point is that most entrepreneurs rarely see getting rich as their principal objective. The founders of Google,

Apple, Facebook and Microsoft all passionately wanted to create a great business, and that objective led to financial benefits for shareholders, and for the leaders themselves, including extraordinary wealth. The strategy was to produce great products. The tactics were less important. They *could* include 'maximising shareholder value' and cutting costs as Tony Hayward and Fred the Shred were to do, but the objective was always a grander vision than just the pursuit of money. Kay writes of unpleasant, egotistical, loud-mouthed business leaders who sound like the fictional Gordon Gekko in Oliver Stone's 1987 film *Wall Street*. 'The most garish publicist for this management style,' Kay writes, 'was Al Dunlap, who noisily proclaimed the cause of shareholder value through the 1990s, acquiring the nickname "Rambo in Pinstripes."'

Dunlap's book is called *Mean Business*. That atrocious pun gives you an idea of someone who revelled in his own ability to suck air from a room. The book cover features a picture of 'Rambo in Pinstripes' with two dogs. Kay writes:

> [Dunlap] describes his philosophy: 'If you want a friend, get a dog. I'm taking no chances, I've got two' … Dunlap had no patience with any view of business corporations except as machines to generate money for stockholders and most importantly for Dunlap himself. In the end, he was forced out of his post at Sunbeam, the appliance manufacturer … The corporation went bankrupt.

Kay's key point is that we want our leaders – in business, politics or any other field of achievement – to appear to believe in something bigger than themselves, and in something more than exercising power and making a personal fortune. If a leader's 'Who am I?' story is so egotistical that 'Who are we?' means we are dupes or servants of the great leader, then 'What is our common purpose?' will be reducible to doing the leader's bidding so he can prosper. It is a leadership story which is disastrous, repulsive and doomed to fail. Those who turned money-making into the 'priority' or key objective have produced many of the muddled corporate messes of the past twenty years: Enron, Sunbeam, RBS, Lehman Brothers, Northern Rock, Bear Stearns, Drexel Burnham Lambert, Salomon Brothers, BP and so on. All these corporate mistakes have echoes of the 'Greed is good' leadership story of the fictitious Gordon Gekko in *Wall Street*, and Gekko was himself based on the real life Ivan Boesky, a 1980s corporate raider. Boesky was quoted as telling students, 'I want you to know that I think greed is healthy. You can be greedy and still feel good about yourself.' Boesky was eventually jailed for insider trading.

What NOT to Do: do not let the brilliance of your tactics confuse you as to your true objective.

One apparently minor What NOT to Do footnote to the Goodwin story particularly interests me. In late 2009 it was reported that he had for a time hired a journalist called Phil Hall to help rebuild his reputation. Hall is, among other things, the former editor of *Hello!* magazine. The link between one of the key players in the greatest financial crisis since the 1930s and the archetypal 'froth of life' magazine is perfect for the world of globalised gossip and trivia. It also demonstrates the scale of Fred Goodwin's failure to understand even his own best interests. All Phil Hall or any spin doctor can do is to help a leader cut still more stones, to build the same wonky cathedral. If Fred Goodwin or Tony Hayward truly want to rehabilitate their reputations, they need to understand the storytelling power of admitting mistakes, and follow the examples of Reagan and Clinton, or of Angelina Jolie in the next chapter. Journalists – like most of mankind – love stories about redemption, the prodigal son, the lost sheep returning to the flock. As the authors of *YES!* put it:

> If you've found yourself in a position where you've made a
> mistake, you should admit it, and follow up with an action plan

demonstrating that you can take control of the situation and put it right. Through these actions, you'll ultimately put yourself in a position of greater influence by being perceived as not only capable, but also honest.

Apologising and admitting error is a technique which works, though it is presumably unlikely to be adopted readily by those of the Ozymandias/Rambo in Pinstripes persuasion, especially when they have cultivated a reputation for infallibility. It raises that other problem in storytelling: not being authentic.

Not Being Authentic

One of the more embarrassing examples of What NOT to Do is William Hague. When he became leader of the British Conservative Party in 1997, Hague was faced with the same kinds of problems David Cameron was to deal with successfully during his leadership a few years later. To be fair, the period from 1997 onwards was probably too early for any Conservative leader to make much of a difference to an exhausted and demoralised party. But at least Hague grasped the problem. He is an able and intelligent politician. He understood that after the Thatcher–Major years the Conservatives were seen as a divided and 'nasty party', as one prominent Tory, Theresa May later put it: dull, stodgy, out of date and out of touch. Hague tried to look and sound different, but his shock of the new did not have quite the desired effect. On one occasion he wore a very un-Conservative baseball cap to the multicultural Notting Hill carnival. He played up his Yorkshire roots and boasted that as a young man he used to drink more than a dozen pints of beer a day. These attempts to humanise himself and begin the process of changing the party's leadership story were seen as at best laughable and at worst as desperate contrivances. Hague lost the next election and his leadership of the party.

Unlike Margaret Thatcher, Bill Clinton, Deng Xiao Ping or Tony Blair, Hague did not prepare the ground well enough, or perhaps he was simply too early in trying to change a party which had not really come to terms with defeat. In any case, as we have seen, leaders need to embrace traditions if they are about to abandon them. The authors of *YES!* put it this way:

> In the same way a painter will prepare a canvas before painting, a medical professional will prepare surgical equipment before operating and a sports coach will prepare her team before a match, a persuasive appeal requires preparation too. And sometimes such preparation requires us not only to consider how to pitch our message but also to pay attention to previous messages and reactions. As the saying goes, the best way to ride a horse is in the direction the horse is going. Only by first aligning yourself with the direction of the horse is it possible to then slowly and deliberately steer it where you'd like to go. Simply trying to pull the horse in the desired direction immediately will wear you out – and you'll probably just upset the horse in the process.

Deng Xiao Ping moved the horse of the Chinese Communist party by first talking of Socialism with Chinese Characteristics. Bill Clinton created the New Democrats only after embracing Franklin Roosevelt as his great hero. For all his talents, William Hague upset the horse by trying to go too hard too fast and in a way which did not seem authentically Conservative.

What NOT to Do: don't be so desperate for change that you look desperate.

Even Bill Clinton, whose peculiar genius in these matters should not be underestimated, occasionally demonstrated What NOT to Do. In May 1993, on a visit to Los Angeles in Air Force One, Clinton had his hair cut in the presidential plane by a hairdresser called Cristophe. Cristophe typically charged $200 a time, but he was an FOB – a Friend of Bill – and so waived his usual fee. There was outrage when this story leaked out because – or so it was widely reported – the president had held Air Force One on the LA airport tarmac while he was having the presidential hair seen to by a Beverly Hills hairstylist, inconveniencing thousands of passengers. The story of 'Hair Force One' came to lead the American TV news. The president's press aide at the time was Dee Dee Myers, who later was to become a consultant to the TV series *West Wing*. This is an account she gave to America's PBS television network:

> …here was this, you know, populist 'putting-people-first' president … basking in the perks of his new power sitting on the runway … air travellers be damned … that thing dominated the news for at least three days … it becomes such a symbolic thing. You … have to be careful of these things that become metaphors.

The Clinton team abjectly apologised for all the inconvenience they had caused. But as a 30 June 1993 *Newsday* article reported, the story of inconvenienced passengers was a myth: 'According to Federal Aviation Administration records obtained through the Freedom of Information Act, the May 18 haircut caused no significant delays of regularly scheduled passenger flights – no circling planes, no traffic jams on the runways. Commuter airlines that fly routes reportedly affected by the president's haircut confirmed they have no record of delays that day.'

The president of the United States had apologised for an inconvenience that he had not caused. Why? Because the storytelling problem, as the Clinton team understood it, was not about facts but about perception, specifically the perception of lack of authenticity, that Clinton was a phoney man of the people. Most of us have no idea whether a warship should cost $2 million or $2 billion, but everyone knows that $200 is a lot to pay for a haircut.

What NOT to Do: do not engage in conduct which undermines the core of your leadership story.

Only Connect ...

Dee Dee Myers contrasted this with another What Not to Do moment based on an embarrassing error made by Clinton's predecessor, George H. W. Bush. Bush Senior was aware that after eight years as vice president and almost four as president he did not 'connect' with many ordinary voters. Early in 1992 when I followed Pat Buchanan's campaign for the Republican nomination to New Hampshire, Buchanan supporters fired searchlights at the sky and claimed they were 'looking for' George Bush because he was so often abroad. The president indeed had a successful record in foreign policy, but he was criticised for not understanding how much the American people were hurting during the 1991–92 recession. Buchanan called his own supporters 'peasants with pitchforks', the clear suggestion being that they were storming the palace of the out-of-touch grandees of the Bush family. Buchanan supporters retold an old joke about the differences between George Bush and God: 'God is everywhere. George Bush is everywhere except the United States of America.'

By February 1992 Bush's advisers were well aware of their storytelling problem. They fixed it so that he could be filmed 'in touch' with ordinary people, in a supermarket. It was, of course, a staged event. It took place at the National Grocers Association convention in Orlando, Florida. One of the exhibits was a checkout scanner. *The New York Times* wrote that Bush 'emerged from 11 years in Washington's choicest executive mansions to confront the modern supermarket ... he grabbed a quart of milk, a light bulb and a bag of candy and ran them over an electronic scanner. The look of wonder flickered across his face ...'

'This is for checking out?' Bush was quoted as saying, making it sound more like a question than an observation. Later he told the grocers in typically clipped Bush-speak, 'Amazed by some of the technology.'

The report pointed out that supermarkets had already been using scanners for some twenty years. Bush, anyone reading the report or watching the TV footage would have concluded, was completely out of touch. One US website, Snopes.com, which is devoted to debunking such stories, noted that 'it was easy to paint a picture of him as someone who no more knew how to handle the economy than he knew the price of a carton of milk or a loaf of bread. All that was needed was a hook to hang the picture on, and Bush's encounter with a scanner … provided it.'

Dee Dee Myers remembered it clearly:

> I think George Bush not knowing how a grocery store scanner worked … became a metaphor for an out-of-touch president and Bill Clinton sitting on Air Force One getting his hair cut while people around the country cooled their heels and waited for him, became a metaphor for a populist president who had gotten drunk with the perks of his own power … It took him years to overcome that … when I left the White House … I would travel around and go, 'How many of you know the president got his hair cut on Air Force One?' Every person in the audience would always raise their hand. And how many people know that it's really not true, the way the story was reported?

> Almost no one.

What NOT To Do: do not underestimate the power of negative stories told about you. Even if they are untrue, they need to be dealt with (Clinton) or suffer the consequences (Bush.)

Mr Potatoe (sic) Head

If the What NOT to Do lesson is not to give the media the hook on which to hang you, Bush's vice president Dan Quayle proved to be a champion at throttling himself. I first met Quayle when he was a senator from Indiana, and interviewed him mainly on national security issues. He was affable and well briefed, but gaffe-prone. During one interview with me Quayle was clearly confused by the difference between Iran and Iraq. Being dim has, of course, never been a bar to high political office. In the

1980s, one of the magazines popular on Capitol Hill used to run an annual competition to find the stupidest member of Congress. One year the winner was a Republican who was so stupid that when named as the stupidest member of Congress he actually called a news conference to deny it.

Quayle's missteps were legendary. White House journalists joked that as vice president Quayle was George Bush's 'impeachment insurance' because he was so stupid no one would ever try to remove Bush from office if Quayle were to succeed him. At a staged photo-opportunity Quayle tried to get a schoolboy to spell the word 'potato'. The boy spelled it correctly. Quayle told him something was missing, and corrected him, adding an 'e' to make it 'potatoe'. In 1989 I heard Quayle give a speech on the twentieth anniversary of the moon landings by *Apollo 11*. The *Apollo 11* team – including Neil Armstrong and Buzz Aldrin – were there, as was President Bush and his wife Barbara. Quayle opened his remarks by addressing the president, First Lady and 'my fellow astronauts'. Another story has it that when Vice President Quayle went to Latin America he said the visit was so interesting he regretted not studying Latin at school. This story, as far as I can tell, is actually untrue. But like Bush with the supermarket scanner, Quayle had destroyed his own credibility. The myth was all too believable. Once such a 'pre-story' is written – lateness in the case of Clinton, laziness in the case of George W. Bush, meanness in the case of Dick Cheney, stupidity in the case of Dan Quayle, being out of touch in the case of George H. W. Bush – it takes a great deal of work to change that perception. The important point is to try to understand your weaknesses, attempt to mitigate them, and on no account give your enemies further examples of the counter-story they are already desperate to tell. But of all the What NOT to Do mistakes a leader can make, the worst in my view is to let your enemies define who you are and what you stand for. That's your job. If you can't do it, you're not really a leader. That's one of the reasons Senator John Kerry is a loser.

Swift Boated

In the American presidential election of 2004 George Bush faced the Democratic Party nominee Senator John Kerry. Kerry, apparently, had a distinguished Vietnam War record, serving in a 'swift boat'. His bravery was recognised by the US military command in Vietnam. He was awarded three Purple Hearts and a Silver Star. Kerry later came out against the Vietnam War, which, you might say, showed another kind of courage, in standing against a war in which he had fought. His opponent, George Bush, meanwhile, was in favour of the Vietnam War, although not so much in favour that he actually took part in it. Bush spent his Vietnam War military service facing whatever dangers lurked in Texas, defending his home state in the Air National Guard. And yet it was *Kerry's* Vietnam record, not Bush's, which became the political issue in 2004. It was *Kerry* who was torn to shreds by supporters of President Bush in a move which was both audacious and also devastating.

A group of 'swift boat' veterans questioned Kerry's life story and heroism, undermining, as we have seen with Barack Obama and others, not his policies but his character and personal story. This proved fatal because Kerry never managed to rebut the counter-story. In contrast, in January 2012, when the Republican candidate for the presidency Newt Gingrich was challenged in a televised debate in South Carolina on CNN about allegations made by his ex-wife regarding his adultery, Gingrich responded furiously. He accused the CNN anchor John King of sleazy journalism and turned the question of his personal morals into an articulate attack on the media. Kerry, the decorated veteran, failed to show real storytelling ability on his war record. Gingrich, the adulterer, showed considerable storytelling ability when demolishing this most damaging charge against him. Kerry's ineptitude was such that the phrase 'to be swift-boated' has become American political slang for a devious, ferocious and destructive attack on the leadership story of an opponent.

What NOT to Do: if the very core of your leadership story – 'Who am I?' – is being destroyed, not to fight back looks like weakness. It is.

Gordon Brown

Gordon Brown's leadership story illustrates a different point. It shows what happens when a man from the old media age of the twentieth century encounters the 'froth of life' journalism of the new media age of the twenty-first and it overwhelms him. Brown was Tony Blair's one-time friend, colleague, rival and finally successor. He was never a 'froth of life' kind of guy. He was prime minister when Blair stepped down in 2007 until he lost the 2010 election. Brown is an excellent example of What NOT to Do because he had a powerful personal story – 'Who am I?' – which he failed to tell in a way which proved attractive to ordinary voters. He let his enemies define him, as Kerry did, and never responded adequately. He lost, as Kerry did.

There are broadly two views in British politics about Gordon Brown. The counter-story is that he was possibly the worst British prime minister in living memory, presiding over the economic disaster of 2007–10, a charmless, bullying individual who never connected with the British electorate. The other view, explained to me eloquently by Baroness Shirley Williams, a Liberal Democrat, is that Brown will be judged much more favourably by history than he was by British voters in 2010. Baroness Williams told me that Gordon Brown was a towering figure who kept Britain out of the euro, helped lead the world away from economic disaster in 2008–9 and whose leadership was appreciated internationally but not by British voters. History, she believed, might eventually smile on the dour Scot.

Here is the Gordon Brown 'Who am I?' leadership story. He is the son of a Church of Scotland minister and was a prodigy at Edinburgh University, a political activist who wrote his PhD thesis on the Scottish Labour leader James Maxton – a thesis which was published in book form. Historians have told me his academic work is quite admirable. He had been 'hothoused' in an experimental education project while a teenager, and was accepted to study history at Edinburgh University at the age of sixteen. Edinburgh is one of the best universities in the world. During a school rugby match Brown suffered a blow to the head which left him with a retinal detachment. Several operations failed to correct the problem and he is blind in his left eye. Later he was to notice similar symptoms in his right eye. His sight is poor. At the age of forty-nine he married Sarah Macaulay, a leading PR strategist. They had a daughter, Jennifer Jane, on 28 December 2001, who sadly died just over a week later of a brain haemorrhage. They have two other children, John Macaulay Brown and James Fraser Brown. James Fraser has been diagnosed with cystic fibrosis.

Most readers will agree that every part of this story is compelling and unusual, but while Brown and his aides spoke endlessly about his 'thrifty' Scottish image, they never emphasised the prime minister's poor eyesight, never joked about it, never referred to it as a handicap, never suggested that perhaps it explained why he looked a bit funny on television – which he often did. He was nearly blind and could not see audiences clearly. Brown valued his privacy and his family life. He was rarely photographed with his children. To his credit he did not see them as political ornaments in the way that other politicians of the twenty-first century sometimes do. His wife, Sarah, is talented, clever and charming, a great political asset, but Brown's image was of a grumpy bully. During the leadership debates in the 2010 election his blindness in one eye meant he always had to take the same position on the stage otherwise he would not have seen his opponents. A better storyteller would have remarked that he saw more clearly with one eye than his opponents with two. But Brown was an appallingly bad storyteller.

It was only when as prime minister in 2009 Gordon Brown started to write personal letters to the families of British military personnel killed in Afghanistan and Iraq that his sight problems – which were never really a secret but never publicised either – became important to Britain's tabloid newspapers. The mother of one soldier complained that Brown had misspelled her son's name. Rather than being praised for taking the time to write personal letters, Brown was pilloried for a misspelling. It was a great opportunity for Brown to engage with the hearts of the British people by admitting the error and explaining how far he found reading and writing an ordeal. However, he rarely missed an opportunity to miss an opportunity when it came to telling stories.

By the time of the election campaign in April and May 2010, an increasingly desperate Gordon Brown tried to reinvent his 'Who am I?' story, but it was too late. He smiled a lot. His teeth looked whiter. He engaged in some confessional media appearances to show off his 'human' side. He went out to meet 'real' people in key constituencies, including a traditional Labour voter called Gillian Duffy, a 65-year-old grandmother from Rochdale, Lancashire. Mrs Duffy bumped into 'Gordon' and complained to the prime minister about a number of things, including immigration. Brown was charming and polite until he got into his official car. Once inside he forgot he was still wearing a TV microphone and described Mrs Duffy as a 'bigoted woman'. The comments were broadcast all over the world, accompanied by Brown's defeated gesture on a BBC radio show when he put his head in his hands as the recording of his supposedly private exchange was played out on BBC Radio 2.

Gordon Brown never fully harnessed the power of stories. He could have argued that Tony Blair or David Cameron were glamorous show-horses while he, Brown, was a workhorse. He could have made light of his partial sight, and converted it into an 'earwig' so that every British voter realised how hard it was for him to do his job. He could have shared the joy he had clearly experienced late in life when he married a wonderful woman and had children he adored. He could, in other words, have tried to fit into the debased world of Junkified journalism, or at least explained why as a dour Presbyterian he was not going to play those silly 'froth of life' games. He didn't. Instead at every possible stage Gordon Brown managed to convey the curmudgeonly image of the sort of Scotsman voters would never mistake for a ray of sunshine. He led Labour to one of its worst ever electoral defeats.

Then, when it was far too late to save his political career and he was quite literally on his way out of Downing Street, something remarkable happened. Gordon Brown let the cameras in on his private life in a way that he had never done before. We saw him with Sarah and their two boys, who clearly adored him as much as he adored them. He, the boys and his wife walked hand in hand as they made their exit. I checked with the BBC's long-serving political staff and this was the best photo-opportunity of Brown that any of them could remember. Nothing in his political life became him like the leaving of it. His successors in power were Prime Minister David Cameron and his deputy Nick Clegg, two men with easy smiles much more in tune with the era of globalised gossip.

In mid May 2010 Gordon Brown was in his constituency in Kirkcaldy in Scotland attending his first public event since his election defeat. It was in the college named after the town's most famous son, the political economist Adam Smith. Uncharacteristically relaxed, Brown joked with students and teachers that after his political failure, perhaps he needed some re-education. 'I was actually thinking of coming in today and applying for the course on communication skills, then I thought I might do public relations, then maybe media management, drama and performance.'

Gordon Brown got it in the end, though perhaps even then his message was tinged with bitterness. A career politician full of the kind of talents which could take him to the top, he did not have the storytelling talents necessary for the twenty-first century, and proved a remarkable example of What NOT to Do.

Leadership Lesson: Learn from your mistakes. Admit them where possible. Do not compound them by giving your opponents the worst examples of a negative counter-story. And defend yourself. If you are not willing to do so, why should anyone else? Most important: if you cannot explain 'Who am I?' others will characterise you according to their convenience, not yours.

Followership Lesson: Be generous when listening to the admission of mistakes from a leader. None of us is perfect. But be aware of Rochefoucauld's observation that we admit small mistakes to hide the larger ones. He's right.

12 Leading Change: The Angelina Jolie Method

Leadership means change. If everything is fine just the way it is, you don't need to change and you don't need leaders to help you do it. We have seen through the examples of Bill Clinton, Tony Blair, Margaret Thatcher and others how storytelling can bring about change to a political party and a country. But we have also noted that many individual leaders find it hard to change themselves, or even to recognise that some things need to be changed in the way they present their character and personality. Throughout this book we have seen why stories are important. We have learned that pre-stories (the prejudices someone may have before they actually meet you) and counter-stories (the negative stories people may tell about you) can be damaging. We have examined how a leader may create his own stories and counter the negative counter-stories told by others. In the previous chapter, I suggested that admitting mistakes and promising to change may be a shrewd strategy for a leader since it often resonates positively with followers. It certainly resonates with journalists, who, since some newspapers try to appear as the modern-day equivalent of our religious guardians, are always hungry for stories of sinners who find redemption. To bring these arguments to a conclusion I would like to consider leaders who offer a clear model for countering negative pre-stories or counter-stories and who have put many of the themes of this book into practice, especially those who have sought some kind of personal redemption. I found the most useful examples not in the White House or in corporate boardrooms, but in Hollywood. And in Dollywood.

Bringing change is risky. As we have learned, one way for a leader to do this is to declare that everything from this point is 'new', while building on those bits of the past which suit their leadership story. This is how Ronald Reagan, Margaret Thatcher, Bill Clinton, Deng Xiao Ping and Tony Blair came to power. It is also how BP reinvented itself as supposedly a green company, 'Beyond Petroleum', until that rebranding exercise came apart after the Gulf oil spill. In some of these cases, leaders were bringing change to the second or third parts of their leadership stories: 'Who are we?' as a group and 'What is our common purpose?' But it is much trickier when a leader has to admit that something is fundamentally wrong with himself or herself as a person. How do you change 'Who am I?' without appearing phoney? How do you admit mistakes, or acknowledge weaknesses and personal flaws? As we saw in the previous chapter, the real problem in getting business leaders to admit faults is that, as Lucy Kellaway says, 'they don't know what their faults are …This denial of flaws is a pity. We like people better when they wear their blemishes openly. It makes them seem more human.'

When I started to think of those people I had met who most bravely took on their apparent flaws and wore 'their blemishes openly', I was struck by how few politicians and business leaders even make an attempt to do this. Clinton admitted to his sexual proclivities, but only after he was caught out. He also dealt with his indiscipline and congenital inability to turn up on time for meetings, but only when he was told by his staff that it was harming his reputation. Ronald Reagan confronted his personal problem of age and infirmity, though, beyond making light of it, this wasn't something he could really change. But at least he was aware that it was a potential problem. One surprising name did come to mind, however –someone who had self-consciously tried to alter what she saw as failings within herself and then spoke to me about it: Angelina Jolie. I make no apology for including Angelina Jolie and other cultural leaders in this book. The lessons they teach are applicable to all of us, and because they are not politicians or corporate titans but public figures who are highly scrutinised by an unforgiving media, they do 'wear their blemishes openly'. They have little choice to do otherwise.

The Prejudice of the Pre-Story

For many years I have interviewed cultural leaders for BBC arts programmes. They have ranged from Nobel Prize winners such as Seamus Heaney to country music stars such as Dolly Parton to literary giants from around the world, including Amin Maalouf, Alaa al-Aswany and V. S. Naipaul. In every case I had to be aware of the pre-story. I knew these great cultural celebrities by name and by reputation long before I met them in person. The novelist V. S. Naipaul, for example, is supposed to be 'difficult'. Perhaps, like the rest of us, at times he can be. I found him delightful, provocative and stimulating. Then there was one of the 'Three Tenors', José Carreras, who along with Placido Domingo and Luciano Pavarotti had made opera much more fun for many people who are not traditional opera fans. I prepared to meet Carreras with a film crew in a Madrid hotel room. Carreras was due at two o'clock, and at around ten minutes to two I said to the producer, 'I bet he's late.'

'Why?'

'Well, you know what opera singers are like.'

'What are they like?'

'Divas and divos. Bound to be late.'

That was my pre-story, or prejudice. Ten seconds before two o'clock the doorbell rang and it was José Carreras, perfectly on time, immaculately dressed, ready for the interview, engaging, charming, intelligent and fun – especially when we talked about the difficulties of an opera singer trying to care for his voice while supporting Barcelona on the football field and yelling himself hoarse. I told Carreras of the conversation I had just had with my producer – that he would be a 'divo' and turn up late.

Carreras responded that such a pre-story about opera singers was common but unfair. Some stars are difficult, Carreras said, but truly successful people cannot afford to be late.

'When I hear the overture play,' he told me, 'I get ready to sing.'

A few months later I was scheduled to meet one of my on-screen favourite actresses, a household name who had better remain anonymous. In this case my 'pre-story' was very positive. I admired her work. But within a few minutes of dealing with her, including tantrums which would have seemed immature in a ten-year-old, I decided that I would rather spend an afternoon with a terrorist murderer than ever have to deal with her again. This screen goddess changed the date and time of the interview whimsically over a period of several days, and then when the interview was finally agreed, refused to come out of her room for almost two hours, until I told her I had instructed the film crews to leave. Even though she turned up in the end, after half an hour of the interview I actually wished that she had not bothered.

At the opposite end of the scale was Dolly Parton. I met her at her home in Nashville, Tennessee, and she showed me around, including the little chapel where she meditates in the mornings. On one wall there is a large piece of glass etched with tiny angels. On closer inspection the angels all have extremely large chests and flowing blonde hair and look exactly like Dolly Parton herself, only with wings. Dolly Parton had just released an album largely of 1960s protest songs, often with an anti-war message, at a time when the United States was embroiled in the wars in Iraq and Afghanistan. I tried to entice her into discussing politics by remarking that the songs suggested a strong degree of anti-war sentiment on her part, but she rebuffed this argument by saying that they were just good tunes. Well, that was her story. Dolly Parton is one of the biggest employers in the state of Tennessee through her 'Dollywood' theme park, which celebrates the culture of the Appalachians. She brings employment to one of the poorest areas of the United States, and has been active in delivering books to the least privileged children, in the hope of encouraging literacy. I suggested that as a successful businesswoman and household name she should go into politics. It worked for Ronald Reagan and Arnold Schwarzenegger.

'Honey, there have been enough boobs in the White House without mine,' she said. Dolly Parton is famous for saying that it takes 'a heck of a lot of money to look this cheap', and so I finally plucked up the courage to ask her which bits of her were real and which fake.

'It's all fake!' she said.

I tell these stories merely to show that we all have pre-stories in our heads, good and bad, about more or less anyone we are planning to meet for the first time. A clever leader, including cultural leaders such as Carreras, understands the negative pre-story and deals with it, in his case by the 'violation of expectations' method. Even before I met her, I knew Dolly Parton would completely confound the stereotype of the dumb blonde, and it is true to say that anyone suffering from that pre-story delusion would soon be reeling from one of the sharpest minds I have ever encountered in any field of human endeavour. However, of all those who changed their pre-story, one woman in particular stands out.

Hollywood Airhead to Humanitarian Activist

I was to interview Angelina Jolie in December 2004 at Pinewood Studios. I had studied her press cuttings, watched her movies, looked at the 'froth of life' magazines and read the gossip, and was unsure whether there was much point to the interview. She sounded like a Hollywood airhead, but with a twist. At the time we met, Jolie was trying to get the United States to sign the international Mine Ban Treaty (1997) to prevent the injuries landmines can inflict on civilians. She had become a campaigner and a UN ambassador on the subject. The issue of landmines – rather than the routine of film promotion – was why she agreed to do the interview, and why (despite my misgivings) I thought it might be worthwhile. I suggested to her that her commitment to an international humanitarian cause was unusual for someone from her background. She grew up in California, the daughter of a famous Hollywood actor, Jon Voight, and she admitted to me that she could have spent her life in shopping malls, on the beach and at parties, unconcerned about the world beyond Bel-Air and Malibu. That, in fact, had been much of her life until she began shooting the film *Tomb Raider*. During breaks in the filming in Cambodia she saw children hobbling on mutilated limbs in the fields nearby.

'How did they get injured?' she asked someone.

'Pol Pot,' was the answer. Jolie said that at first she was mystified. What was a Pol Pot? Some kind of cooking implement? A bomb? A disease? She was instructed not to wander off the set because the undetected landmines made it too dangerous. Then, increasingly curious about this strange world she had entered, she started to do some reading. She found out about Pol Pot's Year Zero – the programme of murder in Cambodia – and the use of landmines all over the country, which made it unsafe to walk in the fields. She also learned about the way Cambodia had been destabilised as a direct result of US policy to try to defeat North Vietnam and the Viet Cong. At that point Angelina Jolie says she decided something had to be done and that she herself would become a campaigner against landmines in Cambodia and elsewhere.

Now, as readers will be well aware, the main followership lesson of this entire book is that stories are not found naturally occurring in the environment. They are constructed. Clearly I was being told a story, and it was one with obvious echoes of that of Diana, Princess of Wales. At the time of her death in 1997, Princess Diana had been a campaigner against landmines, an issue that helped improve her public image which, in the months before her death was as one unkind commentator put it, mostly 'shopping and suffering'. Another had called her an 'upmarket clothes horse.' Diana's commitment to the cause of a landmine ban, like her work on behalf of those suffering from AIDS, was part of her positive leadership story, a story often swamped by the globalised gossip of the tabloids. The echoes of this in Angelina's story were obvious, but it was to turn into one of the tales that humans find most intriguing – ignorance followed by learning followed by redemption, a *Bildungsroman* of sorts. If we break down what I was told, we have what might be called the Angelina Jolie Method for reshaping a personal story. Here's how it works.

Step One: accept, admit and define the problem (even if you do so only to yourself, or privately to your closest friends and advisers). For Angelina, the problem was ignorance and a lack of curiosity about the world. George W. Bush never came to see his lack of curiosity as a problem, and this was one of the key weaknesses of his presidency. Bush was never a stupid president, but he was frequently an ignorant one, lacking any interest in those people who did not share his view of the world. Bill Clinton accepted that his tardiness was a problem, and hired Leon Panetta as his chief of staff to help fix it and bring the organisation and discipline which had been lacking in the Clinton White House. I once asked Panetta if it was true that one of his duties as chief of staff was to get Clinton out of the shower in the mornings when he was late for meetings. Panetta smiled and refused to confirm or deny the story, but other members of the White House staff told me it was indeed true. Clinton – like Angelina Jolie – recognised the problem and changed his ways. Gordon Brown didn't. He never could admit his failure to connect with people on a human level. When he did, it was too late. Margaret Thatcher, as we saw, admitted privately that her stridency was a problem, and set about fixing it. Those behind the London Olympic bid recognised that transport in London was a problem, as was the fact that London had hosted the Games twice before. They defined the problem and set about addressing it as best they could. And so on. Like Angelina Jolie.

Step Two: show intelligence and an open mind to listen to others. Angelina Jolie educated herself. She moved outside her zone of comfort, visiting some grim places to spread her message, including war zones in Africa. Nelson Mandela is another good example of a leader who used education in this way. Mandela was never really a soldier, and yet he recognised the necessity of setting up the armed wing of the African National Council, Umkhonto we Sizwe. He took advice from those who knew what they were doing, and followed that advice, pursuing an armed struggle as well as a political campaign. Bill Clinton followed a similar path when he abandoned the one major promise which had helped him to get elected – the middle-class tax cut. He was open-minded enough to learn from Alan Greenspan at the Federal Reserve and other economic advisers about pacifying the bond market. They were right; Clinton was wrong. But he was right to listen.

Perhaps one of the most highly acclaimed examples of an open mind and the ability to listen to others is John Maynard Keynes. He famously offered the best justification for a leader altering course when he said that when the facts change, he changed his mind. 'What do you do, sir?' was his terse response to a critic.

Step Three (and this is very important): don't just talk about change, actually change your behaviour. Angelina Jolie offered her services as a goodwill ambassador, contacting the UN High Commissioner for Refugees. She then paid her own way to go to war zones and trouble spots including Sierra Leone, Tanzania, Cambodia, Darfur, Chad, Iraq, Libya and Afghan refugee camps in Pakistan. When we met I expected she would be surrounded by some kind of entourage – press and media advisers, agents and the like. She came alone. Like Dolly Parton in her meditation chapel, Angelina Jolie appeared to enjoy simplicity, whatever the supermarket tabloids may say of her lifestyle.

Step Four: let other people know you have changed. If she'd been a political party, Angelina Jolie could have described herself as the 'New Angelina', less self-centred, more informed and far more aware of the world. In fact, during our interview, she all but *did* describe herself as the 'New Angelina'. She shaped her story so carefully that any viewer would come to the conclusion that she had indeed reinvented herself. Part of that strategy meant avoiding the pre-story, the hook upon which she could so easily be hanged. In Angelina Jolie's case, that meant attempting to steer away from 'froth of life' interviews about Brad Pitt and other personal matters.

Step Five: remain good humoured and humble about your failings. Angelina Jolie said to me that in Africa and in other places where she was unknown, she had to describe what she did as a job. Children she met in Sierra Leone would express astonishment that she was paid for 'dressing up' and 'pretending', as they put it. She laughed as she told the story, suggesting that the children were, in fact, truly wise. She accepted in a good humoured way their implicit judgement that her Hollywood stardom is all false, all show, a bit of a con, and presented the story as a shrewd lesson in modesty. Angelina Jolie was clearly able to poke fun at her 'phoney' Hollywood self, which made the rest of her seem more 'authentic'. This is similar in tone to Tony Blair writing about the nonsense of having to memorise shopping lists when he was prime minister, or his comment when signing the Good Friday Agreement that although it was not a day for sound bites, he felt 'the hand of history' on his shoulder – the ability to laugh at one's own image, to be seen not to be too serious about one's flaws. Bill Clinton used the same technique. At the Democratic convention in 1988 he delivered one of the most boring speeches I have ever heard; the only genuine applause came when he said, 'and finally'. In 1992, at the convention in New York, he quipped that he turned up simply to finish the speech he had begun four years earlier. And when Mrs Thatcher addressed the Conservative Party conference after she left office, she made a play on a popular film title, suggesting that 'The Mummy Returns'. It brought the house down. If even someone who was far from being a natural raconteur

– Mrs Thatcher – can find enough laughter in addressing her own failings, then clearly the ability to criticise oneself even obliquely with humour is a hugely valuable story-telling technique.

Inverse Modesty

Angelina Jolie brilliantly spun the story about the 'New Angelina' in my BBC interview and elsewhere. She worked the great trick of inverse modesty. Every time she referred to her former ignorance and selfishness, she was implicitly praising her current wisdom and selflessness. I thought it was a performance of some genius, and I applaud the work she has done to try to get rid of landmines. Her method of bringing change is useful to all of us. Lucy Kellaway is correct when she says that we 'like people better when they wear their blemishes openly', and even more when they laugh at them. Moreover, Angelina Jolie has done well by doing good. Not only does her humanitarian work act as a corrective to all the Hollywood airhead stories or counter-stories, it has also attracted big brand sponsors.

In 2011, Jolie became the face of the Louis Vuitton luggage brand, earning a reported $10 million for an ad campaign photographed by Annie Leibovitz in Cambodia. Of course it would be Cambodia. Angelina Jolie was seen looking perfectly made up, reclining on a boat, not a hair out of place, with the spectacular countryside behind her.

'People are not used to seeing Angelina in this situation,' Louis Vuitton's executive vice president, Pietro Beccari, was quoted as saying. 'I like the fact that it's a real moment. This travel message we give through personal journeys is a fundamental one for the brand.'

A moment's reflection and most of us would agree that there is nothing especially 'real' about the moment when one of the world's best-known actresses is photographed looking glamorous by one of the world's best-known photographers for one of the world's most expensive producers of handbags. The executive vice president may assert that 'personal journeys' are 'fundamental' for his suitcases because the ad campaign in part relies on Angelina Jolie's reinvention of herself as someone with strong emotional ties to the people of Cambodia. To her credit, Jolie is reported to have donated a large slice of her Louis Vuitton fee to charity, almost certainly the Maddox Jolie-Pitt Foundation, which helps community development and conservation in Cambodia.

The phenomenon of admitting errors or blemishes and then prospering from reinvention and redemption has been noted by academic researchers. As we've already seen, the authors Goldstein, Martin and Cialdini cite studies in their book *YES!* which suggest 'that organisations that attribute failures to internal causes will come out ahead not only in public perception but also in terms of the profit line'. When researchers compared company reports which blamed outside factors for poor performance with those in which the organisation itself accepted a significant share of the blame for making mistakes, 'They discovered that ... those that pointed to internal and controllable factors had higher stock prices one year later than those that pointed to external and uncontrollable factors.'

This is the corporate equivalent of the Angelina Jolie Method. Before she made *Tomb Raider* in 2001 she was a relatively obscure young actress. Since 2001 and her reinvention, she has become one of the best-known and best-paid celebrities in the world. It is reasonable to conclude these events are connected. The moral of the Angelina Jolie Method as applied to businesses which admit mistakes is very encouraging: 'If you find yourself in a situation in which you've made a mistake,' Goldstein, Martin and Cialdini say, 'you should admit it and follow up immediately with an action plan demonstrating that you can take control of the situation and put it right ... you'll ultimately put yourself in a position of greater influence by being perceived as not only capable, but also honest.' And yet, as they go on to note, there remains a puzzle: 'So, if taking responsibility for your mistakes and admitting that you're wrong is not only the right thing to do but also right for your company, why is this behaviour such a rarity?'

The answer, at least in the case of political and business leaders, is generally the combination of the factors we have seen in the previous chapter: egotism, embarrassment, the Ozymandias syndrome, the belief that if we blame someone else we will escape censure, and the politician's instinct that being consistent is fundamentally virtuous. It isn't always.

The Consistency Dilemma

So how replicable is the Angelina Jolie Method for other kinds of leaders, and the rest of us? To some extent we have already seen leaders admitting to problems or mistakes, promising a fresh start and then indicating that they have changed. Such a method was actually built into Bill Clinton's political DNA as Saturday Night Bill and Sunday Morning Bill. Throughout his presidency great bursts of energy, risk-taking and enthusiasm were interspersed with heartfelt acts of contrition. But as we have seen, while the sex scandals did indeed damage Clinton's *personal* approval ratings, they never harmed his *job* approval ratings, which always remained above 50 per cent even during the impeachment proceedings. In other words, Americans did not approve of Clinton's moral conduct, but they did approve of the way he ran the country. My own judgement is that Clinton's personal sins and his constant need of forgiveness actually added to his job approval ratings. Every time Saturday Night Bill did something wrong and Sunday Morning Bill seemed so sorry about it, Americans could reflect on the booming economy and relative peace abroad, and then consider that there were worse people who had found themselves in the White House – or, as Dolly Parton might have said, even bigger boobs.

When I have discussed the implications of publicly admitting to making a mistake with political leaders or their staff, they constantly make the same points: the leader should be associated with good news; the staff can handle the bad news; and admitting that the leader needs to change personally opens up what they see as the Consistency Dilemma. They may receive credit for wearing 'their blemishes openly', but that has to be weighed against the opprobrium they suffer for getting things wrong in the first place. The modern combative media plays a part. Journalists, myself included, are apt to look back over a leader's career and find examples of where he has changed his mind in order to use it as a stick with which to beat him.

One leading British politician said that this game of 'Gotcha' means he and others like him are extremely reluctant to admit mistakes openly in the way Angelina Jolie did. Tony Blair's case is instructive. He was clearly wrong over his belief that Saddam Hussein had weapons of mass destruction. He puts that down to faulty intelligence, not an error of judgement. And Blair remains consistent, even adamant, in his refusal to admit the 2003 war against Iraq was a mistake, while he does admit that some parts of the campaign could have been handled better. It is a classic case of Rochefoucauld's dictum about admitting minor faults in order that the major ones may be glossed over, although in Blair's case it did not work. The British public seem to remember Blair's major faults rather than the minor ones. But when I tried to think of examples of political leaders who – while not openly humiliating themselves by admitting mistakes – have shifted their positions so profoundly that they do appear to be putting the Angelina Jolie Method into practice, I turned to some very surprising people: terrorists.

Ulster Says NO!

Terrorists – or freedom fighters, or guerrilla movements if you prefer – have the consistency dilemma at the very centre of their ambitions. They wish to achieve political ends, but they use violent means. At what point do they give up the 'armed struggle' and settle on the political route, without alienating their hard-line supporters who are prepared to kill and die for the cause? Gerry Kelly, now a Sinn Fein leader and government minister in Northern Ireland, was one of the leaders of the Provisional IRA who made that leap. He told me that every 'freedom fighter' in a 'guerrilla campaign' has to realise that outright victory of one side over the other is very unlikely. That means, in the IRA's case, eventually coming to terms with what is achievable, and deciding whether, to secure their objectives, their strategy and tactics have to change. And when that happens, how do leaders like Gerry Kelly, Gerry Adams, Martin McGuinness and others tell a story of change which brings their people with them?

The Good Friday Agreement of 1998 helped to seal the peace process in Northern Ireland. Many leaders, including Clinton, Blair, the former British prime minister John Major and the Irish prime minister Bertie Ahern deserve credit. But so do two other groups notable for their consistent history of stubbornness and resistance to change: the Reverend Dr Ian Paisley's Democratic Unionist Party (DUP) and the IRA, plus its political wing Sinn Fein. The Troubles of Northern Ireland, Ian Paisley and the IRA are about as far away from Hollywood as I can imagine, and yet the opposing sides changed their story following a pattern remarkably similar to that of Angelina Jolie.

Some background: I have known the Reverend Dr Ian Paisley for many years. He is a great creator of 'earwigs', which for decades were always negative. 'Ulster Says NO!' was one perennial Paisley slogan; 'No Surrender!' was another. His Protestant followers would yell, 'No Pope Here!' And when questions of Irish unity or power-sharing with political opponents were raised, Dr Paisley would bellow, 'Never! Never! Never!' Sinn Fein and the IRA were similarly intransigent. They developed the 'ballot box and bullet' strategy towards their sole objective, a united Ireland, and would shoot or bomb their perceived enemies. Sinn Fein would try to break through as a democratic party and talk of a political solution. The twin tracks would, they believed, bring about Irish unity.

Nowadays the leaders of both Sinn Fein and the DUP work together in the Stormont parliament. I grew up partly in Northern Ireland during the Troubles, and I confess I never thought I would see Paisleyites and Sinn Fein sitting in the same room, never mind in the same government. On one occasion, during a Northern Ireland election campaign when the party leaders were invited to the BBC in Belfast, I witnessed Dr Paisley refusing to get into a lift because it contained the Sinn Fein leader Gerry Adams. It has been a long road from not sharing an elevator to sharing power. Gerry Kelly, the former IRA leader who was convicted, among other things, of blowing up London's Old Bailey courthouse and who led the escape from the Maze prison by top IRA commanders known as 'the Great Escape', is now a member of the Stormont parliament. Stormont was originally created by Lord Carson in the 1920s as a 'Protestant parliament for a Protestant people'. Such has been the transformation that another former IRA leader, Martin McGuinness, and Ian Paisley now share so many jokes that they have been nicknamed with typical Ulster humour 'the Chuckle Brothers'.

So – how did it happen?

For decades the Reverend Dr Ian Paisley was widely regarded as impossible to negotiate with, earning him the 'earwig' of 'Dr No'. Like many people of faith, his political genius has always been as a teller of stories with roots in the parables and lessons from the Bible. In conversation with me over the years, Dr Paisley will compare opponents to lost sheep and repentant sinners, he will speak of Good Samaritans, or the lessons of Lot's wife or the walls of Jericho. As we saw in Chapter 10, the authors Thaler and Sunstein recount in their book *Nudge* that one determined individual who sticks fast to his ideas can make others agree with him:'The clear lesson here is that consistent and unwavering people, in the private or public sector, can move groups and practices in their preferred direction.' Early in his political career Paisley helped to lead what was known as the Ulster

Workers Council strike of 1974. It was part of his 'consistent and unwavering' opposition to power-sharing in government between Catholics and Protestants, unionists and republicans. But this is *exactly* the kind of arrangement which Ian Paisley has embraced in the twenty-first century. The crucial difference is that in the 1974 version of power-sharing the Paisleyites and the IRA were left on the outside, shunned as extremists. In the twenty-first century version, they are seen as the voices of their two communities. For years Ian Paisley was 'consistent and unwavering' in saying no to political settlements, until he had destroyed all his opponents on the unionist side as 'sell-outs' and replaced them as the voice of most Ulster Protestants. At that point it was safe to reverse course and for Dr No to become Dr Yes. Paisley's objective was always power, within the United Kingdom. His strategy was intransigence. His tactics included everything from organising strikes and parades to taking part in elections. But when the time came, like all shrewd leaders, he was willing to abandon his tactics and strategy to secure his objective.

From Bullet to Ballot

The IRA's story is the mirror image of the Paisleyite story. The Provisional IRA was born out of the killings and riots in Northern Ireland in 1969. So many young men were politicised that year they became known (without any sexual innuendo) as 'Sixty-Niners'. When I talked to IRA members about the possibility of negotiating a settlement in the 1980s, they would remind me of the leadership story of Michael Collins, 'the Big Fella', the IRA director of intelligence. Collins was sent by Eamon de Valera to negotiate with the British at the end of Ireland's war of independence in 1921. When he signed the treaty with the British, Collins knew he had also signed his death warrant. He was murdered in August 1922 at the age of thirty-one, by fellow Irishmen.

Change, therefore, was just as slow within the IRA as it was within Ian Paisley's DUP. But one small story in which I played a minor part convinced me that change was under way within the IRA and that it was genuine. As I noted, on 25 September 1983 the biggest prison escape in British history took place at the Maze prison just outside Belfast. A total of thirty-eight Provisional IRA members, convicted of crimes which included murder and bombing, broke out of H-7, one of the H-Blocks, the groups of prison cells shaped, as their name suggests, like the letter H. H-7 housed men considered to be among the most dangerous prisoners in Western Europe. Among the leaders of 'the Great Escape' were two Sixty-Niners, Gerry Kelly and Brendan 'Bik' McFarlane.

On 16 January 1986, Kelly and McFarlane were finally captured in Amsterdam. Dutch police found fourteen rifles and 100,000 rounds of ammunition in a related raid. British intelligence sources believed the two men were leading an IRA Active Service Unit and were planning to murder British soldiers across the border in Germany. They were held in a Dutch jail awaiting extradition. I persuaded the BBC to let me make a film about the problems of extraditing the two men. The Dutch authorities were, in effect, being asked to decide upon the legitimacy of the IRA's 'armed struggle'. It turned upon whether the men were common criminals (as Prime Minister Margaret Thatcher argued) or freedom fighters, as the men themselves claimed. I managed to get into the Dutch prison to meet Kelly and McFarlane. The meeting took place through a protective plate glass screen, and McFarlane explained the IRA case to me in familiar terms. He said they should not be treated like common thieves, they were political prisoners. They should not be extradited to continue being oppressed by the British in 'Occupied Ireland'. At the time, they looked like central casting IRA figures – long haired, bearded, Irish Che Guevaras with Belfast accents and scruffy clothes. I produced my report for the BBC and thought nothing much of it for many years.

Then in the late 1990s I travelled to Northern Ireland to

accompany one of the visits by President Bill Clinton to put the seal on the peace process. There had been elections in Northern Ireland for local MPs known as MLAs, 'Members of the Legislative Assembly', at Stormont. Among those MLAs was the man from the Dutch jail who had blown up the Old Bailey in 1973, Gerry Kelly. The IRA leadership had for years been asserting that they would achieve power or victory using 'the ballot box and the bullet', or sometimes 'the ballot box and the Armalite'.

This 'earwig' was trumpeted repeatedly by the *Republican News* editor Danny Morrison, who was a very adept writer, editor, propagandist and phrase-maker. He said of the British government after the 1984 IRA bomb which nearly killed Prime Minister Margaret Thatcher: 'We only have to be lucky once. You have to be lucky every time.' The British press and politicians frothed over the 'ballot box and bullet' strategy, focusing on the word 'bullet' without understanding the significance of what the IRA leadership was actually telling them. The important word was not 'bullet'. It was 'ballot'. The IRA was telling a new story, aimed not at the British but at their own supporters, many of whom grew up believing that democratic politics would not get them anywhere. McGuinness, Adams, Morrison, Kelly and others wanted to change the IRA's leadership story while maintaining the public fiction of being 'consistent and unwavering'. They began to place increasing emphasis on the electoral process which was eventually to give them international legitimacy and finally power.

When I arrived at the Stormont parliament after the Good Friday Agreement was implemented, Gerry Kelly walked down the steps, saw me and smiled.

'Hello, Gavin,' he said in a cheerful Belfast accent. And then more confidentially, 'Could I have a word with you?'

We walked away from the group of reporters. Gerry Kelly said it was good to see me after all those years and we talked a little of our meeting in the jail in Holland. Then he got straight to the point.

'Tell me,' he said, 'do you think I should smile more on television?'

I was astounded.

'Smiling a bit more can't hurt,' I replied eventually. 'Can it?'

Then I asked him why he had put the question. It turned out that some of his family thought he looked too serious, too grim and forbidding, when he appeared in TV interviews. He has since become an accomplished TV performer, as well as someone who has tried to mediate in conflicts around the world, as far away from Ulster as the Philippines, using his violent past to help bring about peace in a way which many people consider admirable. As a result of that short conversation I was convinced that Gerry Kelly was genuine about changing himself, and because he was so admired within the IRA I was also convinced that the IRA itself was therefore genuine about the peace process. It might actually work.

There were of course some obvious differences from what I have called the Angelina Jolie Method. In Northern Ireland, nobody admitted publicly to making mistakes. When I subsequently interviewed Kelly, Adams, McGuinness and other IRA leaders, the closest they got to an act of contrition was when they told me that they 'regretted' casualties and loss of life. Not one of them, to my knowledge, has apologised for their own role in orchestrating killings which have claimed several thousand lives. Neither has Ian Paisley apologised for stirring up Protestant mobs and sowing sectarian hatred between the Protestant and Catholic communities. But rather like the story of Nelson Mandela's years in jail in Robben Island, Gerry Kelly's time in prison, and that of other IRA leaders, uniquely qualified him for a leadership role, and ultimately to be trusted to embrace the peace process without being labelled a 'sell-out'.

Something similar is true of Ian Paisley. Forty years of saying no meant that there was a degree of trust from his supporters when he finally said yes. Like Nixon in China, or Yitzhak Rabin trying to make peace with the Palestinians, or Mandela appealing for racial tolerance, sometimes only someone with a history of rock-solid opposition to something can effectively change enough to seal the deal and bring people with him.

The former IRA leader Martin McGuinness joined the government of Northern Ireland as deputy first minister, and worked with Ian Paisley and his successor as first minister, Peter Robinson. McGuinness went on to run for election as president of Ireland. Gerry Kelly worked for McGuinness and became his party's spokesman on justice and policing, a former terrorist now an expert on law and order. The ironies are obvious.

There were five steps in the Angelina Jolie Method outlined earlier:

- Step One: accept, admit and define the problem (even if you do so only to yourself, or privately to your closest friends and advisers).
- Step Two: show intelligence and an open mind to listen to others.
- Step Three: don't just talk about change, actually change your behaviour.
- Step Four: let other people know you have changed.
- Step Five: remain good humoured and humble about your failings.

Each of these steps applies to the stories of change within the IRA and Ian Paisley's loyalists. The warring parties clearly understood that no one was winning, nor could win outright, the battle for Northern Ireland. They accepted, admitted and redefined the problem. They listened to others, including Bill Clinton and his special envoy Senator George Mitchell, who explained that peace would mean everyone could claim victory, a catalyst for change without humiliation. Then the IRA and DUP changed their behaviour. In the IRA's case, they implemented a ceasefire and agreed to the destruction of weapons. In Ian Paisley's case, he reined in his rhetoric and began to treat Sinn Fein as the legitimate elected representatives of his fellow citizens rather than the modern equivalent of the Anti-Christ. The Good Friday Agreement was itself the document which publicly took us to Step Four, letting other people know the warring factions had changed. And in Step Five, the reputation of the Chuckle Brothers speaks for itself. Laughing with former enemies while attempting to build a peaceful and prosperous life for your children is a leadership story I like.

Leadership Lesson: Telling a compelling story of change is one of the most important things a leader can do. It demands a degree of self-criticism, though not necessarily of public humiliation. Leaders who admit mistakes may find that they are more trusted than before.

Followership Lesson: Perhaps we all need to cut leaders a bit of slack when they change their minds or their behaviour. Journalists in particular love the game of Gotcha!, figuring out inconsistencies in what a leader says now with the way they have acted in the past. This is fair game, but when the leader explains that his or her thinking has evolved, perhaps we should remember the words of Ralph Waldo Emerson: 'A foolish consistency is the hobgoblin of little minds.'

Postscript: Timing is Everything

In the spring of 1995, a couple of years into his presidency, I arranged an interview with President Clinton at the White House. I have a photograph of that meeting on my desk as I write. The picture reminds me how an adept leader will fit the stories he or she tells to capture whatever is necessary for the spirit of the times, and change that story when necessary.

The moment in the photograph came after a bit of slapstick comedy. The first two years of the Clinton presidency were full of hope and promise, but by 1995 the administration was in trouble. The saxophone-playing young president had created, at least according to his spin doctors, a new court of Camelot in an administration filled with America's best and brightest. But all those echoes of John F. Kennedy were undermined by the president's lack of discipline and poor timekeeping, combined with a fairly mediocre White House staff which included Clinton loyalists, long-time supporters and Arkansas cronies. What seemed charming and fresh about Candidate Clinton was un-professional and even rude in President Clinton. Sometimes at White House events he would keep dignitaries waiting for up to an hour. When the press corps was bored (quite often, actually) we would bet when on 'CST' – Clinton Standard Time – he would actually turn up. On one occasion I checked my watch and found that Clinton was forty-seven minutes late. I asked a US Air Force colonel who was sitting near me whether the military men present would approve of the Commander-in-Chief's timekeeping. The man smiled and murmured 'when we say the attack begins at dawn, we don't mean dawn plus forty-seven.'

My White House interview was fixed for 2 p.m. in the Roosevelt room near the Oval Office. It is a magnificent room filled with memorabilia of Theodore Roosevelt and Clinton's hero, Franklin D. Roosevelt. I had two cameras and two TV crews, a set-up rather like the Zardari or Thatcher interviews I described earlier. One camera was on the president, the other on me. The junior White House staff on these occasions are usually fussy and nervous, and nervousness is contagious. At about five minutes to two my crews switched on the lights they had carefully arranged, and unfortunately blew the fuses in the Roosevelt room. The lights went out. Panic followed. The White House staff started to fret loudly, and of course my crew was extremely embarrassed. We all wanted to fix the problem as quickly as possible.

'Don't worry,' I said calmly, attempting to take control. 'Don't worry. He's always late.'

As the words left my mouth, the room went quiet. For a second I was proud of the calming effect my take-charge attitude had produced. Then I heard a familiar voice behind me.

'Who is always late?'

It was the president of the United States, bang on time, hugely enjoying my embarrassment. The photograph captures the immediate aftermath.

Throughout this book I have tried to offer lessons from some of the best known leaders in the world on how to tell stories. I want to end by suggesting that all leadership story-telling demands a sense of timing – and by 'timing' I mean something more than punctuality in Clinton's case. Yes, Bill Clinton did improve his punctuality, but that was merely one sign that he had been forced to recognise that the time was right to improve the sloppy running of his administration. Clinton, as we saw, suffered an electoral disaster in the Congressional elections of November 1994, and was forced to understand that to survive and be re-elected he had to re-write the script of his own leadership story. He began by weeding out some of the amateurs in the White House.

In 1994 Clinton brought in the experienced Leon Panetta as chief of staff. Panetta ensured that the president's day was, miraculously it seemed, properly managed in fifteen-minute segments. Before Panetta's arrival the White House was at times so chaotic that one leading presidential adviser took several months to obtain a proper White House Secret Service pass. It was bizarre to watch this badly organised but senior adviser (a person I had to deal with quite often) stand in line every day to go through the Secret Service controlled gates when a foreign journalist like me, with the proper accreditation, could breeze through in seconds. The impression of sloppiness was extremely damaging, although by the end of 1994 Clinton had got the message. His sudden discovery of punctuality was just one of the more obvious ways through which he tried to tell a fresh story in tune with a new urgency and a new way of working within the White House.

When Greg Dyke became director general of the BBC in 2000 he had a similar problem. Dyke worried that his predecessor, John Birt, had come to seem too aloof from the creative heart of broadcasting. Staff complained that Birt was one of 'Them,' the 'Boss Class' a 'Suit' not one of 'Us' – the producers, directors, photographers, writers, technicians, reporters and other broadcasters. Dyke, who nowadays lectures on the subject of leadership, often speaks about how he tried to change the story of what a director general is for and what that person is like. Visiting a BBC broadcasting centre outside London, for example, Dyke would ask before he arrived for the name of the receptionist. He would then turn up without fuss, and without much of an entourage, walk up to the desk and say: 'Hello, Mary, I'm Greg Dyke. How are you?' Typically he would ask where he could make himself a cup of tea, and perhaps ask the receptionist if she would also like one. Such simple courtesies were planned, but not phoney. They played to Dyke's personal strengths – gregarious, affable, generous and un-stuffy. Stories about his behaviour soon became part of the Dyke legend. At White City, then a fairly new BBC building, Dyke arrived for an important meeting and noticed that the rather splendid glass-enclosed atrium was empty. He asked why no one sat there to read the papers or have a coffee break. Nobody knew the answer. Dyke persisted with his questions on the empty atrium, in between running a corporation with more than 20,000 staff and an income of around £3 billion a year. Eventually someone told him it was a health and safety problem, some bureaucratic matter involving fire regulations.

'Fix it,' Dyke said (although possibly using stronger language, for which he was also well known). Next time I go to White City, Dyke told his underlings, I want to see people sitting in the atrium. It happened. Staff loved him for it. Dyke turned an apparently minor matter into a campaign called – in typical Dyke-speak – Cut the Crap. It is difficult to overstate the effect on a large organisation of someone who sounded like he actually cared about his staff, cared that they were happy and understood that fixing minor irritations had a disproportionate effect on morale much greater than the size of the problem itself. He changed the story of BBC leadership for the twenty-first century, just as Clinton realised the time was right to change his administration's story in 1994. Dyke's immediate predecessor, John Birt, was a cool headed technocrat and engineer who had to face very different challenges. At the end of the twentieth century the BBC needed to embrace the digital future, and also had to avoid alienating a political class who – from the Left and the Right, Labour and Conservatives – often concluded that the BBC was their enemy. After Birt, for whom the very survival of the BBC was the core challenge, Dyke had very different problems for different times. He had to revive the creative heart of a broadcasting organisation demoralised and sometimes baffled by all the structural changes. One of the core skills of leadership, in other words, is not just to recognise the need for change but to have the story-telling skills of a Clinton or a Greg Dyke, to bring about change by telling a story appropriate for the changing times. Clinton did it for himself. Dyke did it for an organisation. It is even possible to do it for an entire nation.

The first woman Chancellor of Germany, Angela Merkel, is telling the story of a new country created in 1989 after a century of catastrophes. The most powerful woman in the world is trying to find a new role for the most powerful country in Europe, at a time of profound economic crisis, while ensuring Germany does not repeat the mistakes and bullying of the past. As we have seen for so many leaders, her own story helps. Chancellor Merkel is exceptional in a number of ways. Brought up in the former East Germany she runs a country dominated by the economic power of the West; a northerner and a Lutheran, her government is dependent upon votes from the more Catholic south. And she is a woman in the still very male world of German politics. Merkel tries to keep her private life private. As we have seen, that may be an admirable trait, but it is very difficult for a successful modern politician to sustain any notion of privacy while winning elections in our celebrity-obsessed culture. From the little that has been made public about her private life, we know that she tries, as much as possible, to cook her husband's breakfast in the mornings. It is one of her concessions to keeping a 'normal' family life, and also in keeping with Merkel's image as the nation's *Haus Frau,* full of commonsense German values. She lives fairly simply, practising Lutheran virtues – *sparsam, seriös, ehrlich, ernst* – thrifty, serious, honest and earnest in her daily life, at least as far as we know.

Angela Merkel rarely talks to foreign journalists. She had never taken part in any broadcast interviews for the British media since becoming Chancellor in 2005 and even some German diplomats thought that she spoke no English. In March 2012 I told her aides that I was making a film about the relevance of Lutheran values for the political leadership of Germany today, 500 years after the Reformation. It is a mark of the importance of those Lutheran values to Germany and to Frau Merkel, that based on this brief conversation, Chancellor Merkel agreed to meet me in her offices in Berlin – the *Kanzleramt*. On the way to the meeting I kept thinking about the surprising contradictions in her position. Politically Angela Merkel (in tune with the values of her country) is desperate to be a good European. But in economic terms she is Lutheran to the core. Even those Germans who are Catholic, who belong to other religions or who are atheists, share the commonsense values associated with Luther. They, and Merkel, prize thrift, responsibility and good behaviour. In principle Merkel believes that those who are profligate or who take financial risks and lose their money should not be bailed out by others, which is why her dilemma over what to do about the Eurozone crisis has been so acute.

Merkel's generation grew up in a Germany destroyed by Hitler and divided by Stalin, a place where she knew the fear of the secret police, the *Stasi*. In some respects that personal story means that Angela Merkel is the perfect German leader for these times, able to articulate the political story Germans now want to hear about their past difficulties and their future role in the twenty-first century. Since 1945 the guiding foreign policy principle of Germany has been to have zero problems with its neighbours, and that means a reluctance to be seen to be bossy. But since the financial crisis, Europe is desperate for leadership, even though in Germany the word for 'leadership' is difficult for many to use. It is the F-Word – *Führerschaft*. The historian Michael Stürmer says that even in this new century the obvious echoes of Hitler, *der Führer*, blight the German consciousness. There are inevitable consequences for the kind of leadership Germany can offer in the twenty-first century, the kind of leaders Germans want, and therefore the kind of leadership stories appropriate to these difficult times. Merkel understands this perfectly. In some ways she embodies the dilemma in her quiet, consensus-building leadership style.

When I met Angela Merkel in Berlin's ultra-modern *Kanzleramt* – a stunning, airy building full of enormous windows overlooking the River Spree and the historic Reichstag, she displayed every one of the story-telling characteristics necessary to begin to create a new narrative for a new Germany which fits the twenty-first century European *Zeitgeist*. Merkel welcomed me in a very homely, but businesslike fashion. She reminded me – in perfect English – that it was very rare for her to give an interview to a foreign journalist. (It was also a violation of expectations that she spoke in English. Merkel always uses German for interviews and public events. None of my German friends knew she spoke English at all.)

Angela Merkel offered a vision of a kinder, gentler German future. Her sense of timing is that the German leadership story for the twenty-first century has to be different from the past – interconnected, interdependent, sharing values and freedom, speaking for *European* principles as common ground between old rivals rather than any notion of 'German principles', a low-key style of story-telling which lives up to Merkel's homely nickname – 'Mutti' – mummy.

The stories I have told briefly here, therefore, of Clinton, Dyke, Merkel – and those of many others throughout this book, are attempts to show how accomplished leaders recognise that something has to change in the stories they are telling and in the stories which are being told about them. All three have many diverse leadership qualities, but their success in bringing people with them, in creating and keeping their followers, is based on one quality above all: the indispensable ability to tell a compelling story.

Lessons from the Top – Sixteen Tips from the Top

I want to end with a summary of the tips which I find most striking and useful when considering successful leaders. I hope they will remind you of the observations in this book and help guide any reader, or any leader, to create a story about themselves, their organisation and their purpose, a story which seems right for the times.

1. Engage your listeners. It does not matter how you do it, so long as you do it.
2. Every leader tells a leadership story in three parts: 'Who Am I?' 'Who Are We?' and 'What is our Common Purpose?' You must learn to answer the 'Who Am I?' question adequately, or the others do not matter.
3. Remember the Earwig. All successful leaders create their own memorable way of answering the 'Who Am I?' bit of the leadership story succinctly. Think of it as the headline you would like to see attached to your name, or the epitaph that would fit on your tombstone.
4. The STAR moment. Give them Something They Always Remember. Think of Bill Gates opening a jar filled with mosquitoes while talking about malaria to a room filled with potential donors.
5. Strive for a Five. Remember the actor's technique. People want you to talk to them as equals, 'just like us,' not talk down to them from the height of a Ten, or even talk up to them, from a lowly One.

6. Don't be so desperate for change that you change and look desperate. By all means tell people how your thinking has developed, but be careful to explain any changes with respect for the past, including your own.

7. The Golden Rule: Objective, Strategy, Tactics. If you order your priorities it will help you think through the message of the stories you are trying to tell.

8. Authenticity is more important than truth. Honesty is still the best policy, because if you tell the truth, you don't have to remember anything, but a story which *sounds* authentic is one which will be believed even if – as with the biographies of many leaders – some of the details have been massaged.

9. Humour works. From Osama Bin Laden to paramilitary leaders in Northern Ireland to Barack Obama, humour is humanising.

10. Menace works. We have all had a boss who radiates an air of menace which, as long as it is not too intimidating, can be motivating. As US Secretary of State James Baker III once said of American policy towards Saddam Hussein after Iraq had invaded Kuwait: 'We've got a carrot and stick policy. And the carrot is, if he pulls out, he doesn't get the stick.' Menace combined with humour like this is an especially memorable story-telling device.

11. Always counter the counter-stories about you. If you don't defend your reputation, who will?

12. Live the story, don't just tell it. Nothing annoys people more than discovering the stories that you tell do not match up to the way you act. In the theatre this is called 'dramatic irony.' In real life it is called hypocrisy.

13. Build learning from mistakes into your story. Re-write the script for new times, and apologise for the past where necessary. Bill Clinton made a career out of it. Greg Dyke did it at the BBC. Angela Merkel is doing it for Germany.

14. People understand character better than policies. That's why

a trivial story well told is always better than a profound story badly told.

15. Repeat yourself. Tell your story, tell it and tell it again. Drill the 'earwig' and the STAR moment into the brains of your listeners.

16. Repeat yourself. Tell your story, tell it and tell it again. Drill the 'earwig' and the STAR moment into the brains of your listeners. (And again ...)

Above all, stories matter. We all tell stories. We all listen to stories. People remember stories told *by* you and *about* you. They define who you are in the minds of others, for good or ill. The only person who can make sure people remember the best stories about you, is you.

Good luck.

Acknowledgements

I would like to say thank you to everyone at Toby Eady Associates especially Toby Eady himself who, as always, was encouraging from the very start. Jamie Coleman read my earliest draft, talked through the ideas and the structure and offered unfailingly good advice. The team at Profile have been extraordinary. Daniel Crewe in particular was meticulous in offering suggestions and questioning assertions, plus also in gently reminding me that at some point the fun of writing the book (which has been enormous) meant eventually completing the project. Thanks also to Penny Daniel, Ruth Killick, Niamh Murray and Valentina Zanca for their enthusiasm, help and advice. I would also like to thank Charlotte and James Esler for their help with some of the research and for their detailed comments on the manuscript.

I would, of course, like to thank all the leaders and their helpers whom I have met over the years for keeping me entertained, amused and on occasions informed by their wonderful story-telling which, quite often, turned out to be based in fact.

Above all I would like to thank Anna for her advice, support, comments and commonsense, and her extensive review of the manuscript and her suggestions.

Any errors or omissions in the final product are mine – but I would be happy to read comments e-mailed to gavin.esler@ yahoo.co.uk and if corrections are necessary I will make them when I can.

Further Reading

I have found a number of books, newspapers, magazines and other sources invaluable. I have referred to most of them in the text. But for those interested in further reading, here are some of the books which I found most useful.

Abdullah, King of Jordan, *Our Last Best Chance* (Allen Lane, 2011)

Adair, John, *The Leadership of Muhammad* (Kogan Page, 2008)

Aldrich, Gary *Unlimited Access* (Regnery Publishing 1996)

Al-Qasimi Sultan bin Muhammad, *My Early Life* (2009) Taking the Reins (2012) both Bloomsbury

Atwan, Abdel Bari, The Secret History of al-Qa'ida (Saqi Books, 2006)

Blair, Tony, *A Journey* (Hutchinson, 2012)

Bush, George W., *A Charge to Keep* (William Morrow, 1999)

Brown, Ben, *Three Days in May* (Faber, 2011)

Churchill, Winston, *The Second World War* (Cassell, 1949)

Cialdini, Robert, *Influence* (HarperCollins, 2007)

Clinton, Bill, *Between Hope and History* (Random House, 1996)

Crick, Michael, *The Boss* (Pocket Books, 2003)

Davies, Nick, *Flat Earth News* (Vintage, 2009)

Esler, Gavin, *The United States of Anger* (Michael Joseph, 1997)

Flynt, Larry, *One Nation Under Sex* (Palgrave MacMillan, 2011)

Frafman Ori and Rom, *Sway* (Virgin, 2008)

Frum, David, *The Right Man* (Random House, 2003)

Giddens, Anthony, *The Third Way* (Polity Press, 1998)

Gifford, Jonathan, *History Lessons* (Marshall Cavendish Business, 2010)

Gingrich, Newt et al, *Contract With America* (Times Books, 1994)

Goldsmith, Marshall, *What got you here won't get you there* (Profile, 2008)

Goldstein, Noah et al, *Yes!* (Profile, 2007)

Green, Mark and MacColl, Gail, *Ronald Reagan's Reign of Error* (Pantheon, 1983)

Greene, Robert, *The Art of Seduction* (2003), *The 33 Strategies of War* (2007) and *The 48 Laws of Power* (2000) all Profile Books

Hare, David, *Stuff Happens* (Faber, 2004)

Haslam, S. Alexander et al, *The New Psychology of Leadership* (Psychology Press, 2011)

Holland, Heidi, *Dinner with Mugabe* (Penguin, 2008)

Jenkins, Roy, *Churchill* (Pan Macmillan, 2001)

Isaacson, Walter, *Steve Jobs* (Little, Brown, 2011)

Johnson, Michael, *Goldrush* (HarperSport, 2011)

Kaletsky, Anatole, *Capitalism 4.0* (Bloomsbury, 2010)

Kantor, Jodi, *The Obamas – A Mission, A Marriage* (Allen Lane, 2012)

Kay, John, *Obliquity* (Profile, 2010)

Kouzes, James and Posner, Barry, *The Leadership Challenge* (Jossey-Bass, 1995)

Kurtz, Howard, *Spin Cycle* (Simon and Schuster, 1998)

Leith, Sam, *You Talkin' to Me?* (Profile, 2011)

Levitin, Daniel, *This is your Brain on Music* (Atlantic, 2008)

McKee, Robert, *Story* (Methuen, 1999)

McRae, Hamish, *What Works* (HarperPress, 2010)

Maraniss, David, *First in his Class* (Simon and Schuster, 1995)

Mason, Todd, *Perot – An Unauthorized Biography* (Dow Jones Irwin, 1990)

Mazower, Mark, *Dark Continent* (Allen Lane, 1998)

Mearsheimer, John, *Why Leaders Lie* (Duckworth Overlook, 2011)

Moore, Jim, *Young Man in a Hurry* (The Summit Group, 1992)

Morris, Dick, *The New Prince* (St Martin's Press, 1999)

Noonan, Peggy, *What I Saw at the Revolution* (Random House, 1990)

Palin, Sarah, *Going Rogue* (Harper, 2009)

Obama, Barack, *The Audacity of Hope* (2006); *Dreams from My Father* (2007 – first published in USA 1995) Canongate

Powell, Colin, *A Soldier's Way* (Arrow, 1995)

Powell, Jonathan, *The New Machiavelli* (The Bodley Head, 2010)

Salecl, Renata, *Choice* (Profile, 2010)

Thaler, Richard and Sunstein, Cass, *Nudge* (Penguin, 2009)

Turner, Ted, *Call Me Ted* (Sphere, 2008)

Van Vugt, Mark and Ahuja, Anjana, *Selected* (Profile, 2010)

Woodward, Bob, *The Agenda* (Simon and Schuster, 1994)

Index